X.media.publishing

Corinna Jacobs

Interactive Panoramas

Techniques for Digital Panoramic Photography

with 179 Illustrations and a CD-ROM

Springer

Corinna Jacobs
Sommerhalde 13
71672 Marbach
Germany
info@interactive-panoramas.com

Translated from the first edition of the German "Digitale Panoramen" (Springer-Verlag 2004, ISBN 3-540-00300-2) by Jeff Parrish, Göppingen, Germany. Updated by the author.

ISSN 1612-1449
ISBN 3-540-21140-3 Springer Berlin Heidelberg New York

Library of Congress Control Number: 2004109053

Springer is a part of Springer Science+Business Media
springeronline.com

Printed in Germany

Cover design: KünkelLopka, Heidelberg
Typesetting and data preparation by the author
Printed on acid-free paper 33/3142 Re – 543210

Preface

Interactive panoramas have a captivating effect in almost every application imaginable: whether they are integrated in a personal homepage or professionally used in architecture, in museums or in company or product presentations. Written in a comprehensive, yet easy-to-understand format, this book details all of the necessary steps involved in panoramic photography: from the production of digital and analog picture sequences, to "stitching" using appropriate software tools, all the way to publishing interactive panoramas on the Internet. The book introduces the concept of producing cylindrical and spherical panoramas and explains how to link individual panoramas to create virtual tours. The production of interactive object presentations – or so-called object movies – also is described. Software products that receive mention include REALVIZ Stitcher, VR Worx and PanoTools, with attention also being paid to publishing Internet-ready video formats using QuickTime VR, PTViewer, VRML, iPIX and HotMedia.

Regardless if the digital pictures are taken with a panoramic camera, a standard or fisheye lens, or using the single-row or multi-row technique: this book offers practical tips and tricks for every alternative. Detailed comparisons of the individual techniques make it easier to decide on the appropriate method for specific goals. This useful information adds an exciting dimension to panoramic photography and leads to high quality results that speak for themselves.

This book is recommended for beginners, as the fundamentals of digital and panoramic photography are clearly explained at the beginning. The experienced photographer or media creator also will find value, as special topics including object photography for the production of object movies are treated.

Beginners should, in any case, start with chapters 1 through 3, where the basics of panorama technique and photography are introduced. Chapter 4 is primarily written for experienced users, as it focuses on special correction methods. Chapter 5 provides tips for selecting suitable equipment. Chapters 6 and 7 introduce the production of cylindrical and spherical panoramas. Chapter 8 deals with the production of object movies, with chapter 9 describing how to link multiple panoramas and additional media to create virtual tours. In chapter 10 you discover how interactive panoramas and object movies can be published to the Internet.

Some of the terms and special expressions used are explained in a glossary at the end of the book. The individual processing steps taken with the software introduced are explained in detail in order to aid comprehension. The respective functions in the software menus are printed in *italics*.

References to the CD are indicated with this CD icon

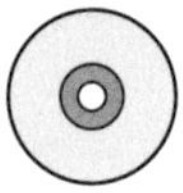

This book comes with a CD including sample files and demo versions of the software. Several chapters in the book refer to the bundled CD; these references are noted by the CD icon. The CD includes copies of the same pictures that are shown in the respective chapters in the book. In addition to the pictures, partially processed project files using the respective software are included to aid workflow comprehension. You will find these pictures and project files in the "Workshop" section of the CD; the folders are named analogous to the corresponding chapters in the book. The "raw pictures" included also can be used in conjunction with other software products (offering similar features) for test purposes. This is relatively easy for object movies, with all of the programs introduced here having the capacity to create such movies using the single-row and multi-row techniques. When it comes to producing cylindrical panoramas, the raw pictures also can be easily stitched using all of the programs introduced. Only when spherical and cubic panoramas are desired are some programs not able to process "normal" and fisheye pictures or pictures from panoramic cameras. Chapter 12 provides a table view of the functions included in the individual software products.

In order to be able to view all interactive panoramas and object movies, you will need the QuickTime plug-in, the iPIX plug-in and a VRML viewer (e.g. the Cortona player); additionally, Java should be activated in your Web browser. Refer to chapter B.1.7 and the readme file on the bundled CD to learn where you can download the required plug-ins. A number of software manufacturers kindly provided us the installation file for their plug-in. You will find these files in the "Viewer" section on the CD.

Demo versions of almost every software product introduced in this book can be downloaded from the manufacturer Web sites. The links are listed in the respective chapters so that you can download the software for testing purposes. A few manufacturers have authorized us to include trial versions of their software programs, which can be found in the "Demo versions" section on the book CD.

Software products are improved and updated all the time. As such, it is highly recommended that you pay a visit to the respective manufacturer's Web site prior to installing their program(s) from the book CD. It is possible that more recent versions of the software are available here.

I would like to thank all of the companies and institutions that supported me in writing this book:

Amazing 3D Graphics, Apple, IBM, iPIX, iseemedia, Kaidan, Marc Kairies Panorama Systeme, New House Internet Services, Pano-Maxx, REALVIZ, Roundshot, Seitz, Spheron, Studio Gruppe Vier, Sun Microsystems, HdM Stuttgart University of Applied Sciences, University of Southern California, VR Toolbox

I also would like to thank everyone who was there to give me advice and provide support on various topics:

Peter Beck, Helmut Dersch, Stephen Elzenbeck, Hans Friedrich, Jürgen Gemmrich, Bernd Häußermann, Marc Kairies, Tim Kondermann, Torben Ohme, David Roman, Johannes Schaugg, Frank Schmidt, Andrea Sojka, Joachim Vollmer, Marcus Weiß

A special thanks go out to Springer-Verlag, with editor Jutta-Maria Fleschutz and producer Gabriele Fischer. Last but not least, I would like to show my appreciation to Julia Merz from KünkelLopka for the cover design and to Jeff Parrish for providing the English translation.

Marbach, June 2004 **Corinna Jacobs**

Table of Contents

1. Introduction

1.1 The fascination of panoramic art

The history of panoramic art has its roots in the 18th century. The panorama was registered for patent in 1787 by Robert Barker in London. At that time, panorama was a new form of painting, with sweeping pictures painted on the inside of the walls in buildings specially designed for such art. These so-called rotundas tapered off in the form of a dome at the top, whereby the panoramic depictions reached a height of up to 15 meters. Sophisticated illumination and special painting techniques played to the imagination of the observer standing on a platform at the center. The aim here was to create the perfect illusion. Popular motifs included current and historical views of cities, war portrayals and distant lands. Panoramic painters first used the camera obscura to depict motifs on site, then branched into photography. These depictions served as the basis for panoramic painting. One of the early panoramas from Robert Barker can be viewed on the Internet at: http: // www.ex.ac.uk/bill.douglas/collection/panorama/barker.html [status: May 12, 2004].

Some historical panoramas have survived the years and still can be visited. "The Battle of Gettysburg", for example, which made its debut back in 1884, today can be seen in the Gettysburg National Military Park. More information on this panorama can be found at: http://www.nps.gov/gett/gettcyclo.htm [status: February 14, 2004].

Another panoramic war portrayal open to the public is "The Battle of Atlanta". If you would like to take in this panorama in person, point your browser to: http://www.atlantanation.com/cyclorama.html [status: March 15, 2004].

The New Yorker Metropolitan Museum of Art exhibits "The Palace and Gardens of Versailles" painting. This panorama was completed in 1819 by John Vanderlyn and depicts the Castle of Versailles. More information on this panorama can be found at: http://www.metmuseum.org/works_of_art/viewone.asp?dep=2&viewmode=0&item=52.184 [status: March 12, 2004].

The panorama of Jerusalem (Cyclorama of Jerusalem) employs a biblical theme. Here, Parisian Paul Philippoteaux paints the crucifixion of Jesus on one side, while the other side depicts the city of Jerusalem with surrounding scenery. This panorama has been on display in Sainte-Anne-de-

Beaupré, Canada since 1895. More information on this panorama can be found at: http://www.cyclorama.com [status: February 14, 2004].

Today, such grandiose panoramic settings continue to mesmerize audiences. A panorama of Alice Springs, which was painted in six months by artist Henk Guth, has been on exhibition since 1975 in Australia. Put together from 33 pieces of Irish linen, the painting depicts the central Australian landscape. More information on this panorama can be found at: http://www.panoramaguth.com.au/panorama.shtml [status: May 2, 2004].

Smaller sized panoramas have always had a certain fascination about them as well. When photography was invented in 1839, it didn't take long for the panoramic concept to quickly spread over to this new medium. Indeed, the first ideas for developing a panoramic camera surfaced in record time. As soon as 1843, Austria's Joseph Puchberger patented a camera with a rotating optical system, whereby the lens could be turned via a hand crank while shooting. At the time, Puchberger's camera used daguerrotypes and reached a horizontal field of view (FOV) of 150 degrees. This technology was further developed by Kodak, which unveiled the world's first panoramic camera in 1899 – the humbly named "Model No. 4". This model had a more compact design than earlier inventions, which gave rise to a wide variety of applications. Later on, there were cameras with a fixed lens that, due to their short focal length, likewise were capable of taking panoramic shots. Such cameras often were used to document large societal festivities, which is why they also were referred to as "banquet cameras".

Since then, the technology of panoramic photography has continued to progress. Today's panoramic cameras include Noblex cameras with a rotating lens, Seitz Roundshot cameras with a swivel motor and digital scanning cameras from Spheron. These special cameras can cost up to US $ 20,000, which is why they only should be purchased by professional photographers. Additionally, such cameras generally are limited to taking panoramic pictures and cannot be used for standard shots.

There are, however, more economical ways to get into panoramic photography. Special software can converge conventional pictures on the computer to create digital panoramic images, which then can be printed out on photo paper or converted to interactive panoramas for viewing on a computer screen. With interactive panoramas, the observer sees only one section of the entire panorama. Via special viewer software, the mouse can be used to move in various directions to create an experience that simulates reality. The panorama can be enlarged and minimized to get a closer view or a more distant view of a particular section. Many virtual tours have so-called "hot spots", or areas of the picture that are linked with additional interactive functions. Hot spots can include sounds, music and text, or even direct the viewer to other panoramas in order to virtually explore a bigger area, such as a complete building. Interactive panoramic technology continues to become more advanced, with the next chapter showing the current level of development in this sector.

1.2 Panoramas on the Internet

The Web now holds a wide variety of different forms of panoramic presentation. The following gives you a brief overview of these forms, with each section containing a link to a Web site for a representative example. As the Internet is a very fast moving medium, it is quite possible that one or more of the printed links no longer exists or has been moved. Should this be the case, the bundled CD contains various examples of cylindrical, spherical and cubic panoramas under "Workshop" as well as virtual tours and object movies in the respective folders.

Version 5 or greater of the QuickTime plug-in is required to view the panoramas. You can download the QuickTime player at http://www.apple.com/quicktime/download [status: March 10, 2004].

Java also should be installed and activated in your browser of choice (download at http://www.java.com/en/download/manual.jsp [status: March 10, 2004]).

Cylindrical panoramas

This type of panorama currently is the most popular one used on the Internet. Vertical travel is limited in cylindrical panoramas. An example can be found at:
http://www.kaidan.com/nightri.html [status: March 24, 2004]

You can view examples of this type of panorama on the CD under \Workshop\06 Cylindrical panoramas

Spherical panoramas

With spherical panoramas, you have unrestricted view of the image in both horizontal and vertical directions. An example of this type of panorama can be found at:
http://360vr.com/ptvr/anasazi.html [status: May 8, 2004]

You can view examples of this type of panorama on the CD under \Workshop\07 Spherical panoramas

Cubic panoramas

Cubic and spherical panoramas appear very similar for the observer, as both formats allow swiveling in the horizontal and vertical directions. Here, a cubic projection is used in place of a spherical format. An example of a cubic panorama can be found at:
http://www.apple.com/quicktime/gallery/cubicvr [status: March 12, 2004]

You can view examples of this type of panorama on the CD under \Workshop\07 Spherical panoramas

Object movies

An object movie is a "reversed" panorama, whereby the object rotates on a turntable and is photographed by a camera in a fixed position. An example of an object movie can be found at:
http://www.apple.com/hardware/gallery [status: March 8, 2004]

You can view examples of this type of panorama on the CD under \Workshop\08 Object movies

The stereo and macro panoramas described in greater detail next represent special forms of panoramic presentation.

Stereo panoramas

Stereo panoramas are 3-D panoramas produced using two cameras set up next to each other at a width that correlates to the gap between the eyes. The three-dimensional effect becomes visible when a pair of red-green or red-blue glasses are worn. Polarizing filter glasses also can be used, as is the case in IMAX 3-D movie theaters. An example of a stereo panorama can be found at:
http://www.outline.be/quicktime/musee3d.html [status: April 2, 2004]

Macro panoramas

Macro panoramas are 360° views of very small quarters in which there is no room for a traditional photo set. Here, a reflective metal ball is used that is placed in the center of the scene. The image reflected off of this ball is then photographed and turned into a panorama. The term "macro panorama" can be misleading, as it involves the depiction of micro worlds. The name comes from macro photography, where small objects can be enlarged by way of close-up pictures. An example can be found at:
http://home.no.net/dmaurer/~dersch/html/Micros.html [status: March 25, 2004]

Panoramas with sound

Panoramas can be combined with background sound. There is also directional sound, which only can be heard from a specific area in the panorama. Here, the viewer perceives dynamism and motion, although fixed images are used. An example of directional sound can be heard at:
http://www.pbs.org/wnet/newyork/hidden/coneyisland/mermaidpano.mov [status: March 8, 2004]

Panoramas with video

Here, a video track is integrated in one or more areas of the panorama, making the viewing experience much more lively. An example can be found at:
http://www.vrhotwires.com/beetle-pano.mov [status: April 8, 2004]

All of the panoramic forms presented here can be linked to virtual tours. The integration of additional functions such as sound or video depends on the form of publication selected.

Virtual tours

In virtual tours, several individual panoramas are linked to each other using hot spots. When a hot spot is clicked in the panorama, the viewer is brought to the next area of the tour. Such "virtual walks" can include real or 3-D pictures. In general, all panoramas and object movies also can be created using computer generated pictures.

An example of a photorealistic tour can be found at:
http://www.soh.nsw.gov.au/virtual_tour/vrtour.html [status: May 2, 2004]

For an example of a 3-D tour, point your browser to:
http://www.alteredearth.com/vr/cubicvr/shaft1.htm [status: May 2, 2004]

You can view examples of this type of panorama on the CD under \Workshop\09 Virtual tours

1.3 Panoramic forms – Projection

The word projection is used to describe how the perspective of panoramic pictures is changed by software in order to present a realistic display of the panorama on a computer screen. The convergence of the individual pictures – known as "stitching" – is assumed by a software application designed to merge the pictures and display the necessary curvature of space through projection. Three different forms of projection are used in the panoramic production process:

- Cylindrical
- Spherical
- Cubic

The most frequently used form of projection continues to be cylindrical, however spherical and cubic panorama formats are becoming increasingly popular on the Web.

1.3.1 Cylindrical projection

With this type of projection, the panoramic picture basically winds around a cylinder, in the middle of which the observer stands. Here, the picture is slightly convex, which makes a more realistic impression on the observer. Some Java viewers and many panoramic depictions made with Flash are more simplistic in their approach. A panoramic filmstrip is moved to the right or the left behind a cut-out window, depending on the position of the mouse. This little trick makes the panorama appear flat when compared to the slightly convex, "real" cylindrical projection.

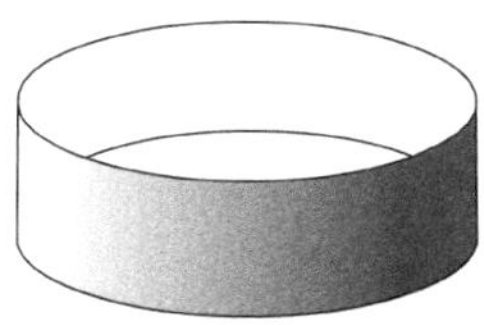

Figure 1.1
The panoramic picture is cylindrically projected

This type of projection can depict a vertical angle of up to 120°. Cylindrical projection is best suited for motifs, where the upper and lower parts of the picture are not very important and can be factored out.

Figure 1.2
Cylindrical panoramic picture with limited vertical angle

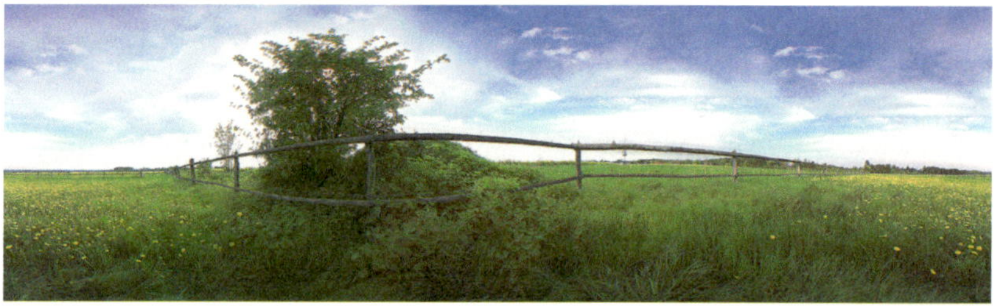

1.3.2 Spherical projection

Figure 1.3
The panoramic picture is spherically projected

Spherical projection differs from cylindrical projection in that the vertical pivoting range is unlimited. The underlying spherical – or equirectangular – panoramic picture has a 360° horizontal and a 180° vertical scope, which is why the aspect ratio here is 2:1. As its name implies, these pictures are projected in spherical format and the observer finds himself optically in the center of this sphere. The respective viewer corrects the horizontal and vertical distortion so that the observer can experience the picture without any falsification.

Spherical panoramas are suited for the majority of motifs, unless the creator consciously wants to shift emphasis away from unaesthetic ceiling and floor areas.

Figure 1.4
Spherical panoramic picture with an aspect ratio of 2:1

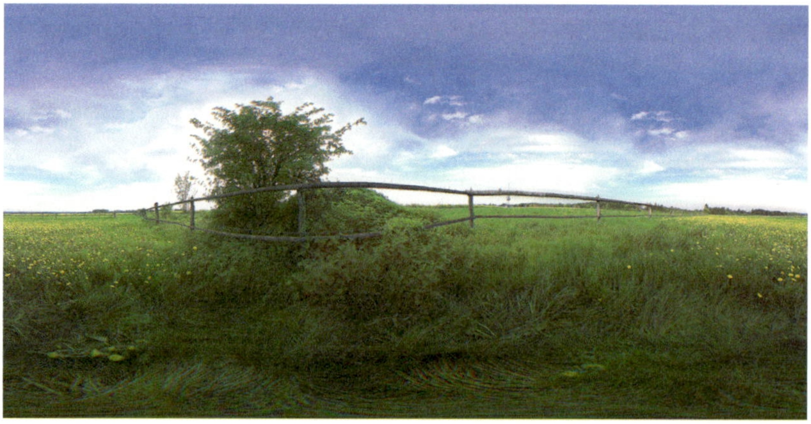

1.3.3 Cubic projection

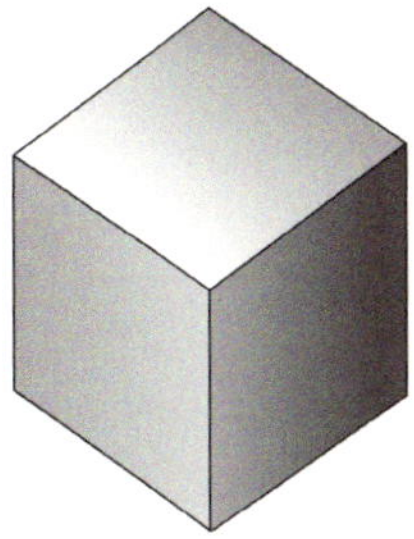

Figure 1.5
The panoramic picture is cubically projected

As with spherical projection, cubic projection places no limitation on the vertical angle. The main processes involved in cubic projection are less complex than those of cylindrical projection. A cube has eight corners and six sides. As such, six quadratic pictures are required for this format. The viewer stitches these pictures to form a cube and distorts the finished product such that the edges of the pictures disappear.

The underlying panoramic picture used for cubic projection has exactly the same dimensions as the picture used for spherical projection, however the former is saved in a different format. Thus, the observer usually cannot distinguish between cubic and spherical projection. If, however, the picture is greatly magnified, the edges of the cube sometimes become visible.

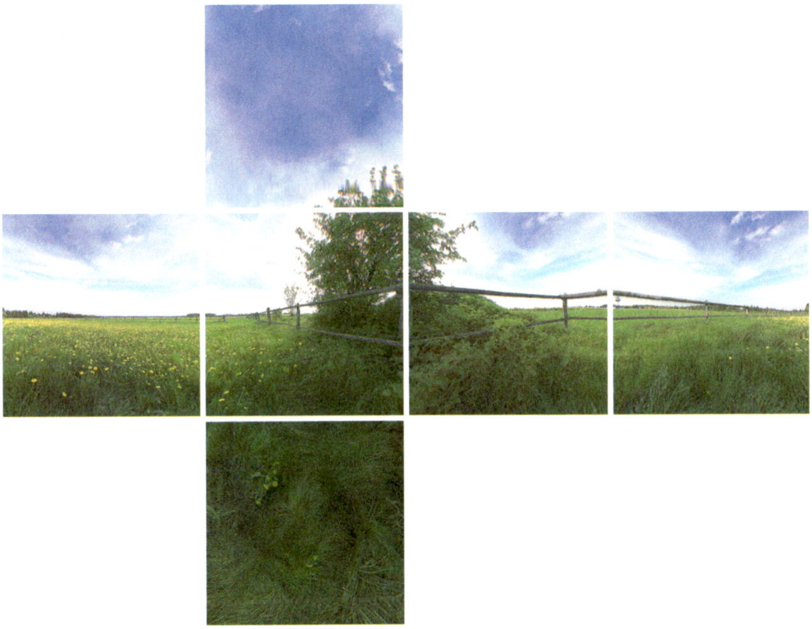

Figure 1.6
The sides of the cube are individually saved

2. Fundamentals

2.1 Production of interactive panoramas

Before we go into greater detail on the various technologies and techniques, here is a brief overview of panoramic production.

2.1.1 Taking pictures with a panoramic camera

The most convenient solution is, of course, to use a special panoramic camera for your shots. The camera either can be analog or digital and works by rotating once about its own axis while shooting the panorama to record the complete environment. For a digital 360° panorama, usually only the two seam edges need to be stitched. Depending on the lens used, the result can be a cylindrical, cubic or spherical panorama.

2.1.2 Taking individual pictures

Another way to create a panorama is to take one or more picture sequences and overlap the individual pictures by a certain percentage. With this method, the camera is turned by a specific amount to the position where the next picture is to be taken until the entire 360° revolution has been completed. The pictures then are stitched to form a panoramic picture using special stitching software. The number of individual pictures and the selected projection format dictate what type of panorama (i.e. cylindrical, spherical or cubic) will result. Here, too, either an analog or a digital camera can be used.

2.1.3 Correcting image distortion

As the pitfalls of most lenses are pincushion and barrel distortion, vignetting and chromatic aberration (see chapter 2.2.3), these errors should be corrected prior to or during the stitching process with appropriate software. Heavily distorted pictures that are not corrected may not be able to be stitched.

2.1.4 Stitching individual pictures

The next step involves stitching the individual pictures to form a panoramic picture. For this, the pictures are projected in the right perspective as soon as the overlapping edges are defined, making it easier to position the images in the overall panorama. The parameters for this projection come from the recording values, which include the lens used, the distance and the number of individual pictures taken. Stitching software normally connects the pictures by overlapping them in order to create a soft, invisible transition.

2.1.5 Retouching the panoramic picture

When creating a spherical panorama, the legs of the tripod or the photographer typically appear in the bottom of the picture at some point. If this area is to appear authentic, retouching is necessary. The procedure for doing this depends on how the scene was shot and what stitching software is used (see chapter 7).

2.1.6 Publication of the panorama

Finished panoramas can be published in a variety of ways, depending on the target group and the format selected. Cylindrical panoramic pictures are well suited for electronic (computer screen) or physical (hard copy) presentation, the latter of which can be printed out on photo paper or professionally developed (see chapter 10.6).

If the panorama is to be digitally published, there are number of ways of doing this, all of which are described in chapter 10. Chapter 13 provides an overview of the different panorama formats and their presentation with viewers.

2.2 Term definitions

This section clarifies a few important terms before we delve into the topic of panoramic production.

2.2.1 Lenses

A wide variety of lenses can be used in panoramic photography. In order to determine the number of pictures required for a panoramic picture, however, it is critical to know the size of the field of view of the lens being used. Chapter 2.2.2 provides more information on the relationship between focal length and field of view. As a general rule, though, the larger the field of view, the fewer the pictures that need to be taken.

As every type of lens has different characteristics, it is important that the lenses be classified. The two main distinguishing categories are standard, or rectilinear lenses, and fisheye lenses.

2.2.1.1 Rectilinear lenses

A right angle depiction lens also is known as a rectilinear lens, whereby rectilinear means that the lens captures straight lines and angles as such. In general, these lenses most often are referred to as "normal", or standard lenses. With respect to the depth of perception of the human eye, these lenses have a focal length ranging from 35 to 50 mm. Rectilinear lenses that can encompass a larger area than that of the human eye (i.e. wide angle lenses with a focal length under 35 mm) often have linear distortion (see chapter 2.2.3.1). The possibilities for taking pictures with these standard lenses are depleted at a focal length of approximately 14 mm. Lesser focal lengths and greater fields of view only can be achieved with fisheye lenses, however these do not have rectilinear depiction.

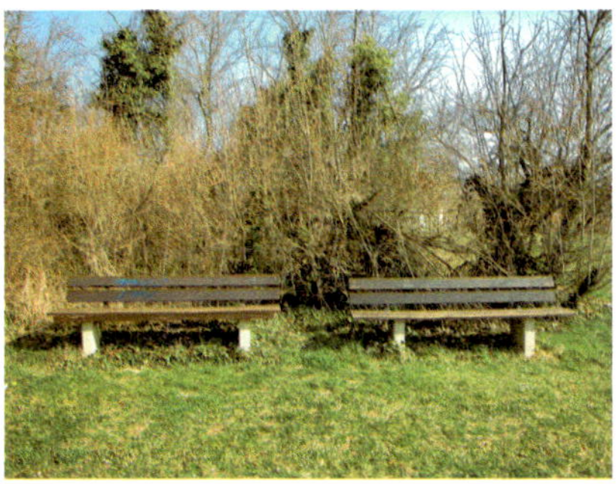

Figure 2.1
Motif captured with a rectilinear lens

2.2.1.2 Fisheye lenses

A fisheye lens is an extremely wide angle lens, whereby the proportions of the scene to be captured are radially distorted in order to achieve the large field of view. This is why all straight lines in the picture are arched outwards. This distortion exaggerates up to the edge of the picture. Only the center of the picture is perceived by the human eye to be correctly displayed. The smallest focal length for this type of lens is 6 mm. Here, a field of view of up to 220° is achieved.

Fisheye lenses also include lenses with circular and full frame depiction. Some digital cameras with fisheye converters provide the option to switch back and forth between these two modes as needed.

Circular fisheyes

If the camera is set to circular mode or a circular fisheye lens is used, a circular shaped picture with black borders appears in the characteristic fisheye dimensions as described above.

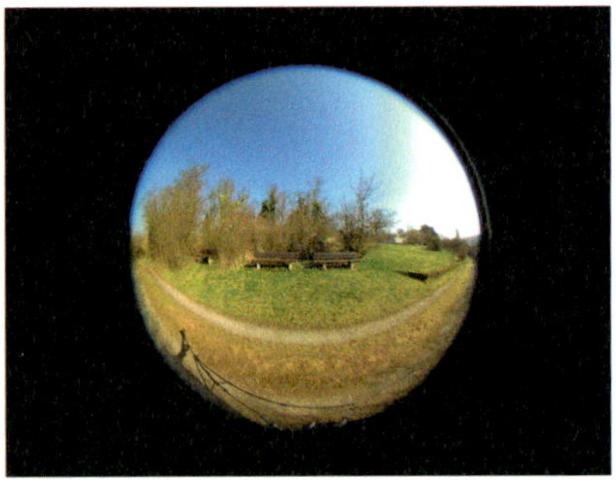

Figure 2.2
Motif captured with a circular depiction fisheye lens

Full frame fisheyes

If the full frame fisheye setting is selected or an appropriate fisheye lens is used, the round perimeter is trimmed off right when the picture is taken. The result is a wide angle picture with square corners and the barrel distortion typical for fisheye lenses.

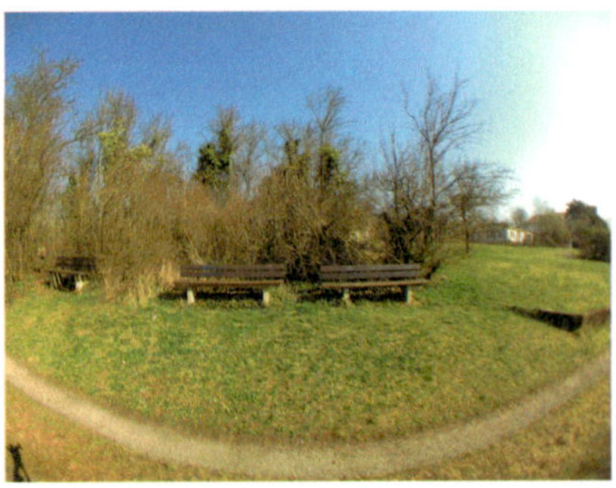

Figure 2.3
Motif taken with a fisheye lens in full frame mode

2.2.2 Focal length and field of view

The distance from the optical center point of a lens to the focal plane is termed the focal length, whereby the field of view defines the picture area of the scene to be captured. With small format cameras, a lens with a 50 mm focal length is typically used. Here, the focal length is only marginally greater than the diagonal width (approx. 43 mm), which produces a field of view of approximately 45° and corresponds to the human eye. Pictures taken with such a lens are viewed by the observer as perspectively neutral. Focal lengths under 50 mm yield a wide angle and allow a larger range to be captured. Focal lengths over 50 mm come in the form of telephoto lenses, which can be used to zoom in on objects. Doing so, of course, limits the field of view.

Most software products that stitch panoramic pictures require the user to enter the field of view or the focal length of the lens used. Some programs, however, automatically determine this value based on the pictures imported. All software applications need this information in order to properly display the projection when stitching. A distinction is made between horizontal field of view (HFOV) and vertical field of view (VFOV). Vertical field of view refers to the vertical stretching of a picture, which can be achieved with a certain lens. Horizontal field of view refers to stretching a picture in the horizontal direction. Both fields of view are given in degrees.

Formulas for calculating the field of view

Camera orientation: Portrait

$$\text{Horizontal field of view (HFOV)} = 2 \cdot \arctan\left(\frac{12}{\text{Focal length}}\right)$$

$$\text{Vertical field of view (VFOV)} = 2 \cdot \arctan\left(\frac{18}{\text{Focal length}}\right)$$

Camera orientation: Landscape

$$\text{Horizontal field of view (HFOV)} = 2 \cdot \arctan\left(\frac{18}{\text{Focal length}}\right)$$

$$\text{Vertical field of view (VFOV)} = 2 \cdot \arctan\left(\frac{12}{\text{Focal length}}\right)$$

The following table gives the field of view associated with various focal lengths for small format cameras. Pictures in portrait format are recommended for interactive panoramas with a large vertical pivoting range. This is why the values in the table refer to a camera positioned for portrait shots. Additionally, these values apply only to 35 mm film. For digital cameras, the focal length multiplier (which is a function of the size of the chip) must be taken into account (see chapter 3.1.2). The exact value of the field of view is important in order to determine the number of individual pictures for a panorama (see chapter 2.2.4).

Field of view as a function of the focal length

Lens type	Focal length*	Field of view (horizontal)	Field of view (vertical)
Fisheye	6-8 mm	180-220°	180-220°
Fisheye	15-16 mm	140-160°	140-160°
Wide angle	17 mm	70°	93°
Wide angle	20 mm	62°	84°
Wide angle	24 mm	53°	74°
Wide angle	28 mm	46°	65°
Wide angle	35 mm	38°	54°
Standard	50 mm	27°	40°
Telephoto	80 mm	17°	25°
Telephoto	120 mm	11°	17°
Telephoto	200 mm	7°	10°

* The information for the focal length is to be treated as approximate values only, as the focal length usually changes for close focus shots. This is why the values generally refer to an infinite range of focus.

2.2.3 Image distortion of lenses

Each lens disk is subject to creating numerous photographic errors, which can take the form of distortion, blurriness and color fringing. As such, each lens is a combination of several lens disks made from various types of glass, which work together to all but eliminate the inherent error potential. Depending on the quality of the lens selected, these photographic errors are more or less perceivable.

2.2.3.1 Linear distortion

Linear distortion is when the straight lines of an object appear arched, an effect caused by the shape of the lens. This effect is less noticeable with landscape shots. With architectural photography or panoramas of interior settings, however, the distortion associated with the shape of the lens is a factor not to be overlooked. Here, a distinction is made between pincushion and barrel distortion. The higher the quality of the lens, the lower the risk of image distortion. Linear distortion errors occur most frequently with economically priced wide angle lenses and zoom lenses or when wide angle adapters are used on digital cameras. With barrel distortion, the straight lines in the picture appear convex. With pincushion distortion, the lines tend to curve toward the center of the picture (see Figure 2.4).

The degree of distortion can be measured based on the deviation of the curved line to a straight reference line. More specifically, distortion is the distance by which the curved line deviates from the straight line with respect to the picture height; this value is given in percent. For digital compact cameras, the deviation value for barrel distortion is approximately 1 percent, with the deviation value for pincushion distortion at around 0.6 percent. Not correcting distortions may lead to problems when converging the pictures later on, depending on the stitching software that is used. REALVIZ Stitcher, for example, can correct distortions during the stitching process (see chapters 6.3.4 and 7.3.2). When PanoTools is used, numerous lens errors can be corrected for individual pictures as well as when stitching a series of panoramic pictures (see chapter 4.1.1).

Figure 2.4
From left to right:
Pincushion distortion
No distortion
Barrel distortion

2.2.3.2 Perspective distortion

Another form of distortion is perspective distortion. Perspective distortion is not the result of an error on the part of the lens, as the perspective is entirely dependent on the position from which the pictures are taken.

It is possible for a stitched panorama to appear imperfect when the perspective is distorted and the vertical lines are not properly displayed. This is the case, for example, when tall buildings are photographed, as the lines can taper off the farther up the shot is made - an effect known as aberrant lines. The greater the inclination of the camera, the more intense this effect. When professional view cameras or shift lenses are used, perspective image reproduction can be influenced by the motion of the optical axis, thus eliminating the distortion. Image editing software such as Adobe Photoshop (see chapter 4.1.2) or PanoTools also can be used to correct perspective distortion. While generally avoided, perspective distortion can be done on purpose in e.g. architectural photography to achieve a certain effect. In this case, the distortion simply is not corrected.

2.2.3.3 Vignetting

Vignetting describes the frequent shading effect that occurs toward the borders of a picture. While the center of the picture is properly lit, the surrounding scene dims with increasing intensity the farther it extends from this point. This type of image distortion primarily affects wide angle lenses. Vignetting is only disturbing when the loss of light to the borders exceeds one stop. The vignetting effect can be counteracted by using a special radial gray filter that is neutral gray at the center and becomes colorless as it extends outward. Vignetting also can be corrected with image editing software such as Adobe Photoshop and PanoTools (see chapter 4.1.3).

Figure 2.5
Vignetting becomes noticeable by the darkened image corners

2.2.3.4 Chromatic aberration

Chromatic aberration occurs when rays of light are refracted differently by a lens (depending on wavelength), leading to loss of a common focal point. The difference in the depth of focus associated with the primary colors red, blue and green is also known as lateral and longitudinal color errors. Chromatic aberration becomes visible with blurriness and color fringing. Telephoto lenses with wide focal lengths and zoom lenses with many lens elements are particular candidates for this type of distortion error. Most lenses are achromatically corrected so that two of the primary colors are focused in a focal plane. This optical system is known as achromat. A lens that is optimized for all three primary colors is the apochromat lens. Chromatic aberration can be corrected with image editing software such as PanoTools (see chapter 4.1.4).

If you are thinking about correcting the image distortion errors caused by a lens, it is recommended that you stitch the individual pictures into a test panorama. If problems arise during the stitching process or the overall display is not what you had in mind, you will know that this additional step is necessary.

Not all image distortion errors need to be corrected

2.2.4 Determining the required number of pictures

In order to ensure that a panorama can be easily stitched, a certain number of pictures is required. The number of required pictures and the degree of overlapping are determined by the field of view of the lens used. A common overlapping value is thirty percent. Every type of lens essentially can be used, whereby fewer pictures need to be taken for a 360° panorama with wider lenses that have a greater field of view.

A horizontal picture sequence usually is needed for a cylindrical panorama; this technique is also known as single-row. If a larger vertical field of view is desired or a spherical panorama is to be produced, the multi-row technique (which consists of several overlapping picture sequences) is used.

The two tables that follow can be referred to in order to find the required number of individual pictures per lens used. Here, the focal length multiplier of digital single lens reflex cameras (see chapter 3.3) must be observed. The focal lengths listed in the tables correspond to 35 mm film. Pictures generally can be taken in landscape or portrait positions. To achieve a larger vertical pivoting range in the panorama later on, it is recommended that the camera be positioned for portrait shots. This especially holds true for cylindrical panoramic production. The table assumes that the pictures will be taken in portrait mode, as this format allows the photographer to keep all downstream production processes open in order to make a cylindrical panorama from a spherical one, for example. The values in the tables apply to panoramic pictures with a 30 percent overlap ratio. In the table for multi-row panoramas, the positive inclination values correspond to upwards inclination, whereas the negative values signal the opposite.

The information in the tables is based on the following equations:

$$\text{Landscape format: HFOV} = 2 \cdot \arctan\left(\frac{18}{\text{Focal length}}\right)$$

$$\text{Portrait format: HFOV} = 2 \cdot \arctan\left(\frac{12}{\text{Focal length}}\right)$$

$$\text{Number of pictures to be taken} = \frac{100 \cdot A}{(100 - B) \cdot \text{HFOV}}$$

A = Final panoramic field of view (here 360°)

B = Overlapping of individual pictures (here 30 %)

HFOV = Horizontal field of view

Number of pictures for single-row takes

Focal length	Field of view	Number of pictures	Arrangement of pictures
15 mm	100° 77°	6	at a distance of 60° each
20 mm	84° 62°	8	at a distance of 45° each
28 mm	65° 46°	10	at a distance of 36° each
35 mm	54° 38°	12	at a distance of 30° each

Number of pictures for multi-row takes

Focal length	Field of view	Number of pictures	Arrangement of pictures
15 mm	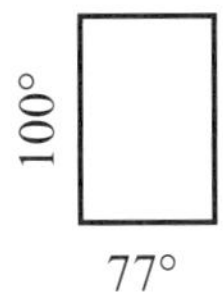	14	• One picture at +90° pitch • Six pictures every 60° at +30° pitch • Six pictures every 60° at -30° pitch • One picture at -90° pitch
20 mm	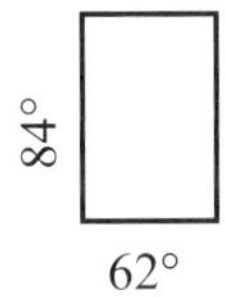	26	• One picture at +90° pitch • Eight pictures every 45° at +60° pitch • Eight pictures every 45° at 0° pitch • Eight pictures every 45° at -60° pitch • One picture at -90° pitch
28 mm	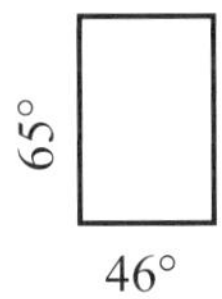	32	• One picture at +90° pitch • Ten pictures every 36° at +45° pitch • Ten pictures every 36° at 0° pitch • Ten pictures every 36° at -45° pitch • One picture at -90° pitch
35 mm	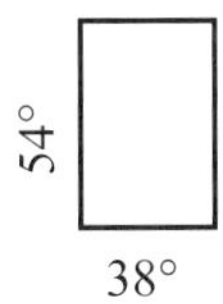	50	• One picture at +90° pitch • Twelve pictures every 30° at +60° pitch • Twelve pictures every 30° at +20° pitch • Twelve pictures every 30° at -20° pitch • Twelve pictures every 30° at -60° pitch • One picture at -90° pitch

A 50 percent overlap ratio can be used in place of the 30 percent figure described here. This provides more picture information for the subsequent editing process, however some stitching programs have difficulty dealing with large overlap ratios. With 50 percent overlapping, the number of individual pictures for a horizontal picture sequence can be determined using a simple rule of thumb. A camera is mounted on a tripod and horizontally turned until a complete circle has been traveled without overlapping (edge on edge). If the number of pictures required for this circle is doubled, the exact number of pictures for a 360° pivot with 50 percent overlap is obtained. This method also is recommended, for example, when the exact focal length of the lens is not known or you don't want to be bothered with determining the number of individual pictures.

Field of view of fisheye lenses

The method for calculating the field of view shown here applies only to standard rectilinear lenses. Fisheye lenses cannot be calculated this way. The technical specifications for the lenses contain the appropriate information on the field of view. This value is used to determine the number of pictures needed for a sphere. For example, an 8 mm fisheye lens has a field of view of approximately 180°. As such, a minimum of two pictures will need to be taken to complete a 360° sphere. Taking more pictures will create a larger overlap area and provide more picture information for stitching and retouching.

2.2.5 Determining the nodal point

When taking panoramic pictures, it is generally necessary to choose the optical center of the camera and lens design – or the so-called nodal point – as the mid-point for pivoting the camera. Not doing so will lead to parallax errors.

Turning the camera around its nodal point can prevent parallax errors

The problem associated with parallax errors can be illustrated with a simple experiment. Close one eye and look for a nearby vertical line as well as a second line behind the first one – for example, the frame of a window in the room and the corner of your neighbor's house. Now tilt your head while continuing to look at both lines. You should notice that the position of these lines in relation to each other has changed. The reason for this is that the optical center of your eyes does not coincide with the rotational axis of your head. The same dynamics are at work when taking a panoramic shot. If the camera does not pivot at the right place, it will be very difficult (if not impossible) to stitch a panorama from these pictures.

Locating the nodal point for the camera/lens combination is one of the most important factors in ensuring a successful panoramic photography session. As the manufacturer typically does not provide the necessary information, the nodal point for the lens to be used must be calculated on your own. It is important to remember that the nodal point changes with the focal length and can have a different position, depending on the design of the lens. More information on the nodal points of various digital cameras can be found on the Internet at: http://www.360texas.com/tips/nodalpts.htm [status: March 10, 2004]. A list of nodal points for several lenses can be found at: http://frog.netperson.net/~wiz/lens_table_1.htm [status: March 10, 2004]. If the value for your camera is not listed there, you can calculate it yourself by applying the following method.

Calculating the nodal point presupposes a design allowing the camera to be swiveled in both horizontal directions above the rotating axis of the tripod. This design can come in the form of a special panoramic head provided by a tripod manufacturer (see Figure 2.6) or your own fabricated device, such as two diagonally opposed micro positioning plates.

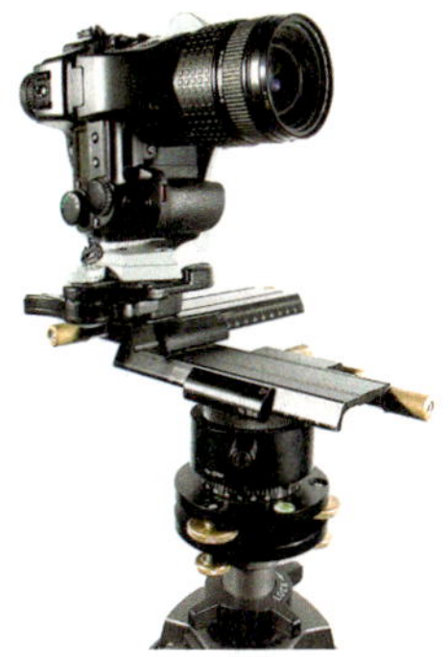

Figure 2.6
Using the panorama tripod head to conveniently adjust the nodal point

Now, locate a nearby and a distant vertical line that can be brought in congruence with each other (e.g. a pillar or post right in front of the camera and the corner of a house farther back). The tripod is erected about one half meter in front of the nearby vertical object so that the object is located exactly between the tripod and the distant vertical object. Then the tripod is horizontally aligned using a spirit level. If the tripod and the panoramic head are to have separately adjusting capability, the tripod is first roughly aligned. Fine tuning is then done on the tripod head.

Once the camera has been mounted on the tripod, the focal length setting to be used for the panoramic pictures is made at the lens. This setting must be able to be reproduced. If you do not have a lens with a fixed focal length, use the maximum wide angle setting of a zoom lens. Before doing this, though, you should be aware of the fact that zoom lenses have poorer optical quality.

The camera is then adjusted such that the horizontal center point of the lens is positioned exactly over the rotating axis of the tripod head. Now look at the view finder or on the connected monitor and focus on the two vertical lines selected. If the optical view finder is not installed above the lens (which is typically the case with compact cameras), it is better to use an LCD monitor. The closer both vertical objects are on the right side of the monitor, the better. The tripod may need to be moved a little and the horizontal position of the tripod head readjusted.

Once the position is okay on this side, the tripod head is turned to the right so that the objects located directly next to each other are just able to be seen on the left side of the monitor. The distance between the objects on the left must appear exactly as great as on the right. If this is not the case, the camera can be moved forwards or backwards to compensate. As a check, swivel the camera back and forth several times. If the distance between both objects remains the same throughout the entire swivel range, the nodal point has been found.

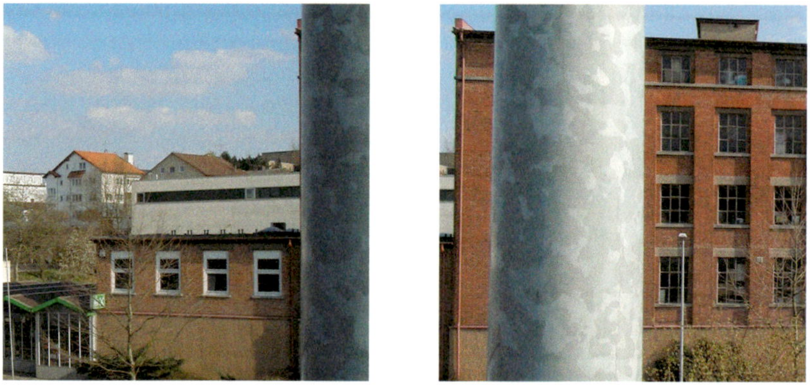

Figure 2.7
The nodal point is not precisely adjusted, thereby changing the distance between both lines

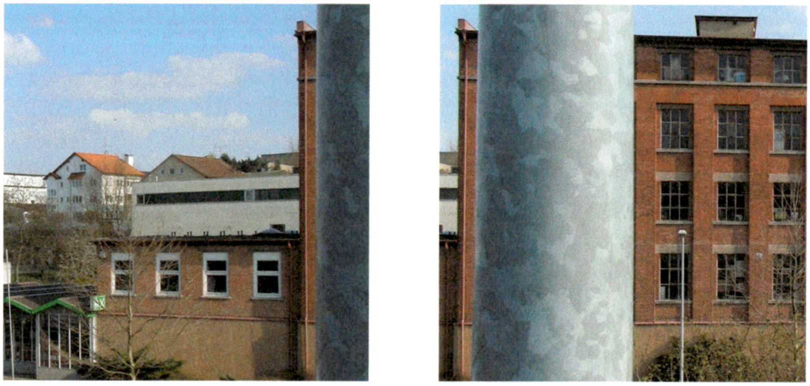

Figure 2.8
The nodal point is precisely adjusted and the distance between both lines does not change

Determining the nodal point of fisheye lenses

The straight depiction of lines makes this method a very easy and common one to use for normal lenses. Due to the radially distorted proportions and curved lines characteristic of fisheye lenses, the distance between both vertical lines usually cannot be determined by looking at the view finder or LCD monitor.

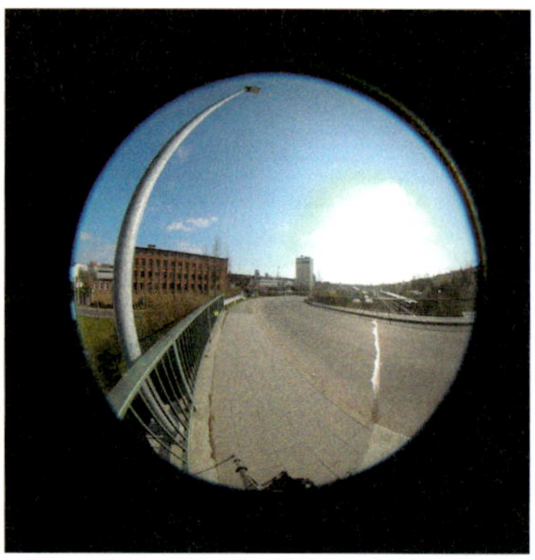

Figure 2.9
The distance between the lines normally cannot be determined for fisheye lenses by looking at the viewer or monitor

The method used for fisheye lenses is quite similar to the method already described for determining the nodal point. With a fisheye lens, it is recommended that a picture be taken in addition to looking at the view finder, as only an enlarged depiction will reveal in detail if the position of both vertical lines has changed over the pan. The camera is positioned on the tripod head such that the front edge of the lens roughly is on the rotating axis. Two pictures are taken in this position – one from the right and left sides. Note this camera position. The best strategy is to take up and log several positions so that the nodal point can be determined on screen by viewing the corresponding picture areas in enlarged format.

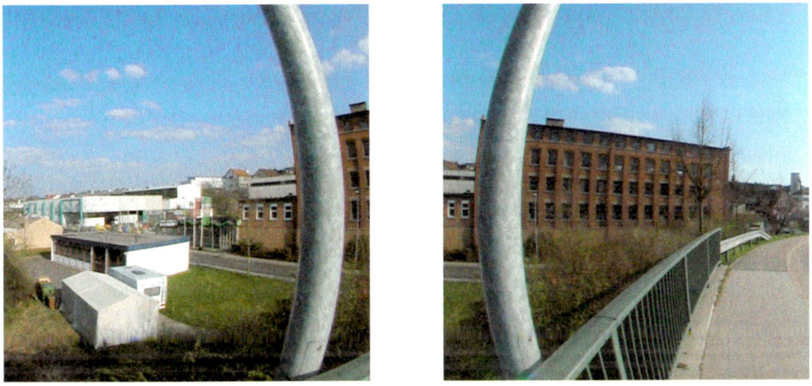

Figure 2.10
The distance between both lines becomes very clear when magnified

For both methods, it is advised that the determined settings be recorded or markings be made on the tripod head. Doing this will eliminate the need to find the right camera position when doing the next panorama shooting.

The nodal point position determined should be noted for both methods

3. Photo technology and techniques

3.1 Differences between analog and digital

When looking for a suitable camera, buyers have the option of choosing between analog and digital technology. Both solutions have their advantages and disadvantages in specific application areas and are explained in more detail in the following sections. Production-related issues are also covered.

With an analog camera, it is imperative that good film be used in order to ensure high quality pictures (see chapter 3.2.1). Generally speaking, higher resolutions can be obtained with analog cameras than with today's commercially available digital counterparts. However, the end resolution is dependent on how the pictures are digitalized. The film either can be brought to a photo developer and digitalized using professional drum scanners, or scanned at home (see chapter 3.2.2).

Here, digital cameras clearly have an advantage in terms of faster production times. Also in cases where many shots need to be taken (such as for a virtual tour), the use of a digital camera is recommended. Instead of using film material to take the pictures, light-sensitive CCD or CMOS chips are used. After the pictures are taken, they are stored in an on-board memory chip and can be downloaded to a notebook computer at any time to check their appropriateness. Now let's compare this production path to that of analog cameras, whose film only has room for a maximum of 36 pictures (at which point new film must be inserted). In order to view the pictures, they first must be developed and digitalized for editing on the computer. High quality digitalization of a large number of pictures is time-consuming and expensive.

Currently, most cameras being used are still cameras, although video cameras also could be used. The problem with today's commercially available video cameras, though, is that they only produce a resolution of 72 dpi for a 1024 x 768 pixel frame. There are also video cameras with an integrated memory chip for taking individual pictures; here, the resolution is a factor of the on-board CCD chip (as is the case with digital still cameras).

3.1.1 Analog technology

Advantages

- Higher resolutions can be obtained than with commercially available digital cameras.
- Analog cameras usually are less expensive than high resolution digital cameras.
- There is a larger selection of high quality lenses for analog cameras.

Disadvantages

- The editing process takes more time than with digital cameras (due to the development process).
- Pictures need to be converted to digital format after development and - more often than not - corrected for color. Retouching dust and scratched areas may be necessary.

3.1.2 Digital technology

Advantages

- Pictures can be viewed on site, making it possible to retake individual shots or an entire picture sequence.
- It takes less time to produce a panorama, as there is no need to develop film.
- Pictures do not need to be scanned and then corrected for dust and scratch marks.
- Immediate display of the image on the built-in screen makes it easier (and faster) to achieve good results.

Disadvantages

- Compared to high-end scans of film material, today's digital cameras traditionally have a poorer resolution.
- Memory chips are considerably more expensive than film. If many high resolution pictures need to be taken, a computer or a mobile hard disk must be brought along to download these pictures at regular intervals (thereby freeing up available camera memory).
- Professional digital cameras with high resolution have a higher purchase price than comparable analog cameras.

3.2 Analog photography

3.2.1 Film material

The three most commonly used types of film material are black-and-white, color negative and color slide film. For interactive panoramas, it is recommended that color film be used, as black-and-white panoramas typically make an impact when special effects are used (such as directly contrasting a historical and a current panorama). An example can be found at: http://www.pbs.org/wnet/newyork/hidden/columbuscircle/cc-pano.mov [status: May 8, 2004]. Choosing color film does not limit your options later on, as a color photo can be converted to a black-and-white image at any time with an editing program.

Color negative film

Color negative film, on the other hand, shows inverted luminance and color values after development. These color negatives are changed into positive paper pictures by an additional step. Depending on the laboratory used, this color conversion process often yields less than perfect color fidelity. For digital image editing and screen display later on, the negative strips or developed paper prints need to be scanned (see chapter 3.2.2). Color negative film has a higher luminance or contrast range than color slide film.

Color slide film

With color slide film, the altered chemical layer of the film material produces an orthochromatic image as early as the development process. This is why color fidelity is greater here. In order to view a color slide, a slide viewer or projector is needed to magnify the image. Color slides also need to be digitalized before they can be edited on the computer (see chapter 3.2.2.3).

Daylight and artificial light film

Once a decision has been made whether to use color negative or color slide material, the next step is to select the color range of the film. Here, a distinction is made between daylight and artificial light film. With daylight film, the ratio of blue to red is adjusted to the color temperature of common daylight (approx. 5600 Kelvin). If this type of film is used in an artificially lit setting, the colors appear warmer and slightly red cast. Artificial light film is just the opposite. This film reacts much more sensitively to blue and balances the color temperature of artificial light (approx. 3,200 Kelvin) to a neutral level. When artificial light film is used in broad daylight, the resulting pictures have a definite bluish cast. In a mixed light setting, it is best to determine what part of the color spectrum is more dominant in the picture and should be prominently displayed.

Film speed (ISO)

Different film speeds are available for each type of film material. Film speed is given in accordance with the International Organization for Standardization, or ISO. The higher the number, the greater the light sensitivity of the film. Film with a greater light sensitivity allows for properly lit shots in unfavorable light settings, however the surface of the film is rougher in texture, which often results in reduced clarity. When enough light is available, a film with a low ISO number should be used because of the finer structure and better picture quality. A 100 ISO film can be sufficient for outdoor shots, however 200 ISO film is recommended for exposures in interior settings so that the darker areas receive appropriate delineation.

Identical film material should be used for a series of panoramic pictures

If more than one roll of film is used for a panorama or object series, it must be ensured that the same film material is used for all exposures. Otherwise, unpleasant differences in color may result.

3.2.2 Scanners

Before pictures taken by an analog camera can be further processed, they first need to be digitalized. This either can take place directly in the laboratory following development, or at home with your own scanner. This chapter explains the differences between the various types of scanners and offers a brief overview of the technology used in the scanning process.

3.2.2.1 How scanners work

A scanner is equipped with light-sensitive sensors. A light ray emitted by a sensor scans the text or picture, the reflection of which is then recorded by the sensor and converted into digital information. During this process, the image is broken down into individual picture elements, or pixels. The brightness and color information created for each of these pixels is transferred to the computer. Only when this digital information has been received by the computer can the picture(s) be edited.

3.2.2.2 Scanning resolution

Scanning resolution is given in ppi or dpi

Scanning resolution generally is simplified to mean the number of pixels per inch, or ppi, with which the image is recorded. Dots per inch, or dpi, is another form of measurement frequently used. A linear scan line consists of a series of light-sensitive elements. The resolution of a particular scanner is the sum of the pixels recorded per line in one direction. The more pixels per line, the higher the resolution. The resolution in the scanning direction, however does not need to be identical to the resolution defined by the scan line. This is why many scanners are categorized as having such resolutions as 600 x 1,200 ppi. Here, the lower resolution in the one direction is mathematically increased by interpolation so that the picture has the right aspect ratio and does not appear distorted.

Scanning resolution should not be set too low or too high

When choosing your scanning resolution, remember that higher resolutions improve the quality of the picture. A high pixel count also has certain disadvantages, such as large file sizes and increased editing times. Once the intention of a picture is known, it makes little sense to scan at a higher resolution than necessary. The right scanning resolution can be determined based on the resolution of the output. Most scanner software allows you to directly enter the output size and resolution, from which the required scanning resolution is then automatically calculated.

3.2.2.3 Types of scanners

Color scanners come in many designs and sizes for a wide variety of applications and needs. Different models operate differently and deliver varying levels of quality, which makes selecting the right unit a task not to be underestimated.

The most affordable models currently on the market can be purchased for less than US $ 100, while professional scanners cost US $ 6,000 and more. Between these two extremes is a broad range of intermediate scanners that continues to gain market share and deliver astonishing results capable of achieving professional picture quality.

Hand scanners

Hand scanners are manually operated

Mobile hand scanners are small and attractively priced. They are operated by hand and therefore do not produce the accurate results characteristic of flatbed scanners. These scanners are swept across the image much like using a computer mouse. Digitalizing larger images requires several sweeps. A steady hand, uniform sweeping speed and an edge to guide the scanner are needed in order to produce useable results. The advantages of the hand scanner are mobility and low price.

Feed scanners

Feed scanners feature a pull-in mechanism similar to that used in fax machines

This scanner type has greater accuracy than hand scanners, as it is equipped with a paper infeed. Just like with a fax machine, images are automatically pulled in and then scanned. Feed scanners can handle widths of up to 9.8" (25 cm). A A4 page be scanned in lengthways at a resolution of 200 to 800 ppi.

Photo scanners

Photo scanners typically are feed scanners

These devices are feed scanners, however they are used exclusively for scanning photos, from passport pictures to panoramic formats up to 4 x 11.5" (10 x 29 cm). Depending on the model, 35 mm slides and negative strips also can be scanned.

Flatbed scanners

Flatbed scanners scan images similar to that of a copier

Here, the image is placed face down on a glass plate. This method not only allows photos and pictures to be scanned, but also larger items such as books and newspapers. As with a photo copier, the images must be positioned flat on the glass plate so that the scan can reproduce the correct clarity. The lowest possible resolution of such devices is around 300 x 600 ppi, with the upper limit currently at 8,000 x 8,000 ppi. Such high imaging quality, however, is not attributed to the physical resolution, but the interpolated resolution of these scanners.

Many flatbed scanners have optional or integrated transparency units with which slides and negatives also can be scanned. The downside, however, is that the resolution typically is less than ideal for such small images, with the result being a lower density range than that offered by film scanners specially designed for this purpose.

Slide and film scanners

Film scanners are specifically designed to optimally scan the format of the respective film material

When scanning slides and negatives, it is necessary that the film be illuminated from the back. These specialized film scanners offer this feature and usually are capable of scanning positive and negative film in various formats. The scanning resolution is optimized for such small images and the results are of better quality than slide or negative scans made by the transparency unit of a flatbed scanner. Another advantage that many film scanners have is the option of focusing the unit right at the film level. This improves the scanning result. The optical resolution of film scanners can reach and exceed 2,700 x 2,700 ppi.

There are also film scanners that are equipped to scan APS film. Here, the film cassette is placed in the scanner, which automatically recognizes the type of film (negative or color slide film). Positioning of the pictures is handled by the bundled software.

Drum scanners

Professional drum scanners usually provide the highest quality results

Drum scanners are high performance machines that, due to their high purchase price, traditionally are used almost exclusively in professional reproduction studios to make digital copies of color photographs. In place of CCD sensors, drum scanners have highly sensitive photo amplifiers (so-called photo multiplier tubes, or PMT) that record and amplify color data. The image is fixed to a rotating drum that is swept by a scanning head line for line. Due to the precise mechanics involved, these units attain very high resolutions. It is critical, however, that images be positioned absolutely planar on the drum for correct scanning.

3.2.2.4 Scanner software

The scanner is only one part of the scanning process; the scanner software used and its configuration also play a role in determining the quality of the results. Most of the time, scanner software recognizes and takes into account the various properties of scanned material (such as photos, pictures from newspapers and magazines, graphics and text) right out of the box. The descreening feature can be used to counteract the disturbing moiré patterns that occur with printed images. Here, the user normally can select one of several raster widths. A preview window typically offers the option of sectioning off and magnifying an area of the picture as well as filter functions to manipulate the image right during the scanning process. Most scanner software automatically configures settings such as resolution, contrast and brightness based on the type, size and quality of the image. These default settings can, however, be manually changed for the majority of software products.

The results of a scan are considerably influenced by the scanner software used

3.2.3 Picture CDs

Another way to convert analog pictures to digital format is to go to your local photo developer for a picture CD. If negative film was used, you can ask for a picture CD in addition to the developed pictures. The only drawback, however, is that the resolution for such package deals usually does not exceed 1.3 megapixels. For higher quality digital images, it is better to take selected negatives or slides to a professional laboratory for scanning. Your photo material will be scanned at a resolution of 6 megapixels and higher (on request) by commercial grade drum scanners. After scanning, the pictures are burned to a CD. The cost per scan is around US $ 1.00 and roughly 10 days currently are required for processing.

When looking for a picture CD, close attention should be paid to the varying levels of resolution offered

The above methods for creating a picture CD are offered by Kodak and other companies. At Kodak, the simpler and less expensive route is termed the Kodak Picture CD (http://www.kodak.com/eknec/PageQuerier.jhtml?pq-locale=en_US&pq-path=511 [status: April 27, 2004]). The higher quality, but more expensive option is known as the Kodak Photo CD (http://www.kodak.com/US/en/digital/products/photoCD.shtml [status: April 27, 2004]).

3.3 Digital photography

As the pictures taken need to be in digital form anyway in order to be edited on the computer later on, using a digital camera accelerates and simplifies the production process. When taking digital photos, it is useful to bring a notebook computer to the set, as the shots can be better assessed on a larger screen than on the small camera display. If many pictures are taken – such as is the case with virtual tours – these can be downloaded from the camera chip directly to the computer on site. A notebook also gives you the ability to stitch and see how well the pictures "fit together" without having to leave the premises. When viewing the pictures it is a good idea to leave your set standing, as you may discover that you need to retake some shots.

Resolution

Digital photos have a lower resolution when compared to physical film. This is more of a technicality than anything else, though, as the pictures will be compressed for Web presentation anyway. Nevertheless, a good compromise should be found between resolution and file size. Too high of a resolution can cause the camera and memory card to take extensive amounts of time to save a single picture, which in turn leaves you waiting for your next shot. Too low of a resolution, on the other hand, considerably reduces the picture quality. A good strategy to follow is to select the highest resolution possible (without creating memory problems), carry out all of the necessary steps, then size down the pictures for Web publication. To justify this thinking, ask yourself the following question: Wouldn't it be better to have more material to work with than not enough?

Compression

Additionally, it is recommended that pictures be taken uncompressed. Most digital cameras offer TIFF and/or RAW formats for this. If pictures are taken in JPG format, the compression algorithms used could lead to data (i.e. picture quality) being lost each time the image is saved. The consequence: Important details could be irretrievably lost. In an uncompressed format such as TIFF and with a high resolution, you also have the option of using the pictures for print publication.

Focal length multiplier

If a digital single lens reflex camera with an interchangeable lens designed for analog cameras is used, attention must be paid to the focal length multiplier. The chip found in digital cameras is smaller than actual film. As such, the focal length of the lens is proportionately extended by the amount (factor) that the chip is smaller than the film. The value of the focal length multiplier usually can be found in the technical specifications that came with the respective camera. A common factor is 1.6. In this case, a 20 mm lens would have the optical effect of a 32 mm lens. If a digital camera with an integrated lens is used, it can be safely assumed that the manufacturer has optimally configured the lens system to the size of the chip and that the focal length stated is comparable to 35 mm format. Knowing the exact values for focal length and field of view are paramount when calculating the number of individual pictures for a panoramic presentation (see chapter 2.2.4).

3.4 Tips for taking panoramic pictures

The recommendations given in this chapter primarily are in reference to panoramic photography. Tips for taking pictures of objects can be found in chapter 8.2.4.

3.4.1 General tips

Unlike conventional photography, the challenge with panoramic photography is to ensure that each picture has the ideal amount of illumination and that all of the pictures together accurately represent the environment captured. If pictures are taken exclusively in daylight or artificially lit settings, there isn't a great deal of problems to avoid. When mixed light situations are introduced, however, it is much more difficult to retain a uniform panoramic color scheme.

Select identical exposure settings

It is recommended that identical settings are used when taking all pictures for a panoramic sequence. These settings include the ISO value, aperture and exposure time. With the exposure memory of the camera, all pictures can be conveniently taken with the same exposure settings. This avoids contrasts in illumination between the individual pictures. To this end, it is a good idea to save the exposure level of a picture that represents a good average of the scene's light spectrum. With digital cameras, the white value should be the same for all pictures and manually adjusted if possible.

A large depth of field typically is desired when taking panoramic shots. In order to achieve a high depth of field, a small focal aperture (small aperture = large f-number) should be selected. The level of light is influenced by selecting an appropriate exposure time. Longer exposure times are not problematic, as the camera usually is mounted on a tripod for the panoramic session.

Panoramic series should be filmed either in sunlit or in cloudy conditions

When taking indoor and outdoor pictures with sunlight, there is the risk that the panoramic shots will reveal fluctuations in brightness. This is why it makes sense to film your panorama either in sunlit or in cloudy conditions. Not doing so will introduce varying patches of light in your panorama.

If pictures are taken in sunlight, you should ensure that your own shadow is not photographed as well. Otherwise, this (generally) undesirable effect will need to be removed later on with computer software.

Objects moving in the wind can cause problems

Taking pictures in windy weather brings its own set of problems, as plants can be blown around and be in a different location in each shot. After stitching, the plants appear “blurred” in the panorama. This effect can, of course, be intentional. Usually, however, a clear picture of the setting is favorable, which is why taking outdoor panoramic shots in strong winds should be avoided.

A flash should not be used

A flash should be avoided altogether, as the illumination generated normally is too intense and too targeted. More dispersed illumination is a better alternative and can be achieved by using a flat reflector that amplifies the existing light, or a floodlight with a diffuser. In order to ensure that this additional light does not create an unbalanced effect on the overall panorama, the light must be somewhat broader in scope than the field of view of an individual picture. Thus, the light must be swiveled along with the camera for each exposure.

The range of contrast can be increased with High Dynamic Range (HDR)

If the differences in the level of illumination are so severe that, when taking indoor shots, for example, no distinction can be made among windows through which light shines, a complex but very effective technique known as HDR (High Dynamic Range) can be applied. Here, a series of pictures is taken at various exposure levels for each individual picture. These pictures are then merged using special HDR software to create a single picture that has a high range of contrast. The resulting picture captures the bright and dark areas in great detail (see chapter 4.2).

The camera's position plays a major role in the overall impression made by a panorama

When photographing in interior spaces, it is important that the camera be positioned as centrally as possible in the horizontal and vertical planes. If the tripod is not set high enough, the horizontal plane will appear too low in comparison to the actual plane the observer would experience if they were physically there. Likewise, it is recommended that roughly the same distance be kept between all of the walls. If distances fluctuate too much, this will have a negative effect on the panorama – the mid-point of the scene disappears.

The camera and tripod should not be moved throughout the shooting session

Another point to keep in mind is that the tripod itself never should move during a panoramic shooting. If the pictures are taken from a different pivoting point, it will be very difficult, if not impossible, to complete the stitching process. A camera level will ensure an exact horizontal position. As every movement of the tripod and the camera should be avoided after adjustment, it is beneficial to use the camera's timer feature or a remote control release.

It is advantageous to rotate the camera clockwise, as the majority of stitching programs are configured for editing in this direction. This way, the pictures will not have to be resorted. Although most stitching programs are capable of resorting pictures – even if they already were imported for editing – it is just easier when the right sequence is chosen at the beginning.

Photographing moving objects can lead to problems

Moving picture elements are almost always problematic, as they are in a different position in each picture of the panorama. If, for example, someone who shouldn't be present in the panorama moves in front of the lens, it is best to take several shots from the same camera position. The superfluous pictures can be thrown away afterwards.

Moving objects that are photographed must not be in the overlapping section the pictures, as they will appear faded in or half present after stitching. Equally as problematic are large monochrome areas, which can create problems for some stitching programs. To discover which panoramic technique is best in which situation, refer to chapter 11.

3.4.2 Tips for taking pictures with digital cameras

It is recommended that you take pictures only with fully charged batteries, as the battery compartment is located on the underside of some camera models. This is where the tripod connects to the camera, which should not be moved when taking a series of panoramic shots, as this will necessitate readjustment.

During a panoramic photo shooting, the LCD monitor does not need to be used once settings such as exposure time, aperture and white balance have been configured, unless some of the pictures are going to be taken with alternative settings. The batteries will last much longer with the LCD monitor switched off.

Direct sunlight should be avoided when using a digital camera

When outdoor pictures are taken, there is an inherent risk of encountering problems with direct sunlight. Such light can cause the CCD sensors to overexpose, which is known as "blooming" in digital photography. When this happens, the CCD chips reach a maximum load and the recorded picture information at this point appears white without any other contrast. With extreme overexposure, this excessive load can transfer to neighboring CCD elements and lead to large areas of the picture appearing white. In order to prevent this negative effect, direct sunlight should be avoided. To this end, it is advisable that you wait until the sun is a little lower in the sky or has disappeared behind a cloud, for example. The sun also can be covered up (such as with your hand), however this area will need to be retouched afterwards. The effort is worth your while, as the result typically looks better than an overexposed picture.

3.4.3 Tips for taking pictures with analog cameras

Moving the camera when changing film during a panoramic photo shooting can negatively influence your setup. The worst that can happen is that the pictures you take create problems when trying to stitch them. For this reason, you should always ensure before shooting that not too many pictures have been taken on the roll; alternatively, you can insert a fresh roll for every panoramic session.

4. Special correction methods

4.1 Correcting image distortion

Image distortion usually can be avoided by using high quality lenses. In the event that undesirable errors crop up, there is a good chance that they can be corrected when the appropriate software is used. The following chapter describes the correction options at your disposal for the most frequently occurring image distortion errors. The list of manufacturers near the end of this book includes additional information on image editing software suited to correcting image distortion (see chapter B.1.9).

4.1.1 Correcting optical distortion

Pincushion and barrel distortion characteristic of wide angle lenses can be corrected with a software application called Panorama Tools (PanoTools). PanoTools can be used to fix individual shots as well as an entire series of panoramic pictures. When doing normal stitching with PanoTools, any distortion is corrected such that the pictures are able to be ideally converged to form a panorama. The following explains how linear distortion in individual pictures is corrected.

PanoTools can be found on the CD at the following paths: \Demo versions\Mac and \Demo versions\PC

In order to determine the degree of distortion associated with a specific lens, it is recommended that correction be made with an individual shot based on a reference picture. Once the degree of distortion has been determined for the lens, all additional pictures taken with this lens can be edited using the same correction values. For this correction, it is best to have a picture with a grid pattern, which can easily be created with almost every drawing program. This grid pattern is then shot using the lens to be corrected. Due to the structure of the grid, it can be identified very clearly as to the nature of a distorted area (i.e. pincushion or barrel shaped distortion). In order to ensure a perfect result, it is critical that the camera be exactly positioned when photographing such a grid pattern.

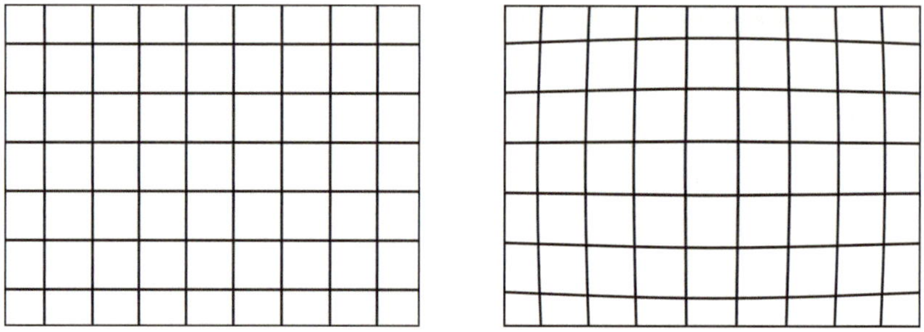

Figure 4.1
Undistorted reference picture (left) and barrel-shaped distortion (right)

Before beginning with the correction process, make sure that the monitor itself is free of distortion. Most models allow distortion to be calibrated via the built-in monitor menu. Here, too, calibration can be done using a grid pattern.

The PanoTools suite has plug-ins for Adobe's Photoshop image editing software. These so-called filters can be used to make various corrections to a picture. The *Correct* filter, for example, can correct linear and perspective distortion as well as chromatic aberration. PanoTools determines the corrective action based on a polynomial function. In order to execute this function, four coefficients are required: a, b, c and d (see Figure 4.3). These coefficients have different values for each lens.

The reference picture with a large number of straight lines is used to determine whether the lens in question tends to produce barrel or pincushion distortion. The most common type of lens error is that of barrel distortion. If the distortion is to be corrected in Photoshop with PanoTools filters, the dialog box is invoked via *Filter > Panorama Tools > Correct*.

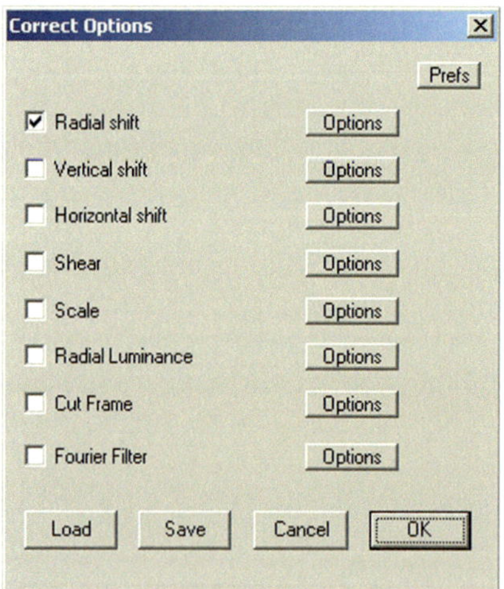

Figure 4.2
Distortion correction via the *Correct* PanoTools filter for Photoshop

This type of distortion requires the *Radial shift* function. An additional dialog box is opened via *Options*.

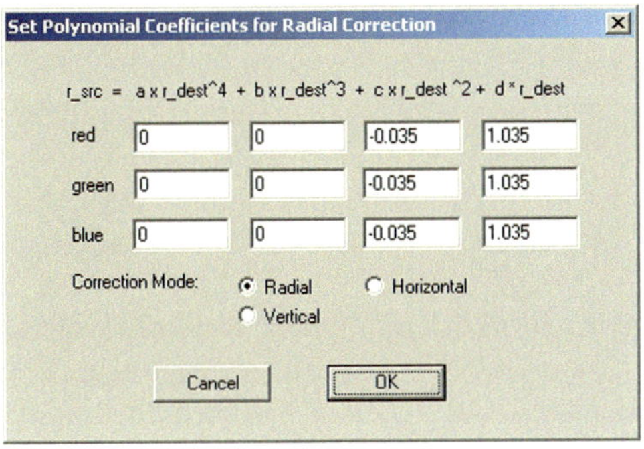

Figure 4.3
Entry of the coefficients "a", "b", "c" and "d" for the *Radial shift* function

In this dialog box, the values for coefficients "a", "b", "c" and "d" can be selectively entered. To correct distortion, the values for red, green and blue each are identically selected. Negative coefficients will correct barrel-shaped distortion, while positive values eliminate pincushion errors. It is recommended that you first change the "c" coefficient and do not alter the "a" and "b" values (i.e. leave them at "0"). If the picture to be corrected is not to be changed in size, the value for "d" must be selected such that the sum of the coefficients "a", "b", "c" and "d" yields the number "1" (a + b + c + d = 1). By *Correction Mode*, *Radial* should be checked. Pressing the *OK* button applies this function to the respective picture. For barrel distortion, you can apply the values from Figure 4.3 for an initial test run and optimize them in additional trials for your specific lens. When the previously curved lines appear straight, the correction of the distortion was successful.

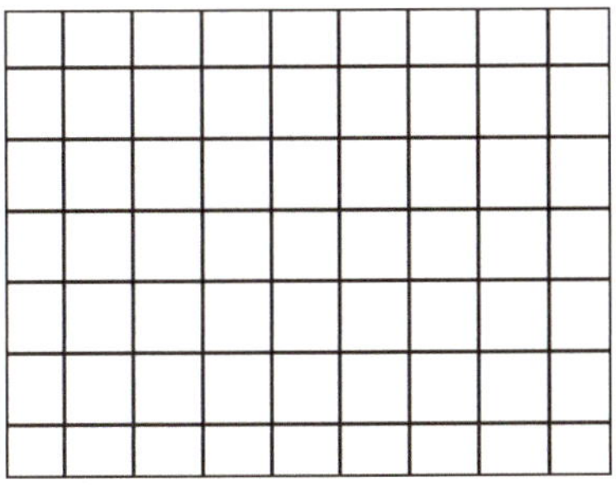

Figure 4.4
The previously distorted picture after the correction using PanoTools

It is advisable to save your correction values so that all additional pictures taken with the respective camera/lens combination can be quickly and accurately corrected.

Additional information on correcting distortion errors with PanoTools can be found at: http://home.no.net/dmaurer/~dersch/barrel/barrel.html [status: March 24, 2004] and http://www.all-in-one.ee/~dersch/barrel/barrel.html [status: March 24, 2004]

4.1.2 4.1.2 Correcting perspective distortion

Perspective distortion, an effect that especially occurs when tall buildings are photographed, can be quickly and easily corrected using image editing software such as Photoshop. Before perspective distortion is corrected, however, pincushion or barrel shaped distortion should be removed (see chapter 4.1.1).

A grid placed over the picture will assist in aligning the lines exactly vertical. In Photoshop, trace to *View > Show > Grid*. The actual perspective correction work is started by tracing to *Edit > Transform*, then clicking on *Perspective*. By depressing the mouse button, the corners of the picture are brought into the desired position.

Figure 4.5
Correction of perspective distortion in Photoshop

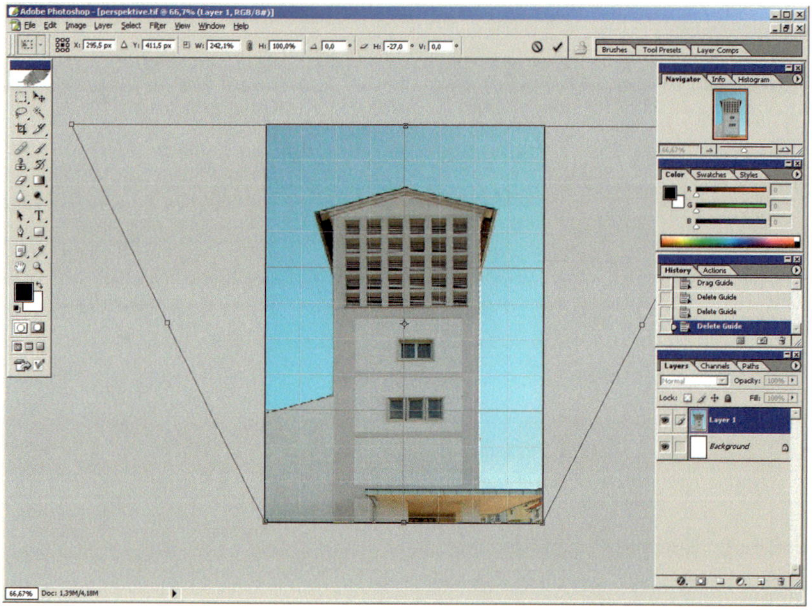

If the theme was captured at a slight angle, the horizontal lines also will need to be corrected. This can be done by tracing to *Edit > Transform > Distort*. Here, the corner of the picture in question is pulled to the desired position with the mouse button depressed until all lines appear straight.

The result of the correction can be seen in Figure 4.6. Correcting perspective distortion isn't always favorable; in many architectural shots, for example, this natural phenomenon is purposely left in for effect.

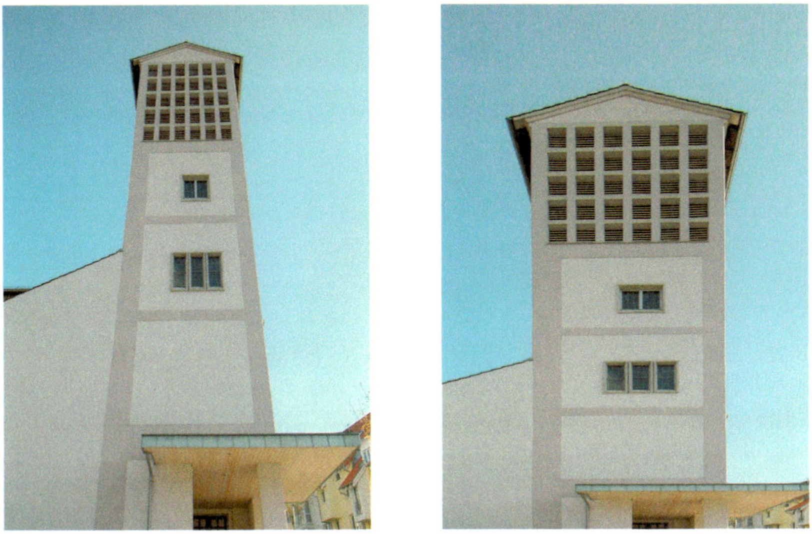

Figure 4.6
Left: distorted
Right: corrected

4.1.3 Correcting vignetting

Vignetting, a shading effect that increases in intensity toward the borders of a picture and is primarily associated with wide angle lenses, can be corrected using PanoTools filters for Photoshop. The *Correct* filter, for example, is capable of treating any undesired vignetting. In order to determine the intensity and scope of vignetting associated with a particular lens, it is recommended that you take a picture of an evenly lit, bright surface.

To correct vignetting in Photoshop, invoke the PanoTools dialog box by tracing to *Filters > Panorama Tools > Correct.*

PanoTools can be found on the CD at the following paths: \Demo versions\Mac and \Demo versions\PC

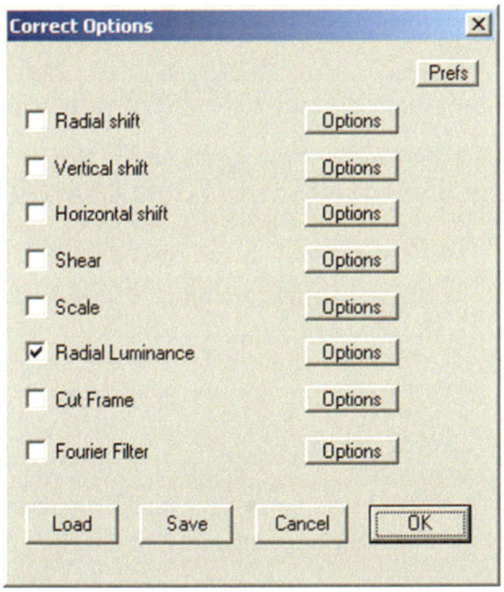

Figure 4.7
Correction of vignetting using a PanoTools filter *Correct* for Photoshop

This type of lens error requires use of the *Radial Luminance* feature. An additional dialog box is opened via *Options*.

Figure 4.8
Entry of correction values for the red, green and blue color channels

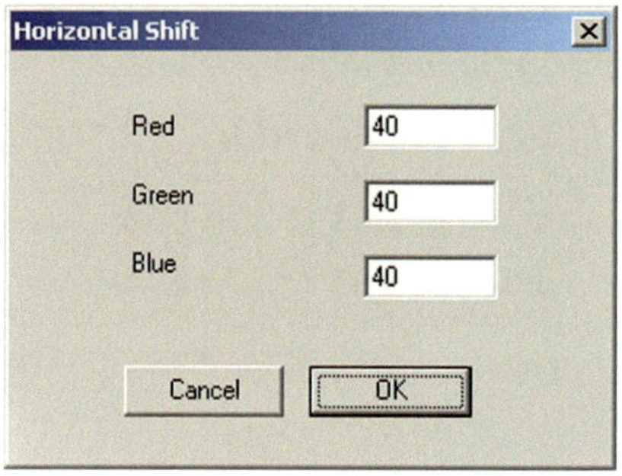

In the *Horizontal Shift* dialog box, the values for red, green and blue can be individually entered. In order to achieve a uniform result, the values for all three colors are identically selected for vignetting correction. The vignetting effect is corrected by darkening the center of the picture and brightening the perimeter. The factor used to make the correction is the half the value that was selected in the dialog box. For example, if a value of 40 is entered, the perimeter is brightened by a factor of 20 and the center darkened by a factor of 20. For an initial test run, you can apply the values from Figure 4.8 and optimize them in additional trials for your specific lens. When the previously darkened perimeter appears balanced with the center of the picture, the correction was successful.

Figure 4.9
Left: with vignetting
Right: corrected picture

It is advisable to save your correction values so that all additional pictures taken with the respective camera/lens combination can be quickly and accurately corrected.

4.1.4 Correcting chromatic aberration

This type of distortion error occurs because shortwave light (blue) is refracted more intensely by a lens than long wave light (red) and the light rays no longer have a common focal point. The difference in the depth of focus associated with the primary colors red, blue and green is also known as lateral and longitudinal color errors. Chromatic aberration becomes visible with blurriness and color fringing, especially in areas of a picture with a high bright/dark contrast. Frequently, however, this color fringing only becomes really noticeable when magnified. Most lenses are achromatically corrected so that two of the primary colors (blue and red) are focused in a focal plane. This optical system is known as achromat. A lens that is optimized for all three primary colors is the apochromat lens. If longitudinal color errors still can be recognized as color fringes in the picture, the distortion can be corrected using PanoTools filters for Photoshop. Before chromatic distortion is corrected, however, pincushion or barrel shaped distortion affecting all three color channels should be removed (see chapter 4.1.1).

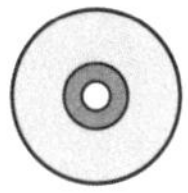

PanoTools can be found on the CD at the following paths: \Demo versions\Mac and \Demo versions\PC

In order to determine the intensity and scope of chromatic aberration associated with a particular lens, it is recommended that you take a picture of a uniform sample with a high bright/dark contrast. This can be a perforated plate lit from the back, for example.

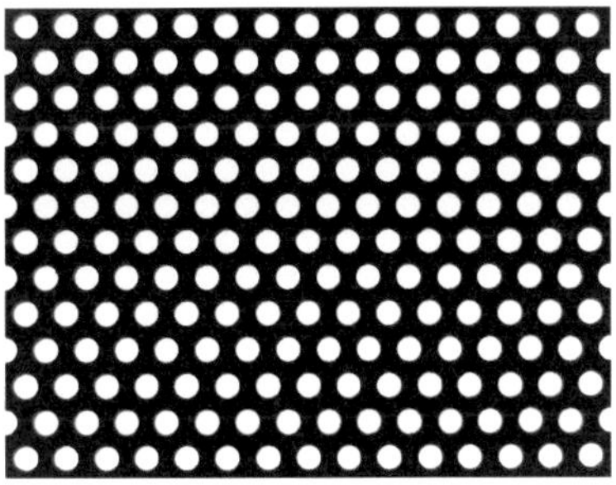

Figure 4.10
Perforated plate with high contrast for determining the scope of chromatic aberration

The scope of the chromatic aberration becomes visible by magnifying selected areas of the picture. To do this, it is best to select an area from the center of the picture as well as from any corner. This way, the magnified display will allow you to easily determine if the distortion travels horizontally, vertically or radially across the picture.

In Figure 4.11, the radial color fringing effect can't be overlooked. The same holds true for the offset red and blue color channels. As such, correction of chromatic aberration for the lens in question should focus on these two color channels and be done in a radial direction.

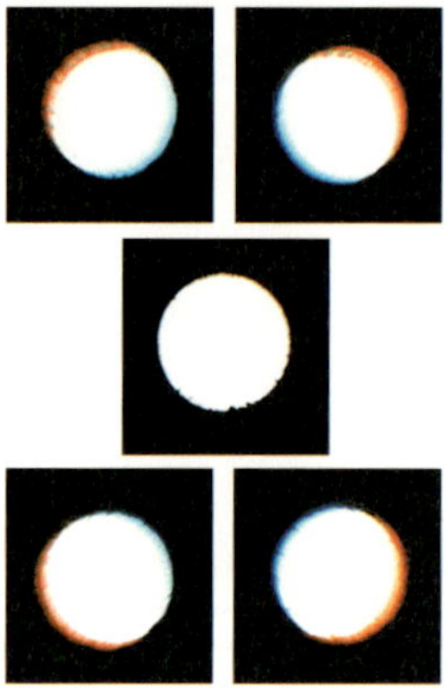

Figure 4.11
Magnifying specific areas of a picture makes the direction of the color fringing evident

If the distortion is to be corrected in Photoshop with PanoTools filters, the PanoTools dialog box is invoked via *Filter > Panorama Tools > Correct*.

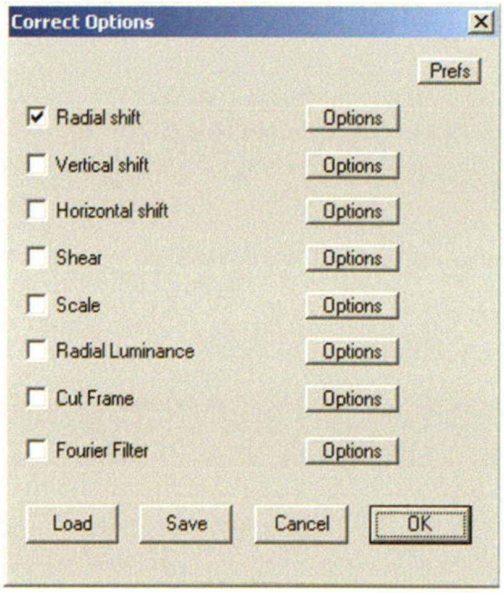

Figure 4.12
Correction of chromatic aberration via the *Correct* PanoTools filter for Photoshop

The *Radial shift* function is needed to correct chromatic aberration errors. An additional dialog box is opened via *Options*.

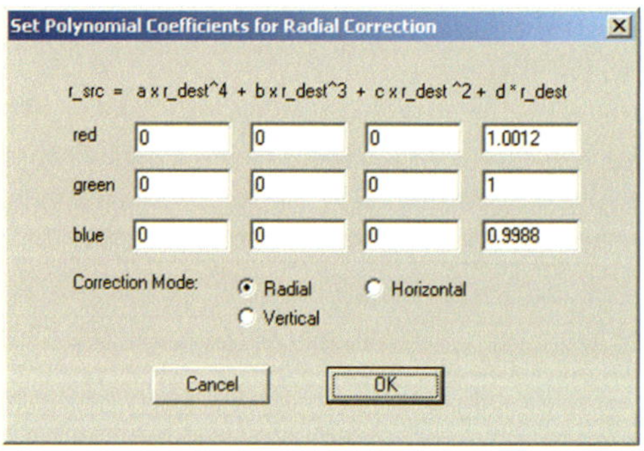

Figure 4.13
To correct color fringing, value "d" is individually changed for each color channel

In the *Set Polynomical Coefficients for Radial Correction* dialog box, the coefficients "a", "b", "c" and "d" can be selectively entered. To correct chromatic aberration, the values for red, green and blue must be selected with respect to the color fringing offset.

In our example (see Figure 4.11), the red color information appears to be slightly "smaller" and the blue color information slightly "larger", whereby these two terms refer to the actual scope of the color channels and not saturation. The scope of the individual color areas is influenced by coefficient "d". If the color channels are not to be adjusted in size, the value for "d" must be selected such that the sum of "a", "b", "c" and "d" yields the number "1" ($a + b + c + d = 1$). If, however, chromatic aberration is to be corrected, it is essential to know the change in size of the individual color areas. In the example, the red color channel should be slightly increased and the blue color channel slightly decreased. Here, the discoloration is corrected using the following values: coefficient "d" is set to "1.0012" for red, "1" for green and "0.9988" for blue. In Figure 4.11, it is quite evident that chromatic aberration appears in a radial pattern. Thus, the *Radial* function should be checked by *Correction Mode*. Pressing the *OK* button applies this function to the respective picture.

For an initial test run, you can apply the values from Figure 4.13 and optimize them in additional trials for your specific lens. When the previous distinctly visible color fringes appear milder and no longer are able to be perceived in the overall picture, the chromatic aberration correction was successful.

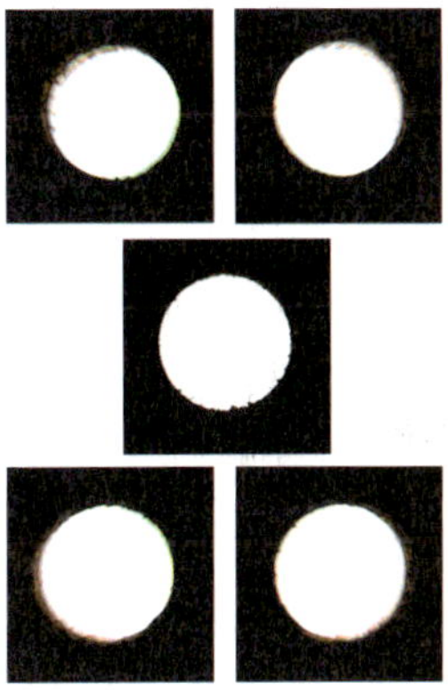

Figure 4.14
The enlarged picture area reveals the corrected chromatic aberration

It is advisable to save your correction values so that all additional pictures taken with the respective camera/lens combination can be quickly and accurately corrected.

4.2 High dynamic range

The dynamic range of a scene represents the range of contrast between the lightest and darkest areas of the picture. Almost all pictures have a high contrast ratio in which the light sources are directly present. A high dynamic range image is a picture that includes a higher range of contrast than that which can be photographed with a digital camera or film.

The HDR technique allows you to realistically portray scenes with a high range of contrast

A frequent problem in photography is that compromises in lighting need to be made when taking shots of a scene with a high range of contrast. When dark areas appear sufficiently lit with a particular setting, bright areas can be overexposed. If, on the other hand, the light exposure is adapted to these bright areas, the dark sections will appear too dark or even black without delineation. In order to avoid this, the high dynamic range technique can be applied. Dynamic range refers to the range of light and dark areas in a picture. High Dynamic Range (HDR) is a technique in which the range of contrast saved on a recording medium approaches the true contrast of a scene. When the HDR panoramic camera from Spheron is used, an automatic range of contrast of up to 26 aperture stops is possible when photographing (see chapter 7.2.1.2).

Panoramic camera with integrated HDR function

In order to extend the real range of contrast of a scene beyond the dynamic range of the film or digital chip, special HDR cameras can be used; alternatively, one can opt for the less expensive, but quite time-consuming method that involves taking a series of pictures at a number of different exposure levels. Here, as many pictures of a scene are taken from the exact same camera position as there are available aperture stops. The more individual pictures are taken, the more accurate the result. As this method would cost a tremendous amount of time for a complete set of panoramic pictures, three or six pictures per picture series should suffice for good HDR results. In any case, the extreme areas (i.e. those areas that are very bright and very dark) should be covered.

High Dynamic Range via picture series and HDR software

These individual pictures can be converged into an HDR picture using special HDR software such as HDR Shop. Other manufacturers of HDR software can be found in the list of manufacturers (see chapter B.1.6). The following explains how an HDR picture is created with HDR Shop.

Before an HDR picture can emerge from a series of shots taken at a particular exposure level, it is recommended that the specific *Camera Response Curve* be determined for each camera. The preset gamma value of 2.2 can be used, however most digital cameras have their own specific value. When the gamma value specific to a particular camera is used, the end result is improved primarily in the display of color. The shots taken to create the HDR picture can be incorporated in order to determine the Camera Response Curve. Tracing to *Create > Camera Response Curve Calibration* brings you to the characteristic curve menu.

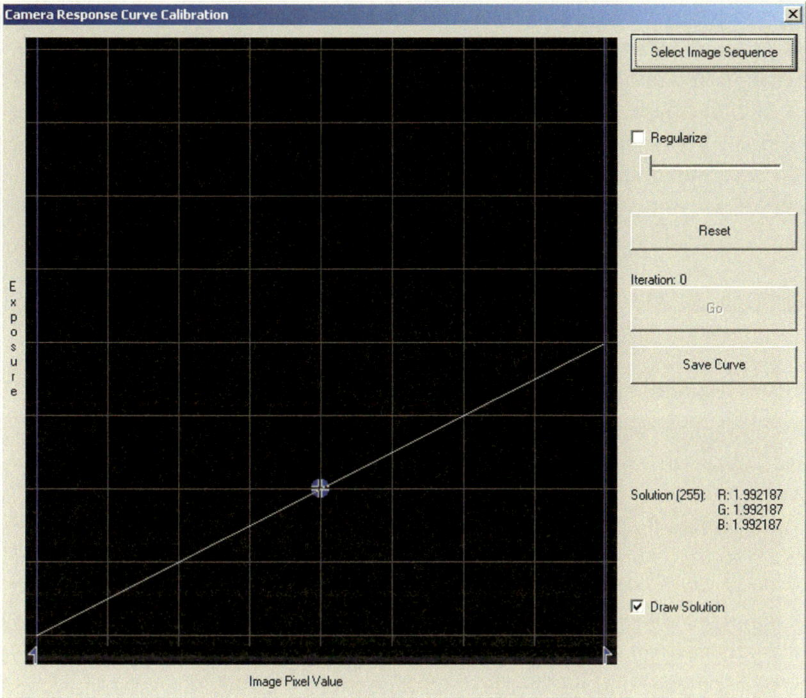

Figure 4.15
The *Camera Response Curve* editing window before determining the characteristic curve

Click on *Select Image Sequence* to access the corresponding submenu, where the relevant pictures can be loaded via *Load Images*.

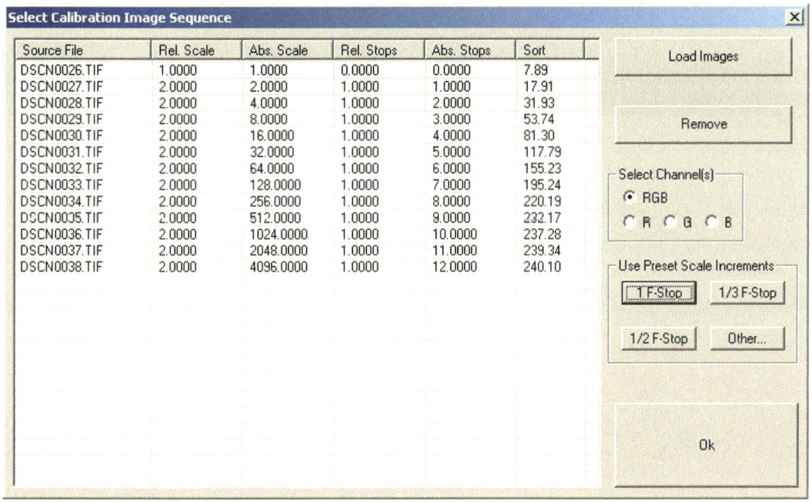

Source File	Rel. Scale	Abs. Scale	Rel. Stops	Abs. Stops	Sort
DSCN0026.TIF	1.0000	1.0000	0.0000	0.0000	7.89
DSCN0027.TIF	2.0000	2.0000	1.0000	1.0000	17.91
DSCN0028.TIF	2.0000	4.0000	1.0000	2.0000	31.93
DSCN0029.TIF	2.0000	8.0000	1.0000	3.0000	53.74
DSCN0030.TIF	2.0000	16.0000	1.0000	4.0000	81.30
DSCN0031.TIF	2.0000	32.0000	1.0000	5.0000	117.79
DSCN0032.TIF	2.0000	64.0000	1.0000	6.0000	155.23
DSCN0033.TIF	2.0000	128.0000	1.0000	7.0000	195.24
DSCN0034.TIF	2.0000	256.0000	1.0000	8.0000	220.19
DSCN0035.TIF	2.0000	512.0000	1.0000	9.0000	232.17
DSCN0036.TIF	2.0000	1024.0000	1.0000	10.0000	237.28
DSCN0037.TIF	2.0000	2048.0000	1.0000	11.0000	239.34
DSCN0038.TIF	2.0000	4096.0000	1.0000	12.0000	240.10

Figure 4.16
The individual pictures from the picture series are loaded

The pictures are automatically sorted according to their average level of brightness, which is given in the table (see Figure 4.16) in the column labeled *Sort*. The *Remove* button is pressed to delete any excess pictures that were loaded. *RGB* remains activated in the *Select Channels* field, as the characteristic curve is to be determined for all three color channels. The scale increment between the individual pictures is selected via *Use Preset Scale Increments*. This increment can be 1, 2 or 3 aperture stops (*F-Stops*) or be individually specified via *Other*. When all settings have been made, click on *OK* to switch back to the characteristic curve control panel. Here, *Go* is pressed to start calculation of the camera's characteristic curve. If the curve does not change after numerous iterations, the process can be prematurely aborted via *Stop*.

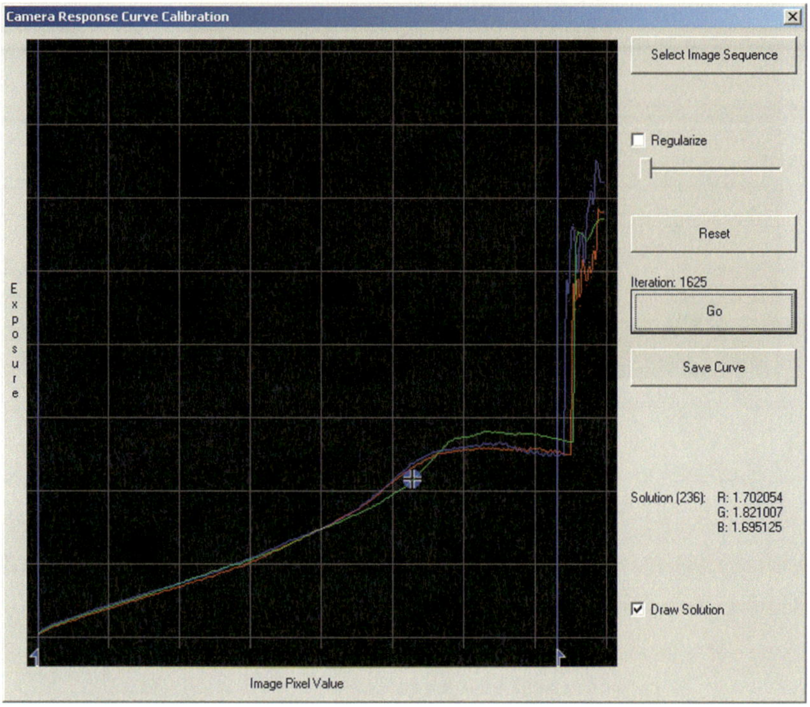

Figure 4.17 The *Camera Response Curve* is calculated based on the individual pictures

If the calculated curve shows severe jags or bumps, correction can be made. Simply execute the *Regularize* function and the corresponding controller, whereby the *Go* button must be pressed again to recalculate. When the curve has been straightened, it is saved by pressing *Save Curve* and can be invoked at any time for subsequent creation of the HDR picture.

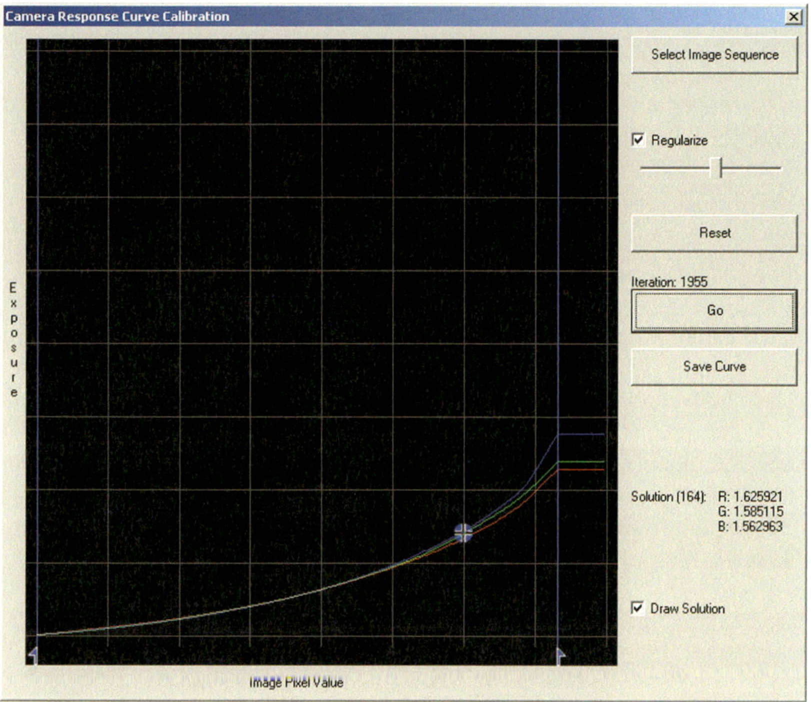

Figure 4.18
The characteristic curve can be optimized using the *Regularize* function

With this *Camera Response Curve*, an HDR picture now can be created from the individual pictures of the picture series. In order to edit this picture series with HDR Shop, the *Create > Assemble HDR from Image Sequence* function is invoked. *Load Images* imports the pictures.

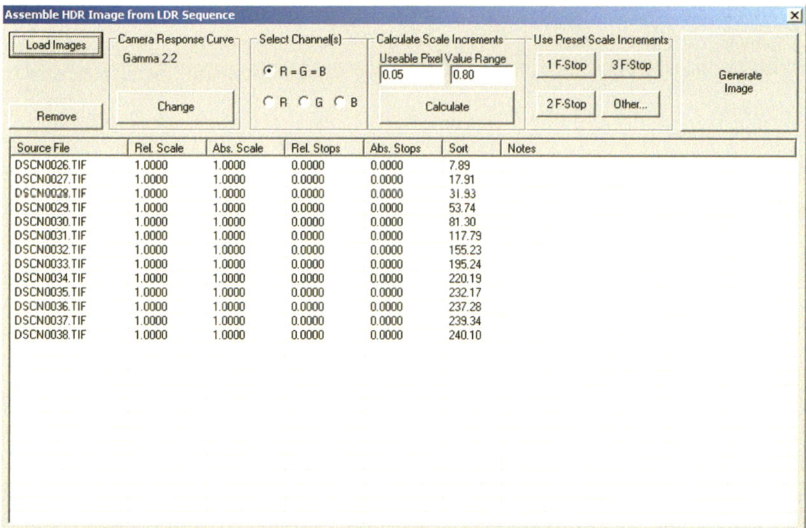

Figure 4.19
The individual pictures of a picture series are imported to create an HDR picture

The *Change* button is pressed to invoke the previously determined *Camera Response Curve.* To create an HDR picture from a picture series, the *Renormalize Curve* checkbox should be activated.

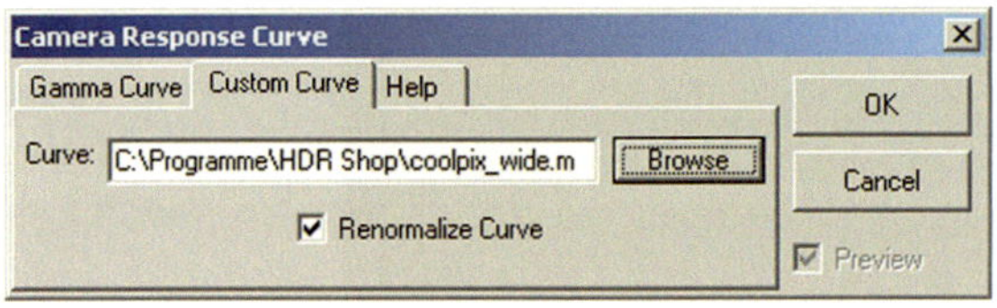

Figure 4.20
The *Camera Response Curve* is loaded when the *Renormalize Curve* function is checked

If the calculation for an HDR picture is to be applied to all three color channels, *R* = *G* = *B* must be selected in *Select Channels*. The scale increments between the individual pictures can be calculated in the *Calculate Scale Increments* field. This function can only work properly with minimal scale increments, otherwise the values need to be manually entered under *Use Preset Scale Increments*. When all required parameters have been defined, an HDR picture is created from the picture series by pressing *Generate Image*.

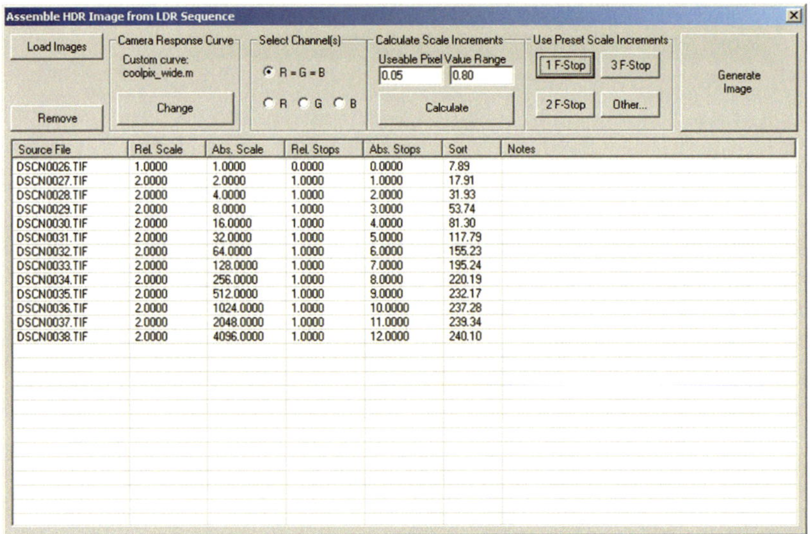

Source File	Rel. Scale	Abs. Scale	Rel. Stops	Abs. Stops	Sort	Notes
DSCN0026.TIF	1.0000	1.0000	0.0000	0.0000	7.89	
DSCN0027.TIF	2.0000	2.0000	1.0000	1.0000	17.91	
DSCN0028.TIF	2.0000	4.0000	1.0000	2.0000	31.93	
DSCN0029.TIF	2.0000	8.0000	1.0000	3.0000	53.74	
DSCN0030.TIF	2.0000	16.0000	1.0000	4.0000	81.30	
DSCN0031.TIF	2.0000	32.0000	1.0000	5.0000	117.79	
DSCN0032.TIF	2.0000	64.0000	1.0000	6.0000	155.23	
DSCN0033.TIF	2.0000	128.0000	1.0000	7.0000	195.24	
DSCN0034.TIF	2.0000	256.0000	1.0000	8.0000	220.19	
DSCN0035.TIF	2.0000	512.0000	1.0000	9.0000	232.17	
DSCN0036.TIF	2.0000	1024.0000	1.0000	10.0000	237.28	
DSCN0037.TIF	2.0000	2048.0000	1.0000	11.0000	239.34	
DSCN0038.TIF	2.0000	4096.0000	1.0000	12.0000	240.10	

Figure 4.21
The exposure parameters are defined prior to creating the HDR picture

You can switch between the individual HDR levels in a preview screen by pressing the plus and minus buttons. The finished HDR picture can be saved in HDR format or in so-called low dynamic range format.

When HDR pictures are created, not only color information is saved for each pixel, but also the sum of the light that meets this particular area. As in reality there is no limitation placed on the quantity of light, these pixel values are saved as floating point numbers. These numbers can have a few or many digits to the right of the decimal point (0.2132947, etc.). For a conventional picture with 8 bits per color channel, the pixel values are saved in whole numbers (0, 1, 2, etc. up to 255). HDR Shop can import and export special HDR formats such as Radiance HDR, Floating Point TIFF (16-bit TIFF), Portable Floatmap (PFM) and Raw Binary Floating Point (FLOAT or RAW). In addition, HDR Shop is capable of editing conventional 8-bit picture formats (or so-called LDR formats) such as BMP, JPEG, TIFF, TGA and PPM.

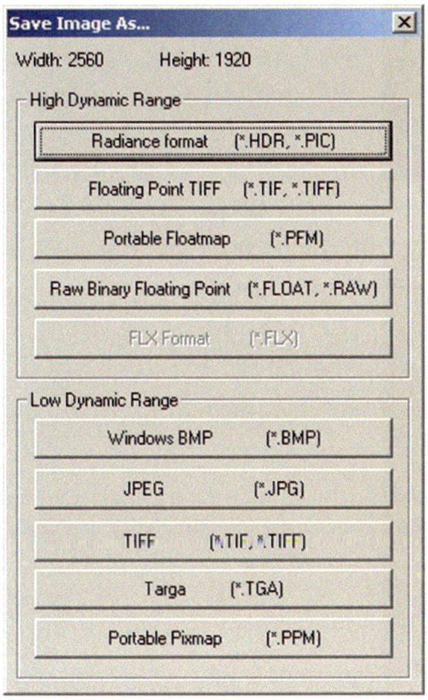

Figure 4.22
HDR pictures can be saved in various HDR and LDR file formats

On the next page, you can see the results of the picture series edited here as compared to an unedited picture. When viewing the picture as a whole, the differences between HDR and LDR are not necessarily apparent right away. Magnifying certain areas of the image, however, definitely reveals the heightened range of contrast in the HDR picture. Unlike the simple replacement of overly bright areas with darker ones, the HDR method genuinely increases the range of tonal value in complete pictures.

More information on HDR Shop as well as how to download the software can be found at: http://www.debevec.org/HDRShop [status: February 26, 2004].

In addition to making the most out of difficult light situations, HDR technology finds application in 3-D scenarios. With computer generated pictures, for example, HDR files can be used to create realistic lighting effects (see chapter 7.2.1.2 and chapter 14).

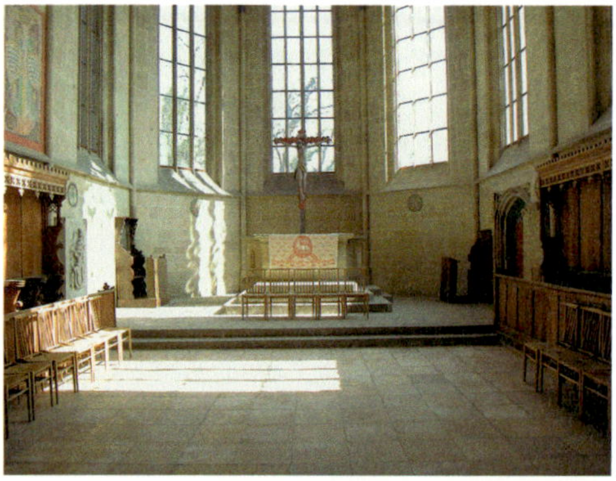

Figure 4.23
Individual picture from the picture series

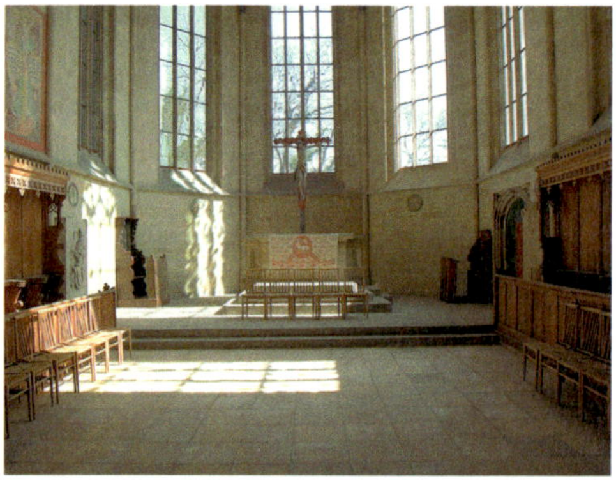

Figure 4.24
HDR picture with increased range of contrast

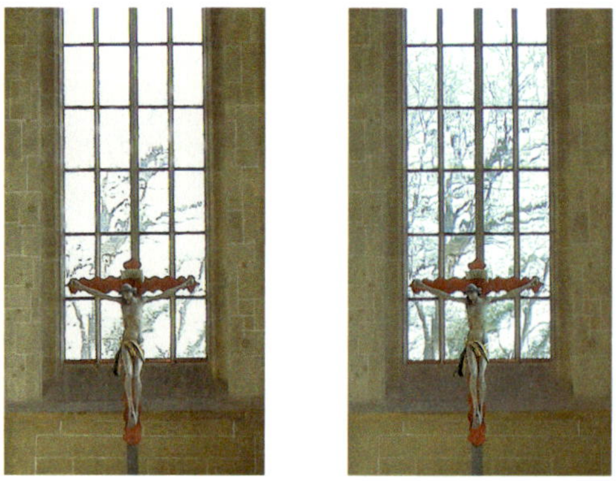

Figure 4.25
Magnified view
Left: normal picture
Right: HDR picture

5. Equipment

5.1 Cameras and lenses

Regardless of the which type of camera you prefer to take pictures with (analog or digital), there are a number of different options at your disposal when it comes to finding a suitable camera for panoramic or object-based photography. It is not absolutely necessary to have a special panoramic camera to create good panoramas; less sophisticated models also allow you to achieve decent results. In the end, what really makes interactive panoramas and object movies striking are the photographer's creativity, the theme/scene selected and the overall effect. The following describes the advantages and disadvantages associated with the respective camera/lens combination.

5.1.1 Compact cameras

Compact cameras typically have a built-in lens and view finder that display the scene in front of the lens slightly offset. In other words, the image seen by the photographer through the view finder is not identical with the one that will be saved by the camera to film or to a chip. Most built-in lenses are zoom lenses that comprise a series of lens disks to form an adjustable lens system. If such a camera is used to take panoramic shots, it is recommended that the lens be set to the maximum wide angle setting. Although image distortion is most prevalent at this setting for the majority of lenses, the focal length is best reproduced.

Advantages

- Compact cameras usually are less expensive to purchase than single lens reflex cameras.
- They more often than not are smaller and lighter than other models.
- Operation is easier for some users, due to the automatic nature of the camera.

Disadvantages

- The view finder displays the scene somewhat differently than the image saved to film or a chip.
- Built-in zoom objectives typically are lower in picture quality than that of fixed focal lengths, which are optimized for a specific value.
- In many models, it is not possible to deactivate all of the automatic features. In panoramic photography, it is important to have the ability to set the flash, exposure and auto focus.

5.1.2 Single lens reflex cameras

Single lens reflex cameras display approximately 95 % of the total image in the view finder. Light is refracted to the view finder by a mirror, which is folded back when the picture is taken so that the light meets the film (or the chip), not the finder. Most reflex cameras allow the lens to be swapped. It is recommended that a lens with a fixed focal length be used, as such lenses have better imaging qualities. In order to achieve a large field of view and reduce the total number of pictures taken for a panorama, it is wise to use a wide angle lens. If only a zoom lens is available, it should be moved to its wide angle setting. Although image distortion is most prevalent here, the focal length is best reproduced.

Advantages

- Lenses normally can be swapped.
- The view finder displays almost all of the image.
- Generally, all necessary settings can be manually as well as automatically configured.

Disadvantages

- The camera can be quite heavy, depending on the camera unit and the lens used.
- The purchase price is almost always higher than that of compact cameras.

5.1.3 Video cameras

A digital video camera can be used in place of a still camera to take pictures for a panorama or an object movie. Oftentimes there are two options available: Either the still shots of the video film are used or the individual pictures are taken using the camera's still mode. If video mode is used, a mere resolution of 1,024 x 768 pixels (currently the standard) is all that can be expected. Additionally, still video shots frequently reveal streaks, which are caused by the interlacing method. Some image editing programs have a de-interlacing feature to remove this unwanted effect. If the pictures are taken in still mode, however, higher resolutions usually can be achieved (depending on the chip used).

Advantages

- As a result of black-and-white balancing, the camera can be perfectly configured to the light situation at hand.
- The display can be used to show a preview of the shot. It is difficult, however, to size up the true level of light based on the display alone.

Disadvantages

- As a general rule, video cameras have a lower resolution than still cameras.
- Some pictures may not have the level of clarity and definition required.
- Digital video cameras typically have a higher price tag than do digital compact cameras.

5.1.4 Panoramic cameras

Special panoramic cameras outfitted with a pivoting lens or a swivel motor can be used to photograph complete panoramas in a single pass. The panoramic picture is produced by literally "scanning" the scene in front of the lens. Most models allow different lenses to be fitted. Here, the vertical field of view is determined based on the focal length.

Advantages

- A panoramic picture can be taken in a single shot.
- Panoramas with a horizontal field of view of less than 360° do not need to be stitched.
- Panoramas with a horizontal field of view of 360° and more require only one seam edge to be processed.
- Depending on the model, differences in the level of illumination of a scene can be balanced out at the time of exposure.

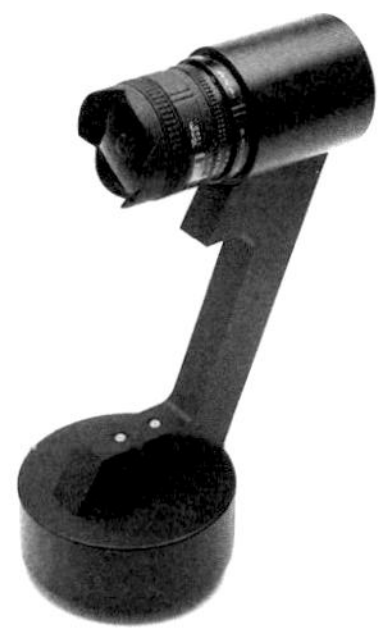

Figure 5.1
Panoramic camera from Spheron

Disadvantages

- The purchase price is quite a bit higher than that of standard digital or analog cameras.
- The cost of processing the wide film format of analog panoramic cameras is higher than that of more traditional sizes.
- For the most part, panoramic cameras are limited to panoramic photography.
- The scanning technique used in digital panoramic cameras leads to the distortion of moving objects.

5.1.5 One shot solutions with a parabolic mirror

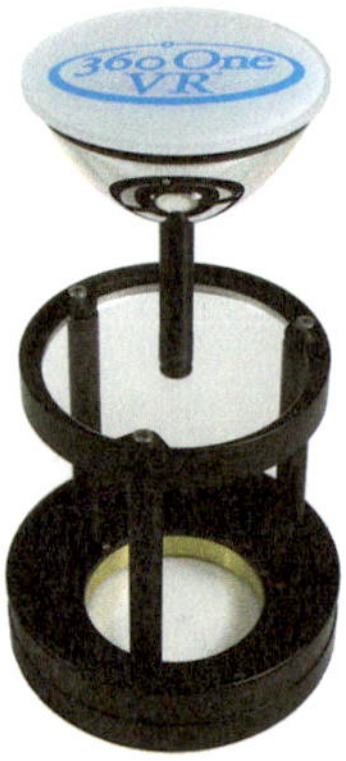

Figure 5.2
One shot parabolic mirror 360 One VR

These curved mirrors usually are attached to the respective lens by way of an adapter and allow a 360° view to be captured in a single shot. This, however, is only possible up to a certain horizontal field of view. As such, the subsequent digital panoramic application of this type of photography is limited to the cylindrical format.

Advantages

- A complete panorama can be photographed at once with a single exposure.
- No stitching is required.
- Moving objects in the scene represent no problem, as they can be photographed with great clarity (depending on the setting of the camera).
- A parabolic mirror and the corresponding camera are all that is needed; your tripod can be left at home.

Disadvantages

- Parabolic mirrors are not compatible with all cameras.
- Their use is restricted to cylindrical panoramas.
- The circular picture that results must be converted to a panorama using special software, otherwise it makes little sense to use the image.
- The resolution of the panorama is restricted to the maximum resolution of the camera chip.
- Parabolic mirrors are more fragile than lenses and, consequently, break more easily.

5.2 Panoramic tripod heads

A number of manufacturers offer special tripod heads for panoramic photography. Such heads are used to precisely set the nodal point and to pivot the camera about it. Most panoramic heads provide the option to control the number of shots taken per horizontal sweep via so-called click stops. With the click stop feature, you do not need to look at the degrees scale on the tripod head after each shot for an interval of 30°, for example, but instead simply turn the camera until it clicks into place. There are several panoramic heads to choose from, which can be broken down as follows:

- Tripod heads manufactured for a special camera and lens combination. These heads typically have markings for the respective lens. Such designs can only be used for a specific camera model.
- Tripod heads that can be adjusted for each camera/lens combination. Adjustable heads normally are a little more expensive, however they have the clear advantage that you can individually set the nodal point for different cameras.

More information on specific models can be found in chapters 6.2.5 and 7.2.4 as well as in the list of manufacturers (see chapter B.2.5).

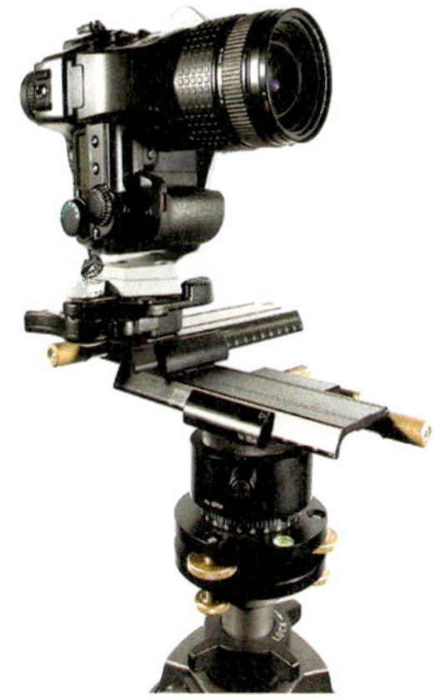

Figure 5.3
QTVR 302 plus tripod head from Manfrotto

5.3 Turntables for object movies

In order to photograph an object movie, a device is needed which can be used to rotate the object exactly around its center point. If the point of rotation used is slightly off center, the resulting motion in the object movie will not be round and the object will wobble back and forth. The simplest solution is to use a turntable from the kitchen, however many of these tables do not have perfect rotation. As such, it is recommended that a turntable specially designed for object movies be used. Such tables are graduated and allow the object to be precisely rotated around a specific value, such as 10°. Both manual and motorized turntables are available, the latter of which are controlled by a computer.

More information on specific models can be found in chapter 8.2.3 and in the list of manufacturers (see chapter B.2.6).

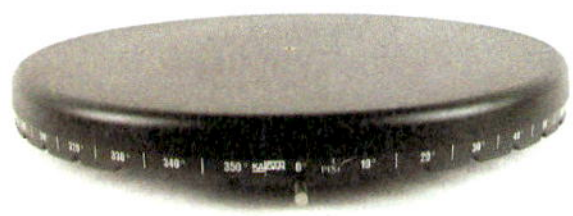

Figure 5.4
Pixi manual turntable from Kaidan

6. Cylindrical panoramas

6.1 Introduction

This form of panoramic presentation allows for a full 360° horizontal sweep. Vertical travel is limited and depends on the focal length of the lens used. Cylindrical panoramas can be photographed using special panoramic cameras. Alternatively, there is the option of taking a number of individual pictures that overlap each other by a certain percentage. This series of pictures is then stitched into a panoramic picture using special stitching software.

6.2 Photo technology and techniques

6.2.1 Panoramic cameras

The camera market currently offers analog and digital panoramic cameras. With analog cameras, application is usually restricted to cylindrical panoramas, whereby the lens used determines the vertical field of view. In addition to cameras capable of a full 360° sweep, there are models that only cover a horizontal field of view of around 150°. As a smaller field of view is less suited to completely depicting rooms and scenes, however, this type of panoramic camera will not receive any further coverage.

An analog panoramic camera is introduced in chapter 6.2.2.1, whereas chapter 7.2.1 shows the digital equivalent for the production of spherical panoramas. There are more models available than just those presented in this book. A selection of manufacturers of panoramic cameras can be found in chapter B.2.4.

6.2.1.1 Seitz Roundshot 28/220

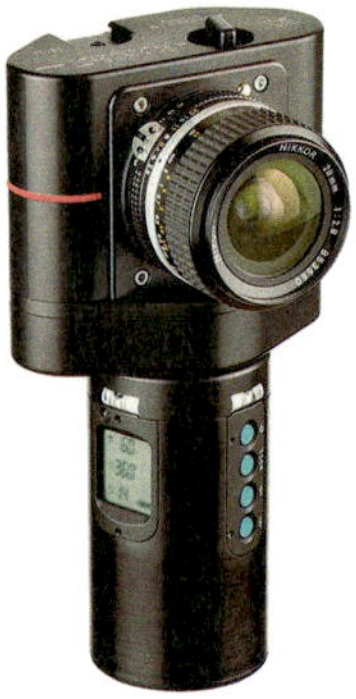

Figure 6.1
Roundshot 28/220

The Roundshot 28/220 analog panoramic camera from Seitz shown here comprises two assemblies (see Figure 6.1). The upper assembly houses the film transport system, with the motor in the lower assembly. During the photo shooting, only the upper assembly moves. When a picture is taken, the shutter opens a small vertical gap. The light that passes through the lens is then projected onto the cylindrical surface of the film material. The turning motion activates the transport system, which moves the film in parallel with the camera as the film is wound around a film core.

The exposure time is controlled by the turning speed and can range from 1/500 to 8 seconds. The horizontal camera angle can be set in stages of 45° up to 999°. At the maximum setting, the camera turns several times around its axis and exposes an entire roll of film. The vertical field of view is restricted to no more than 84°, as the camera is optimized for 28 mm lenses and the use of other focal lengths would be impractical.

Appropriate film material for such an application would be 120 and 220 medium size film. If the wider 220 size is selected, the resulting picture will have a height of 50 mm. The camera also has a delayed start feature with a maximum delay time of 10 seconds. This gives the photographer enough time to get out of the picture before it is taken.

In order to convert a scene captured using this method into an interactive panorama, the pictures first must be digitalized. A scanner will be needed to scan in the shots, whereby the scanner must be able to process a format this large. Appropriate scanners include those with a transparency unit and professional drum scanners. Due to their higher resolution, however, drum scanners are better suited. The Custom Panorama Lab in Boca Raton, Florida, USA has special offers for this particular type of application. More information on the services of this laboratory can be found at: http:// www.roundshot.com [status: February 1, 2004].

Figure 6.2 shows a picture taken using this technique. Refer to chapter 6.3.1 for the additional steps required to produce an interactive panorama.

Figure 6.2
Complete panoramic picture taken using the Roundshot 28/220

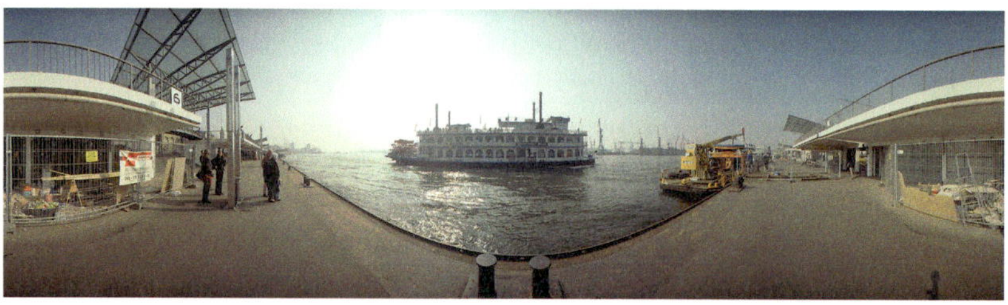

Advantages

- A panoramic picture can be taken in a single shot.
- No stitching is required.
- Moving objects in the scene represent no problem, as they can be photographed with great clarity (depending on the setting of the camera).
- The camera is all that is needed; your tripod can be left at home.
- Due to the high resolution of the analog film, the panorama also can be used for making hard copy prints and enlargements.

Disadvantages

- The camera costs around US $ 3,000 and can only be used for panoramic photography. Traditional shots cannot be taken.
- The medium film format required and the subsequent development are more expensive than the film and developing costs associated with standard cameras.
- The expense of digitalizing panoramic formats is greater than that of normal film.
- The production process takes longer than with digital photography, as there must be sufficient time to develop and digitalize the film.
- The possibilities for interactive panoramas are somewhat limited using the cylindrical approach.

6.2.2 One shot solutions with a parabolic mirror

These curved mirrors usually are attached to the respective lens by way of an adapter and allow a 360° view to be captured in a single shot. This, however, is only possible at a horizontal field of view of up to around 100°.

As only a single picture is taken with the one shot technique, the resolution of the panorama is limited to the maximum resolution of the chip integrated in the camera. The surface of the chip is not fully utilized, however, which is attributed to the fact that the picture is circular in shape. The resulting image is heavily distorted and must be corrected using special software in order to achieve the desired panoramic view. Compared to lenses, parabolic mirrors are not especially robust and tend to break more easily. There are more parabolic mirrors available than the one presented here. A selection of manufacturers can be found in chapter B.2.3.

Figure 6.4 shows a picture that was taken using the 360 One VR one shot parabolic mirror. These so-called "donut" pictures are corrected after the exposure. The software supplied with the parabolic mirror is used to carry out the correction process.

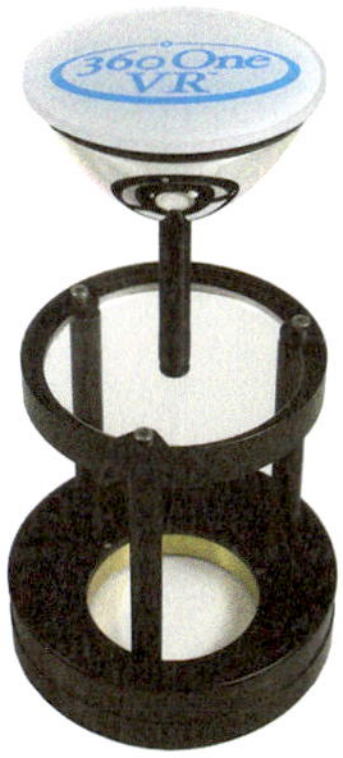

Figure 6.3
One shot parabolic mirror 360 One VR

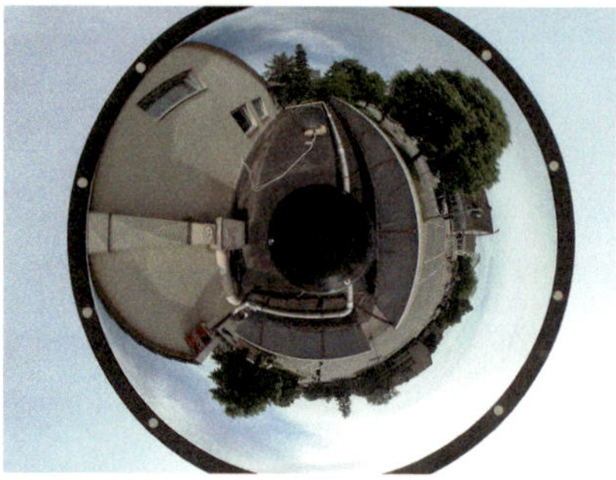

Figure 6.4
Picture taken using the 360 One VR

The panorama shown here was corrected using a software application called PhotoWarp. This software also is capable of creating QVTR movies and cylindrical pictures. More information on the software can be found at: http://www.eyesee360.com/photowarp [status: February 13, 2004]. Figure 6.5 shows a converted cylindrical panorama.

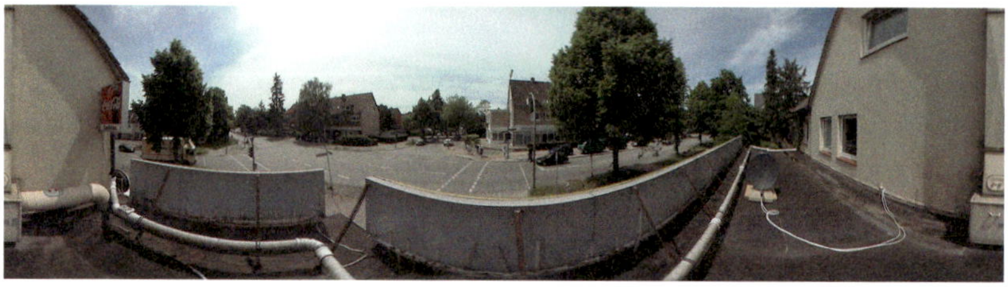

Figure 6.5
Picture converted with PhotoWarp

Advantages

- A complete panorama can be photographed at once with a single exposure.
- No stitching is required.
- Moving objects in the scene represent no problem, as they can be photographed with great clarity (depending on the setting of the camera).
- A parabolic mirror and the corresponding camera are all that is needed; your tripod can be left at home.

Disadvantages

- Parabolic mirrors are not compatible with all cameras.
- Their use is restricted to cylindrical panoramas.
- The picture that results must be digitally converted to a panorama using special software, otherwise it makes little sense to use the image.
- The resolution of the panorama is restricted to the maximum resolution of the camera chip.
- Parabolic mirrors are more fragile than lenses and, consequently, break more easily.

6.2.3 Single-row technique

With the single-row technique, a series of individual pictures is taken, whereby each picture overlaps the next by a certain percentage. Either analog or digital cameras can be used to take the pictures. The number of pictures required depends on the field of view provided by the respective lens (see chapter 2.2.4). For cylindrical panoramas, more than one series of pictures can be taken to increase the vertical pivoting angle. What must be noted here and the equipment that is needed to take advantage of the so-called multi-row technique can be found in chapter 6.2.4.

It is recommended that a special panoramic tripod head be used to photograph a cylindrical panorama (see chapter 6.2.5).

Figure 6.6 shows a series of pictures that were taken using this technique. Refer to chapter 6.3 for the additional steps required to produce an interactive panorama.

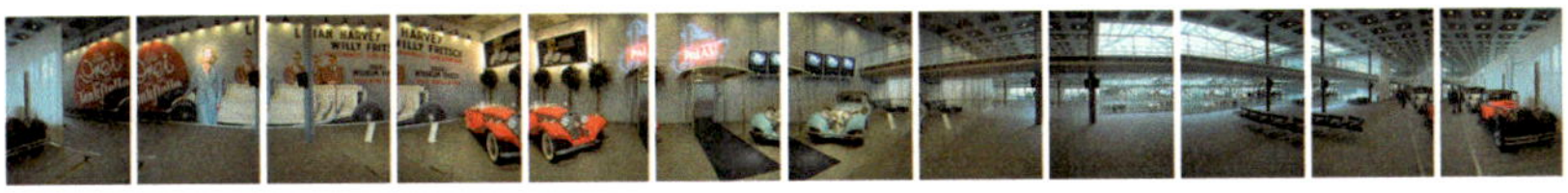

Figure 6.6
Individual pictures of a single-row panorama

Advantages

- The single-row technique does not require special camera equipment; practically any camera and lens combination can be used.
- Compared to the multi-row technique, only a few pictures need to be taken.

Disadvantages

- A tripod with a panoramic head is recommended in order to be able to exactly align the camera.
- Depending on the focal length of the lens, anywhere from 6 to 18 pictures need to be taken.
- The time required for stitching is a function of the number of pictures.
- The single-row technique presents problems when moving objects are introduced. Thus, it cannot be ruled out that such objects will appear incomplete in the panorama.

6.2.4 Multi-row technique

The multi-row technique generally requires that a number of pictures be taken, respective of the field of view provided by the lens. Beginning with the horizontal plane, a multiple series of overlapping pictures is taken. Depending on the number of picture series, a cylindrical or spherical panorama can result. Cylindrical panoramas taken using the multi-row technique usually have a larger vertical pivoting range than those produced with the single-row technique. In order to take advantage of the multi-row technique, a tripod head is required that allows the nodal point to be adjusted horizontally and vertically.

Suitable tripod heads include the Quickpan III from Kaidan and the Roundshot VR-Drive (see chapter 6.2.5).

Figure 6.7 shows two series of pictures that were taken using this technique. Refer to chapter 6.3.4 for the additional steps required to produce an interactive panorama.

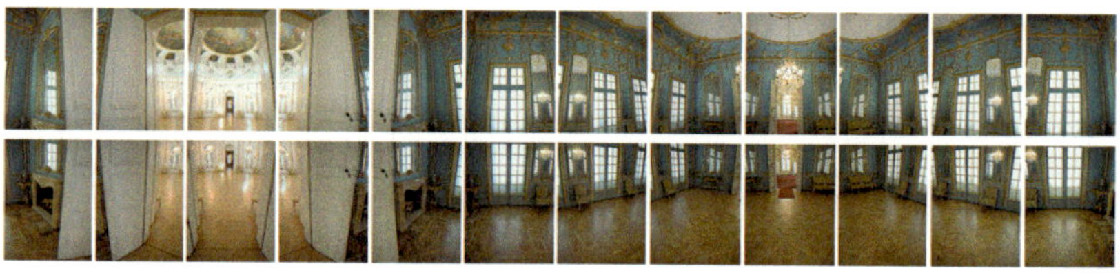

Figure 6.7
Individual pictures of a double multi-row panorama

Advantages

- The multi-row technique does not require special camera equipment; practically any camera and lens combination can be used.
- The high number of pictures increases the resolution of the panorama.

Disadvantages

- A special panoramic tripod is required to exactly align the camera for multi-row shots.
- The relatively high number of pictures increases the amount of time spent photographing and stitching.
- The multi-row technique presents problems when moving objects are introduced. Thus, it cannot be ruled out that such objects will appear incomplete in the panorama.

6.2.5 Tripod heads

A special tripod head is recommended in order to precisely pivot the camera about the nodal point. Several tripod heads are introduced in the following text. Other manufacturers of panoramic tripod heads can be found in the list of manufacturers (see chapter B.2.5).

Manfrotto / Bogen QTVR 302 plus

This tripod head (see Figure 6.8) can be individually adjusted, making it an option for many camera models. The QTVR 302 plus, however, is only suited for cylindrical panoramas.

Figure 6.8
Manfrotto QTVR 302 plus

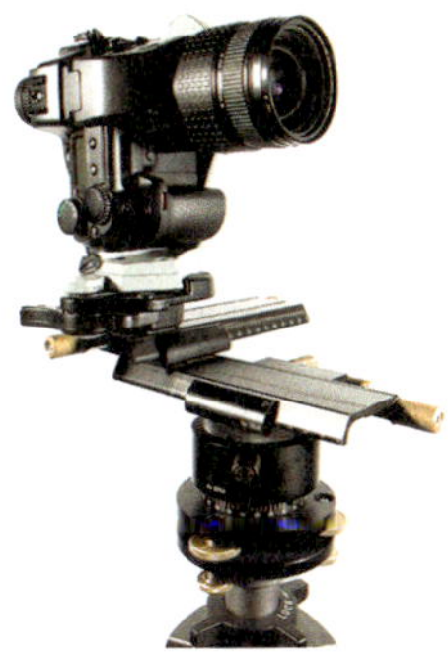

Kaidan QuickPan III CS (Camera Specific)

The QuickPan III CS (see Figure 6.9) is designed exclusively for a specific camera model. This tripod head can be used to photograph cylindrical and spherical panoramas, depending on the lens used.

Figure 6.9
Kaidan QuickPan III CS

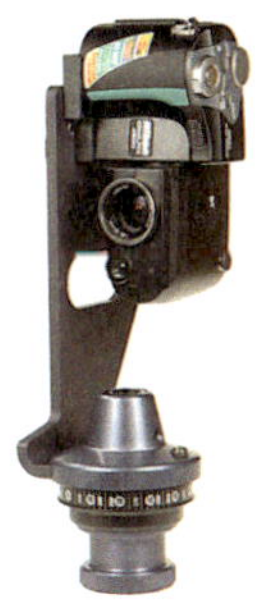

Kaidan Quickpan III

Figure 6.10
Kaidan Quickpan III

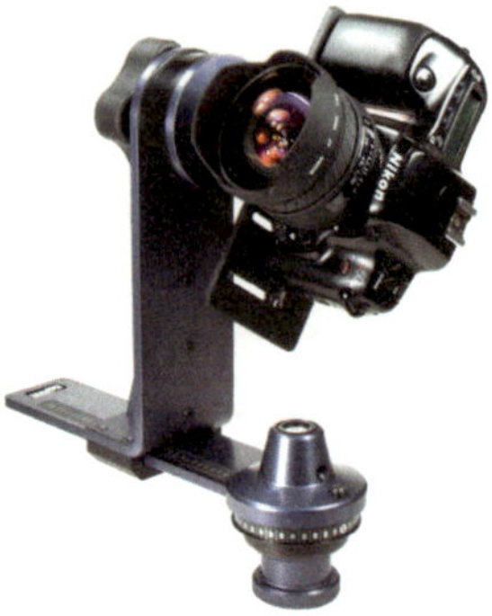

The Quickpan III tripod head (see Figure 6.10) can be individually adjusted and thus is a viable option for many cameras. With this model, cylindrical and spherical panoramas can be photographed using the single-row or multi-row technique.

Seitz Roundshot VR-Drive

Figure 6.11
Roundshot VR-Drive

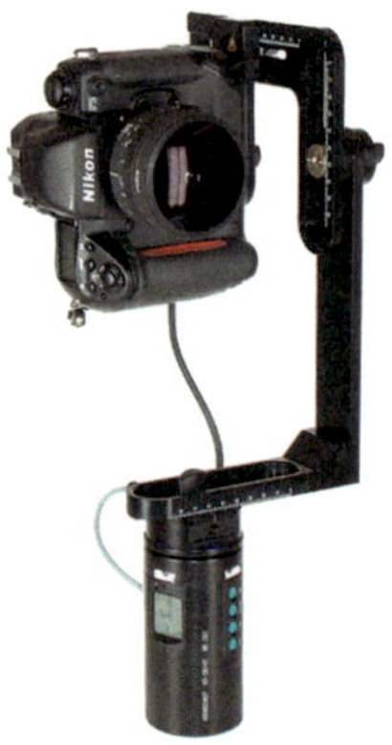

The VR-Drive (see Figure 6.11) is a motorized tripod head designed for single-row and multi-row shots. The unit is individually adjustable and can be used to take cylindrical and spherical pictures, depending on the lens fitted. The motor controls not only the rotational movement, but also the tripping device.

6.3 Stitching software

This chapter introduces a number of software products that can be used to produce cylindrical panoramas. Additional software manufacturers can be found in the list of manufacturers (see chapter B.1.1). A few of the software products are capable of producing cylindrical, cubic and spherical panoramas. As it would be impossible to list all of the applications and their features here, a comparative overview of the software covered can be found as a table in chapter 12.

6.3.1 VR Worx – VR PanoWorx (panoramic picture)

The following explains the image editing process of cylindrical shots taken with panoramic cameras. For more information on photographing such panoramas, please refer to chapter 6.2.1. After the photo shooting is finished, additional steps need to be taken in order to acquire a cylindrical panorama from a panoramic picture.

You will find a demo version of VR Worx on the CD at the following paths: \Demo versions\Mac and \Demo versions\PC

First, you should make any necessary color and brightness changes. This is best done on the complete panoramic picture using commercially available image editing software. After the color correction, the horizontal interface is defined. This must be done, for example, when a 380° format is used for overlapping purposes instead of the required 360°. A prominent area in the overlapping region is located and the superfluous parts of the picture are cut out on the right and left sides.

To learn how such cylindrical panoramic pictures can be published using a Java viewer, refer to chapter 10.2. There you will find more information on viewers as well as the source code used to embed panoramas in HTML files.

An alternative to publishing with a Java viewer is to create cylindrical QTVR movies. Here, VR PanoWorx software can be used to edit the sample panorama.

In VR Worx, the VR PanoWorx program module is called up via the *Create New Project > Create a Panorama* function in *File > New*. To create a QTVR movie from a cylindrical panoramic picture using VR PanoWorx, the *Setup, Blend, Hot Spots, Compose* and *Preview* editing tabs are run through.

First, *Single Panorama* is selected in the pull-down menu by *Source Format* in the *Setup* tab (see Figure 6.12). In *Node Sweep,* the horizontal capture of the shot is defined in degrees. The exact size of the panoramic picture is specified in pixels via *Dimensions*. If the respective picture size cannot be found in the popup menu, custom values can be entered by selecting *Custom* or automatically set by selecting the *Auto* function.

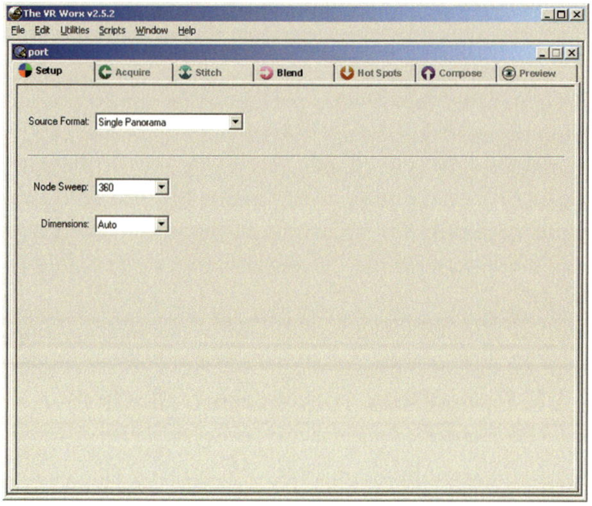

Figure 6.12
The properties of the panoramic picture are defined in the *Setup* tab

The panoramic picture is loaded in the *Blend* tab (see Figure 6.13) via the *Actions > Import* function. The software integrates all of the individual pictures into the existing VR Worx document, which is why VR Worx files are quite large when compared to the project files created by other programs.

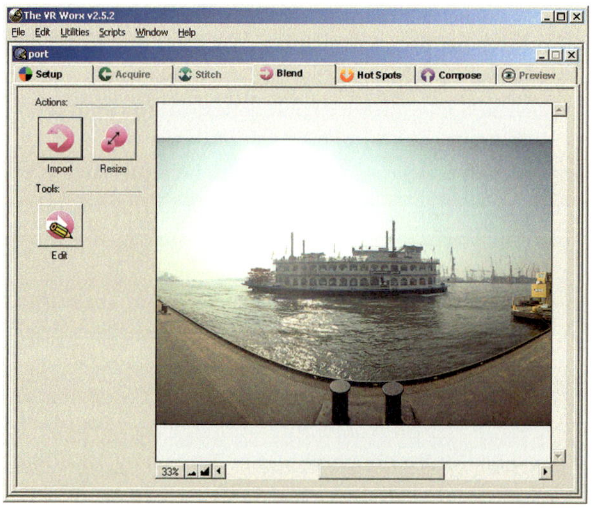

Figure 6.13
The panoramic picture is imported in the *Blend* tab

In the *Hot Spots* editing tab, hot spots can be defined in any desired form using the *Tools* function. Hot spots can be assigned various functions. For more information, refer to chapter 9.3.2.

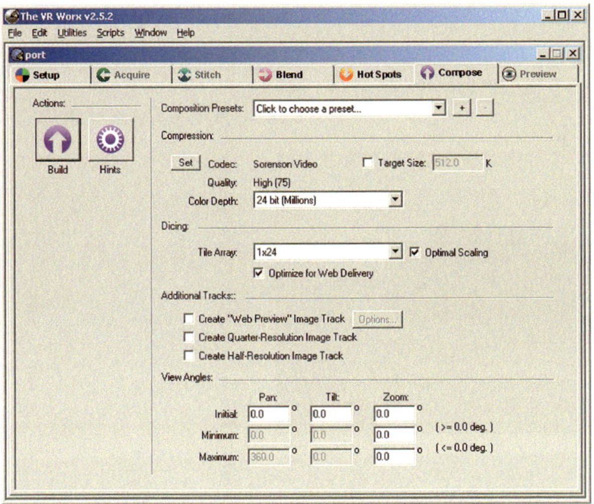

Figure 6.14
The QTVR movie is created and compressed using the selected codec in the *Compose* tab

In the *Compose* tab (see Figure 6.14), the compression codec used can be specified via *Compression > Set*. The default setting is *Photo-JPEG Quality Medium*, however other compression settings also provide good results. Chapter 10.1 provides more information on QuickTime codecs. *Color Depth* is used to specify the depth of color. Here, it is recommended that you apply the preselected *24 bits (millions)*. You can specify a file size by activating the *Target Size* dialog box and entering the numerical figure. The software then will create a QTVR movie that does not exceed your desired file size. In the *Dicing* field, the panoramic picture is divided into quadratic sections (*tiles*) so that only the visible areas of the picture are loaded when playing the QTVR movie. This allows the load placed on the CPU to be kept to a minimum during playback. The more *tiles* are selected, the less memory is required to view the movie. If you are publishing for the Web, the *Optimize for Web Delivery* field should be selected so that "fast start" QuickTime streaming is activated. When "fast start" is activated, parts of the panorama are able to viewed by the user while the QTVR file is being downloaded. It is also beneficial to generate a preview of the panorama via *Additional Tracks*; this allows the observer to see a low resolution version of the panorama during the download process. The part of the picture that is to be seen and the zoomable area for the QTVR movie can be specified under *View Angles*. It is recommended, however, that you do not change these default settings in the *Compose* tab, but instead apply the respective values in *Preview*. There you can define the same parameters and immediately test them on the panorama to see the result. Once all of the settings have been properly configured, the QTVR movie is rendered via *Actions > Build*. The finished movie is then viewed and tested in the *Preview* window (see Figure 6.15).

Figure 6.15
The QTVR movie is tested in *Preview* and saved after defining additional properties

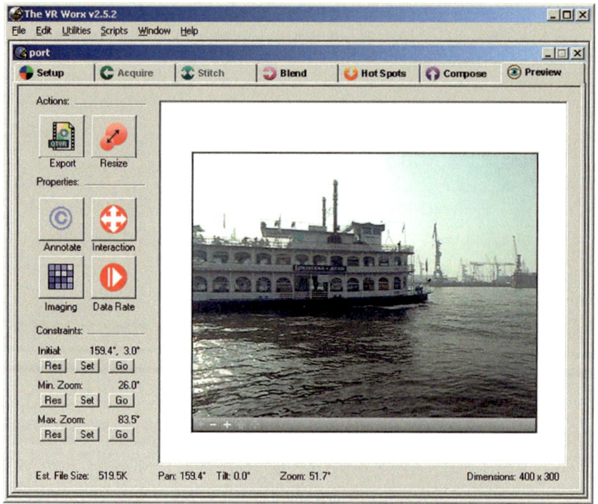

The final size of the window is defined via *Actions > Resize*. Under *Properties > Annotate*, information such as name and copyright can be added to the panorama. *Properties > Interaction* determines the mouse functions as well as the rotational speed of the QTVR movie. *Properties > Imaging* is used to influence the picture quality of the panorama when moving (*Motion*) and not moving (*Static*). With the *Properties > Data Rate* function, the download speed for various connections can be calculated. The part of the panorama that is to be seen when the movie is started is defined via *Constraints > Initial > Set*. The *Constraints > Min. Zoom* and *Max. Zoom* functions are used to set the zoom range accessible by the user for the QTVR picture. When all settings have been configured, the panorama is saved via *Actions > Export*.

You can find the panoramic picture shown here and the cylindrical QTVR on the CD at the following path: \Workshop\ 06 Cylindrical panoramas\ 6_3_1 Panoramic picture

Chapter 10.1 provides information on how to publish QTVR movies. There you will find more information on viewers as well as the source code used to embed panoramas in Web sites.

Advantages

- Easy to use and the individual functions are intuitive in scope.
- The software provides support for importing numerous file formats and scanned pictures can be directly loaded via the TWAIN interface.

Disadvantages

- Only cylindrical QTVR movies can be created; other projection formats are not supported.
- As the picture data are not referenced, but integrated, VR Worx documents are comparatively large (depending on the number of imported files). This is why the book CD only includes the finished panorama for the example shown and not the associated VR Worx document.

6.3.2 VR Worx – VR PanoWorx (single-row technique)

VR Worx software is capable of editing single-row panoramas. The following explains how you can create a cylindrical QTVR movie.

In VR Worx, the VR PanoWorx program module is called up via the *Create New Project > Create a Panorama* function in *File > New*. To create a cylindrical panorama using VR PanoWorx, the seven editing tabs *Setup, Acquire, Stitch, Blend, Hot Spots, Compose* and *Preview* are run through.

First, *Multiple Images* is selected in the pull-down menu by *Source Format* in the *Setup* tab (see Figure 6.16). By *Acquire From,* image sources such as scanners or video cards can be selected. If the required images already are on your computer's hard disk, select *PLUG-IN Image File* here. The *Node Sweep* setting allows you to specify the horizontal sweep, which usually is 360°. *Max Frames* defines the number of individual pictures. In the *Lens Params* section, the focal length of the lens used is entered next to *Length.* The software then automatically calculates the vertical field of view (*F.O.V.*) based on this information. The exact size of an individual picture is specified in pixels by *Image Size.* If the corresponding size cannot be found in the popup menu, custom values can be entered by selecting the *Custom* option.

You will find a demo version of VR Worx on the CD at the following paths: \Demo versions\Mac and \Demo versions\PC

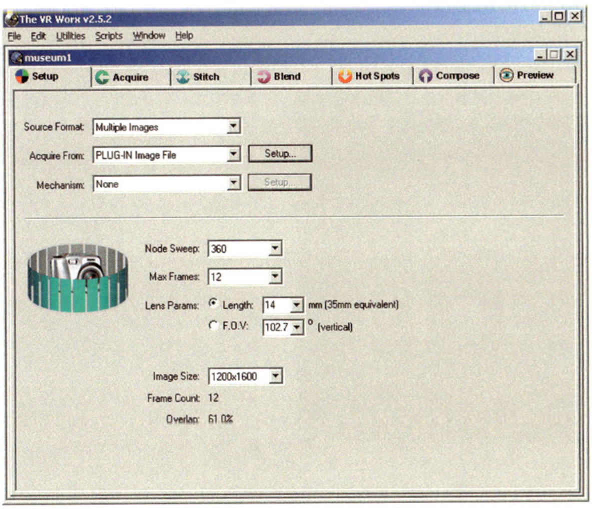

Figure 6.16
The properties of the individual pictures are defined in the *Setup* tab

The *Acquire* tab (see Figure 6.17) includes placeholders for the individual pictures respective of the information you entered in the *Setup* tab. Press the *Multiple* button to import several individual pictures. If some pictures need to be exchanged for others, click on *Clear* to remove the pictures from the window, then click *Single* to import the replacement pictures. *Rotate, Origin* and *Reverse* are used to turn the pictures and/or change the picture sequence. The software integrates all of the individual pictures into the existing VR Worx document, which is why VR Worx files are quite large when compared to the project files created by other programs.

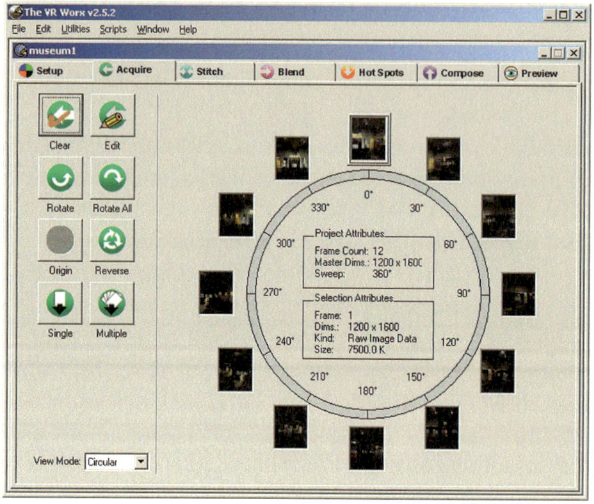

Figure 6.17
Individual pictures are imported in the *Acquire* tab

In the *Stitch* tab (see Figure 6.18), individual pictures can be positioned. Begin by initializing the stitching process so that the panoramic filmstrip can be viewed; to do this, go to *Actions* > *Build.*

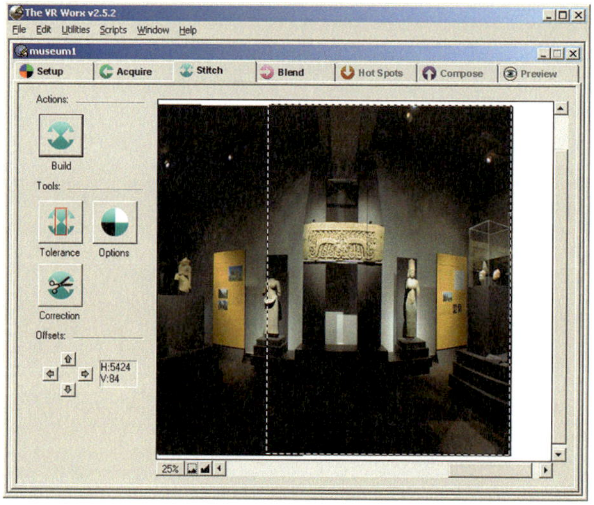

Figure 6.18
Individual pictures are positioned in the *Stitch* editing tab

The position of the individual pictures is then controlled based on the panoramic picture. The position of the pictures now can be changed as required. To do this, click on the respective picture in the filmstrip, which then is demarcated by a dotted yellow perimeter. With *Offsets,* the horizontal and vertical position of a picture can be changed using the arrow buttons. The stitching result can be optimized by *Tools;* here, the vertical and horizontal tolerance ranges for stitching can be set with the *Tolerance* function, for example. Display options can be changed under *Tools* > *Options*. Here, you can set image transition to be transparent, whereby the preset function *Fast-*

er stitching is better suited to editing larger image files. In the *Tools* > *Correction* field, automatic correction (*Auto*) is sufficient for the majority of application scenarios.

In the *Blend* tab (see Figure 6.19), the individual pictures are blended into each other according to the positions defined in the *Stitch* tab.

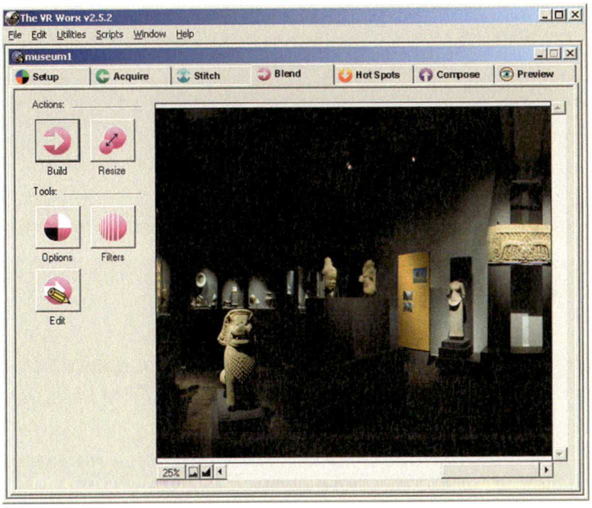

Figure 6.19
The *Blend* function allows the individual pictures to be stitched, or "blended", to create a panoramic picture

Before you start the blending process, however, it is a good idea to specify the size of the overlapping area. The overlapping scope can be set from *Min* to *Max* via *Tools* > *Options*. If you want to have a soft transition between the individual pictures, it is recommended that you select a large value. The blending process is started via *Actions* > *Build*. After the process has completed, the panorama can be viewed as a filmstrip in the same window. The size of the panoramic picture can be changed via the *Actions* > *Resize* function. *Tools* > *Filters* allows you to take advantage of image editing functions such as brightness, contrast and definition for the panoramic picture. If you want to edit the picture in an external editor such as Photoshop, select your program of choice under *Tools* > *Edit*. The panoramic filmstrip can be saved as a special image file prior to making additional editing changes. This, however, is only possible in the *Blend* tab after the individual pictures have been stitched. You have the option of saving the panoramic picture in many common formats (including BMP, JPG, PSD and TIFF) from *File* > *Export*. These filmstrips can be published with a Java viewer (see chapter 10.2) as well as printed out (see chapter 10.6). Additional editing steps are required in order to produce a QTVR movie.

In the *Hot Spots* editing tab, hot spots can be defined in any desired form using the *Tools* function. Hot spots can be assigned various functions. For more information, refer to chapter 9.3.2.

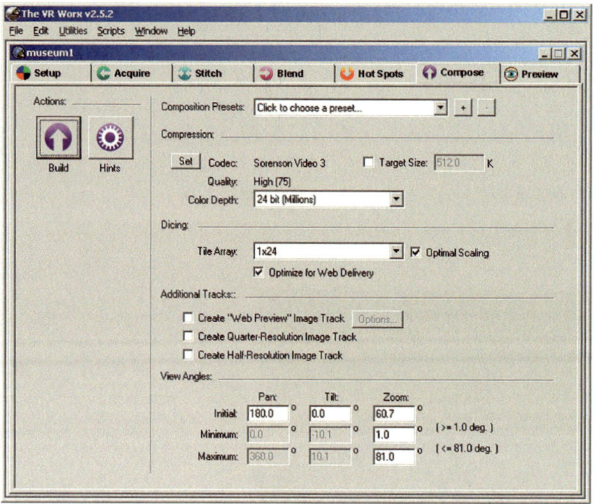

Figure 6.20
The QTVR movie is created and compressed using the selected codec in the *Compose* tab

In the *Compose* tab (see Figure 6.20), the compression codec used can be specified via *Compression > Set.* The default setting is *Photo-JPEG Quality Medium,* however other compression settings also provide good results. Chapter 10.1 provides more information on QuickTime codecs. *Color Depth* is used to specify the depth of color. Here, it is recommended that you apply the preselected *24 bits (millions).* You can specify a file size by activating the *Target Size* dialog box and entering the numerical figure. The software then will create a QTVR file that does not exceed your desired file size. In the *Dicing* field, the panoramic picture is divided into quadratic sections (*tiles*) so that only the visible areas of the picture are loaded when playing the movie. This allows the load placed on the CPU to be kept to a minimum during playback. The more tiles are selected, the less memory is required to view the movie. If you are publishing for the Web, the *Optimize for Web Delivery* field should be selected so that "fast start" QuickTime streaming is activated. When "fast start" is activated, parts of the panorama are able to viewed by the user while the QTVR file is being downloaded. It is also beneficial to generate a preview of the panorama via *Additional Tracks;* this allows the observer to see a low resolution version of the panorama during the download process. The part of the picture that is to be seen and the zoomable area for the QTVR movie can be specified under *View Angles.* It is recommended, however, that you do not change these default settings in the *Compose* tab, but instead apply the respective values in *Preview.* There you can define the same parameters and immediately test them on the panorama to see the result. Once all of the settings have been properly configured, the QTVR movie is rendered via *Actions > Build.* The finished movie is then viewed and tested in the *Preview* window (see Figure 6.21).

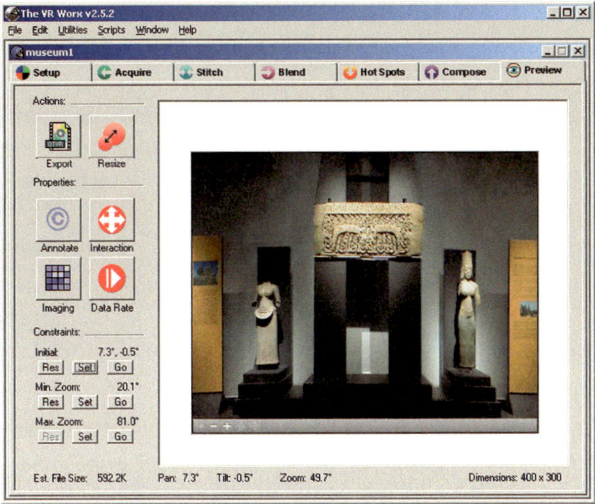

Figure 6.21
The panorama is tested in *Preview* and saved after defining additional properties

The final size of the window is defined via *Actions > Resize.* Under *Properties > Annotate,* information such as name and copyright can be added to the panorama. *Properties > Interaction* determines the mouse functions as well as the rotational speed of the QTVR movie. *Properties > Imaging* is used to influence the picture quality of the panorama when moving (*Motion*) and not moving (*Static*). With the *Properties > Data Rate* function, the download speed for various connections can be calculated. The part of the panorama that is to be seen when the movie is started is defined via *Constraints > Initial > Set.* The *Constraints > Min. Zoom* and *Max. Zoom* functions are used to set the zoom range accessible by the user for the QTVR picture. When all settings have been configured, the panorama is saved via *Actions > Export.*

You will find the pictures and panorama file shown here on the CD at the following path: \Workshop\06 Cylindrical panoramas\6_3_2 VR Worx

Chapter 10.1 provides information on how to publish QTVR movies. There you will find more information on viewers as well as the source code used to embed panoramas in Web sites.

Advantages

- Easy to use and the individual functions are intuitive in scope.
- The software provides support for importing numerous file formats and scanned pictures can be directly loaded via the TWAIN interface.

Disadvantages

- Only cylindrical QTVR movies can be created; other projection formats are not supported.
- As the picture data are not referenced, but integrated, VR Worx documents are comparatively large (depending on the number of imported files). This is why the book CD only includes the pictures and the finished panorama for the example shown and not the associated VR Worx document.

6.3.3 PanoTools – PTGui (single-row technique)

PanoTools can be found on the CD at the following paths: \Demo versions\Mac and \Demo versions\PC

Panorama Tools (PanoTools) consists of several components and is designed to be used for the production of cylindrical, spherical and cubic panoramas. In addition, PanoTools is capable of correcting image distortion caused by camera lenses as well as creating object filmstrips for the production of object movies.

The PanoTools suite comprises the following applications:

- *PTEditor* – a graphical panoramic editor.
- *PTStitcher* – used to stitch panoramas.
- *PTPicker* – graphically depicts the arrangement of pictures.
- *PTStereo* – computes 3-D data from image pairs with different angles of view.
- *PTInterpolate* – gives two pictures from the same scene with different angles of view a common angle of view.
- *PTMorpher* – morphing software.
- *PTAverage* – reduces "noise" in digital pictures and increases the range of contrast (density) of a picture by averaging several images.
- *PTStripe* – combines a sequence of object pictures to create a filmstrip for viewing in an object viewer (see chapter 8.3.1).
- *Panorama Tools for Photoshop* – plug-ins for editing and converting panoramas as well as correcting image distortion errors (see chapter 4).

As PanoTools is not very user-friendly, it is recommended that an add-on program such as PTGui or PTMac is used. This software integrates all of the PanoTools functions in a well organized, easy to understand graphic interface. PTGui runs on Windows, with a comparable product available for the Mac appropriately termed PTMac.

Demo versions of PTGui and PTMac can be found on the CD at the following paths: \Demo versions\Mac and \Demo versions\PC

In the following example, a cylindrical panorama is produced that consists of 12 individual pictures. The 12 pictures were taken in sequence at an interval of 30 degrees.

Creating a panorama using PTGui software requires use of the following editing tabs: *Source Images, Lens Settings, Panorama Settings, Crop, Image Parameters, Control Points, Optimizer, Preview* and *Create Panorama.*

The first step is to import the individual pictures in the *Source Images* tab (see Figure 6.22) by clicking the *Add* button. Here, the *Correct* PanoTools application can be called up as required in order to correct any lens-related image distortion errors. Please note that when this function is used from PTGui, the original pictures will be overwritten; as such, it is wise to make a backup of the respective pictures beforehand. Please refer to chapter 4 for more information on the correction possibilities offered by the *Correct* PanoTools function.

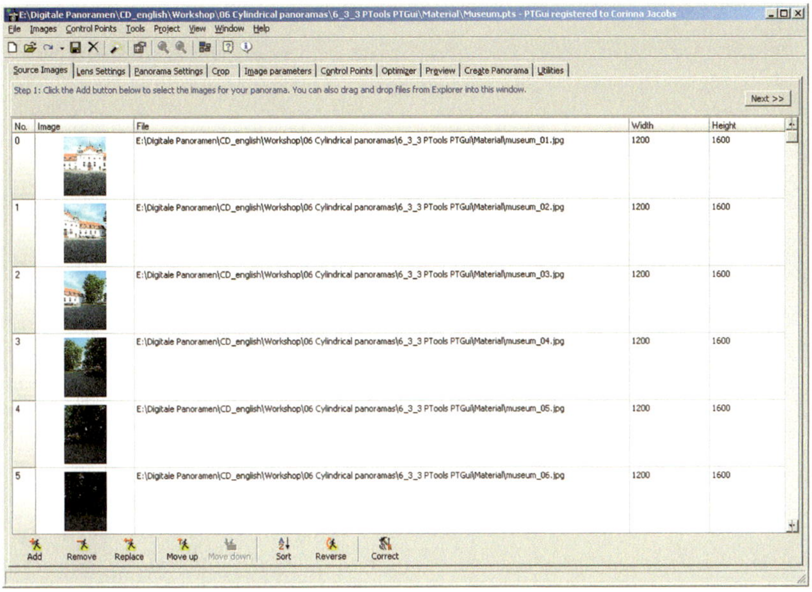

Figure 6.22
Individual pictures are loaded in the *Source Images* tab

In the *Lens Settings* tab (see Figure 6.23), select your lens type in the pull-down menu by *Lens type.* By *Hor. Field of View,* enter the horizontal field of view of the pictures or, alternatively, select a value for the *focal length.* The software then automatically calculates the corresponding parameter value based on one of these two values. If a digital single lens reflex is used, you can directly enter the focal length multiplier value in the *Focal length multiplier* field. Picture data can be integrated under *EXIF,* provided that your camera is supported by the software. In the *Advanced* section, correction values for the lens used can be numerically entered and saved via *Restore defaults.* If you are not aware of the correction values for your lens, simply ignore these fields.

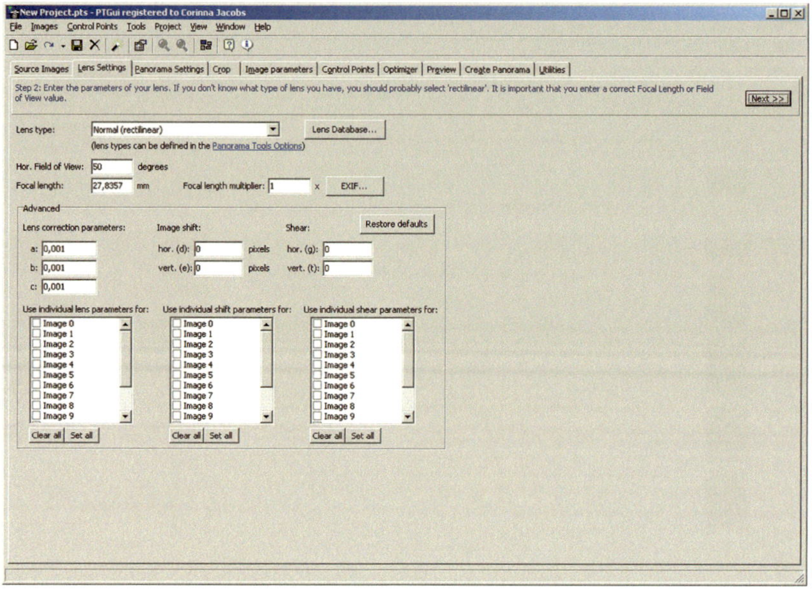

Figure 6.23
Exposure parameters are entered in the *Lens Settings* tab

Settings for the resulting panoramic file are configured in the *Panorama Settings* window (see Figure 6.24). Select the desired file format in the drop-down menu by *File format.* Some of possible formats include *Photoshop with masks* (ideal for retouching later on), *BMP, JPG* and *TIF.* If the *JPG* format is selected, the degree of compression can be set by *JPEG quality.* Projection specifies the form of projection; here, the possible settings are *Rectilinear* (for planar pictures), *Cylindrical* (for cylindrical 360° panoramas) and *Equirectangular* (for spherical 360° panoramas). The horizontal and vertical fields of view of the resulting panorama are defined by *Field of View.* In the *Advanced* section, the overlap width between the individual pictures can be set under *Feather width.* A large value leads to a softer transition, while a small value effects a hard edge. The tonal value range of the panoramic picture can be influenced under *Gamma,* whereby a value of 1 leaves the gamma curve unchanged. *Interpolator* specifies the interpolation method used to converge the individual pictures. The default method – *Poly 3* – brings about good results, without placing an overly large load on computer resources (which in turn leads to long processing times). The *Color correction* function is used to correct differences in color and lighting between the individual pictures. *Correct* is activated in the *Apply color correction* dialog box, at which time you can select a reference picture (via *Anchor image*) to which all other pictures in the sequence are adapted. This function is okay to use for smaller differences; however, if the pictures reveal greater fluctuations in color or lighting, it is recommended that you use a targeted color correction technique provided by image editing software.

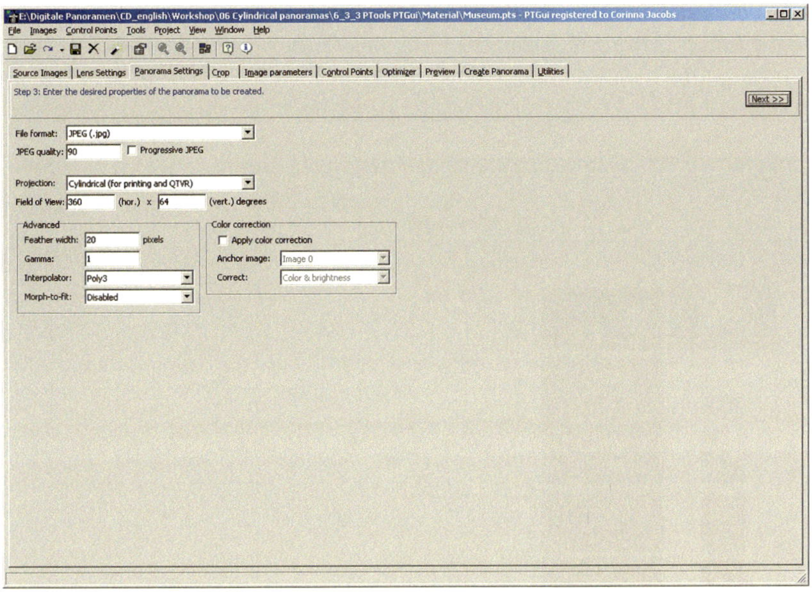

Figure 6.24
Panorama properties are defined in the *Panorama Settings* tab

Individual pictures can be cut, or cropped as required in the *Crop* tab (see Figure 6.25). This function is helpful when using scanned or circular fisheye pictures, as the black perimeter can be factored out to further edit the panorama. The size of the original pictures does not change after this function has been applied. If cropping is to be identical for each picture in a panoramic sequence, press the *Apply to all images* button.

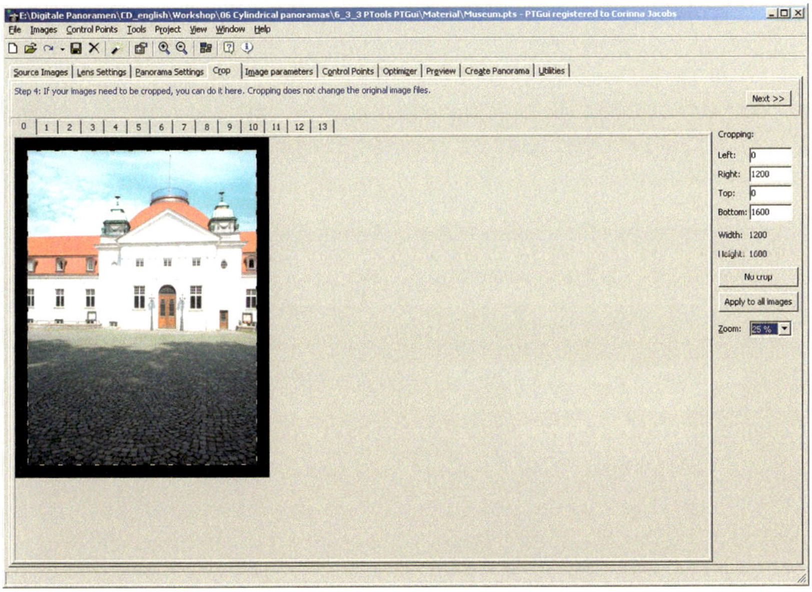

Figure 6.25
Pictures can be cropped in the *Crop* tab

The arrangement of the individual pictures in the panoramic strip is defined in the *Image parameters* tab (see Figure 6.26). You can enter the numerical values for each picture in the table or use the *Panorama Editor* (see Figure 6.27).

Figure 6.26
Individual pictures are positioned in the *Image Parameters* tab

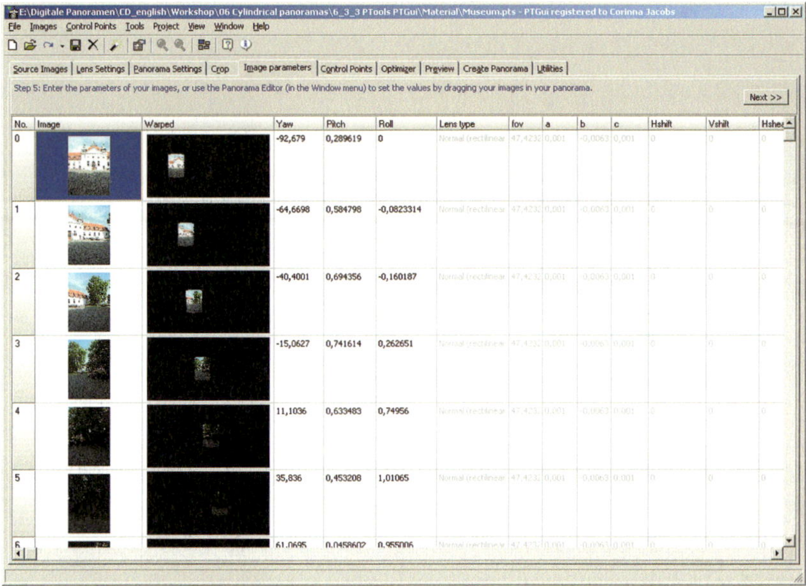

The table shows the pictures scaled down; in *Warped,* the pictures appear according to their arrangement in the panoramic strip. The type of distortion (*warp*) depends on the form of projection (*Rectilinear, Cylindrical* or *Equirectangular*) selected. *Yaw* (horizontal), *Pitch* (vertical) and *Roll* (rotation) define the position coordinates of each individual picture. Instead of numerically entering the coordinates, it is recommended that you use the *Panorama Editor* (see Figure 6.27), which is called up via *Window > Panorama Editor.*

Figure 6.27
In *Panorama Editor*, pictures can be positioned using a mouse

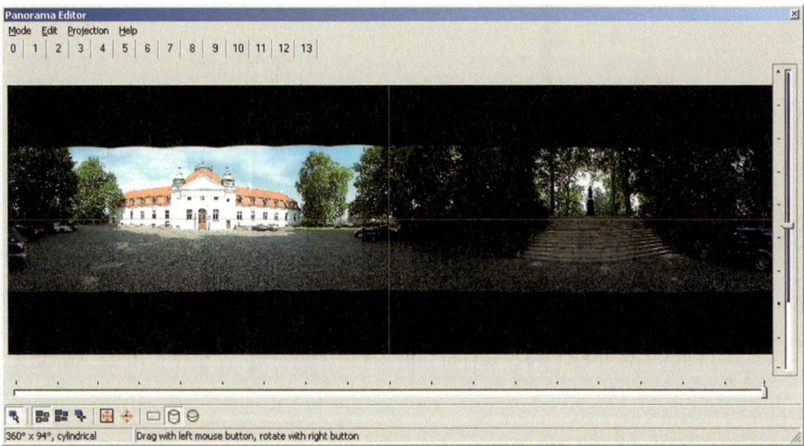

In *Panorama Editor,* the individual pictures in the panoramic strip can be positioned with the mouse. For better positioning, the pictures are displayed in distorted format analogous to the form of projection selected. The settings configured here are applied as position coordinates in the table of the *Image parameters* window (see Figure 6.26).

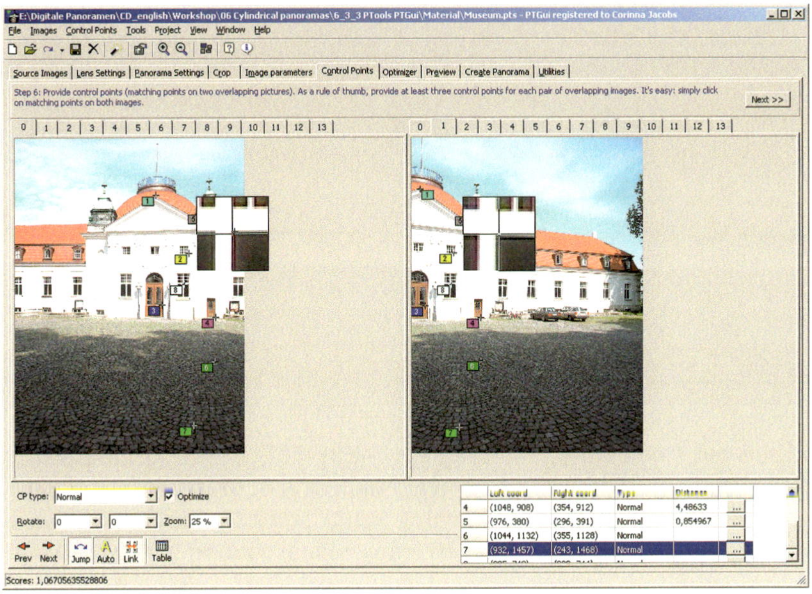

Figure 6.28
In the *Control Points* tab, stitching points are defined in the overlapping area of the individual pictures

The *Control Points* tab (see Figure 6.28) is used to specify individual points in the overlapping area of the individual pictures that are to coincide in the panorama. These points should be distributed as equally as possible in the overlapping area. The more control points are defined, the greater the fitting accuracy. When selecting points, it is advantageous to focus on areas of the picture that are rich in contrast. In the editing window, two neighboring pictures are placed next to each other. The stitching points are set using the left mouse button and appear in the table in the lower right corner of the window. The *Auto* function simplifies the process of setting control points; as soon as you have defined the first point of a control point pair in the left picture, the software automatically jumps to a similar point in the right picture. Once all of the required control points have been defined, the *Next* or *Prev* button is pressed to go to the next overlapping area. When all of the points for all of the pictures have been set, it is time to click on the *Optimizer* tab.

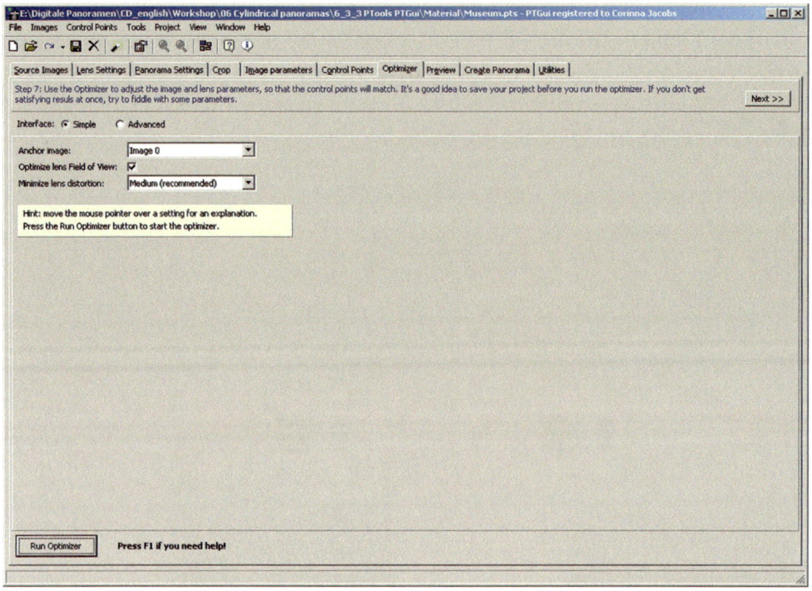

Figure 6.29
In the *Optimizer tab,* parameters are optimized based on the control points

In this tab (see Figure 6.29), the previously defined parameters such as focal length, field of view, position and distortion of the individual pictures are optimized such that the stitching points selected coincide with each other as much as possible. For most application scenarios, the *Simple interface* is sufficient. *Anchor Image* is used to define the reference picture to which all other pictures in the panoramic sequence are adapted. When the *Optimize lens Field of View* checkbox is activated, the values already defined for the focal length and the field of view in the *Lens Settings* tab (see Figure 6.23) are optimized based on the existing pictures. The *Minimize lens distortion* function is used to correct distortion errors. The optimization process is started by clicking the *Run Optimizer* button.

While the optimization process is running, an additional window opens that allows you to track the progress. *Optimizer* shows the average distance between the control points (*average control point distance*). The smaller the number, the better the chance of obtaining a good result. After optimization has concluded, a message window is displayed that informs you of the expected result (see Figure 6.30).

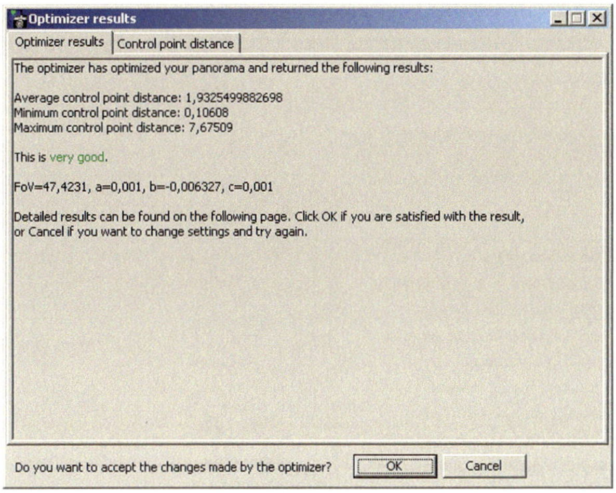

Figure 6.30
The expected result is notified in the *Optimizer results* window

If you are okay with the optimization result, confirm the changes by clicking the *OK* button. If the optimizer does not expect a good result, it is recommended that you delete the control points with a greater difference and redefine them. To do this, refer to the control point list to determine the stitching points in question. The respective points are then changed in the preceding tab, *Control Points* (see Figure 6.28). If you have made any changes, the optimization process should be run through again.

After this, you can see a preview of the panoramic picture in the *Preview* tab (see Figure 6.31). *Width* and *Height* determine the size of the preview picture. If certain pictures should be left out, simply uncheck the respective checkbox in the *Include images* field.

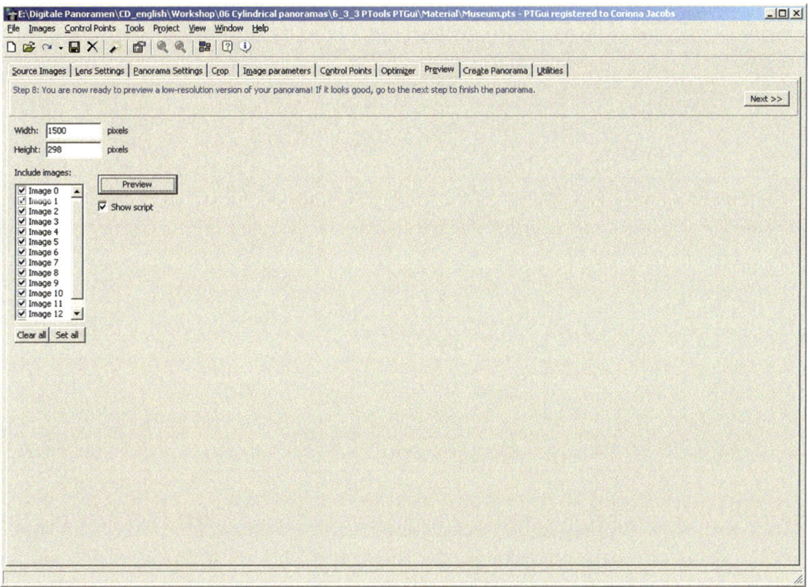

Figure 6.31
You can see a preview of the panoramic picture in the *Preview* tab

The software stitches the individual pictures using a script that can be viewed at any time. This script is displayed by activating the *Show script* dialog box (see Figure 6.32).

Figure 6.32
Script used by PTStitcher (PanoTools application) to process the pictures

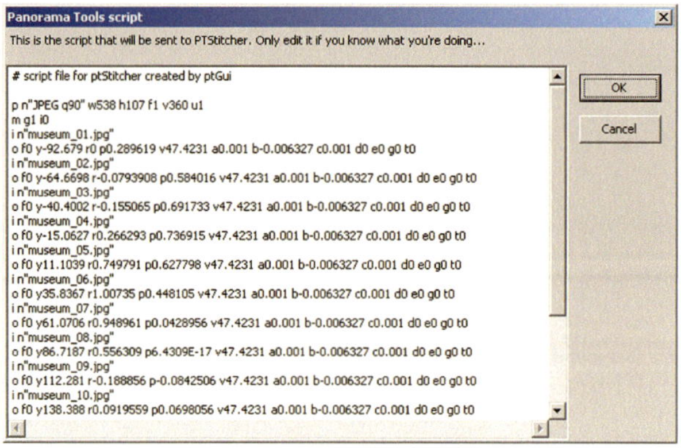

Only advanced users should make changes to the PanoTools script. The preview is started by clicking the *Preview* button. If no preview picture is displayed, it is possible that the path information for the PTStitcher application and the viewers is missing. Without this information, PTGui cannot call up the respective PanoTools functions. Proper configuration can be made via *Tools > Options > Directories & files.*

Figure 6.33
The final panoramic file is created in the *Create Panorama* tab

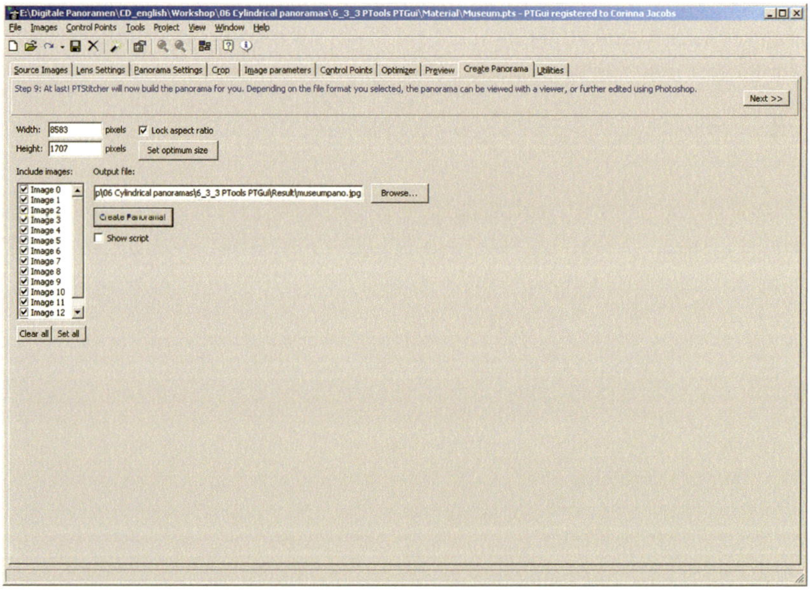

The panoramic picture is created in the *Create Panorama* field (see Figure 6.33). The size of the picture is specified in pixels by *Width* and *Height.* If you have activated *Lock aspect ratio,* the aspect ratio of the panoramic picture remains consistent, even when one of the two values is changed. The *Set optimum size* function triggers the software to calculate the optimum size of the panorama based on raw material (1:1). Under *Include images,* you can include and exclude certain pictures from the calculation process. *Show script* shows the script that is sent to PTStitcher. Clicking the *Create Panorama* button initiates the final stitching process and saves the resulting panoramic picture.

You will find the pictures and the panorama shown here on the CD at the following path: \Workshop\06 Cylindrical panoramas\6_3_3 PanoTools PTGui

Cylindrical panoramic pictures frequently have wavy edges at the top and bottom, which are caused by overlapping several pictures. Thus, an additional editing step is required. At this point, you switch to an image editing program and manually cut the panoramic picture to the desired size. The picture width must not be cut for a complete 360° panorama! After this, you will need to save the panoramic picture. For Web publication, it is best to save in JPG format.

Chapter 10.2 provides information on how to publish these cylindrical panoramic pictures. There you will find more information on viewers as well as the source code used to embed panoramas in Web sites. These flat panoramic strips also can be printed out on paper or professionally developed in a photo lab. For more information, refer to chapter 10.6.

Several of these cylindrical panoramas can be stitched to create a virtual tour. There are a number of different solutions available for such a task, some of which are introduced in chapters 9.3.3 and 9.3.5.

Advantages

- The software is free of charge (freeware).
- PanoTools runs on Linux, Mac and PC platforms.
- The software supports all lens types. Fisheye and rectilinear pictures can be used for stitching.
- PanoTools supports a large number of file formats.
- The software not only can be used for stitching; PanoTools is capable of correcting optical distortions.
- The script, which can be viewed in any text editor, makes the algorithms used very transparent.

Disadvantages

- Large monochrome areas (e.g. the night sky) are difficult to stitch with this software. The overlapping points defined should reveal a high range contrast, as otherwise they cannot be identified as reference pixels for stitching.
- PanoTools is not intuitive for beginners, however add-on programs such as PTGui and PTMac make operating the software easier.
- The filmstrip appears as an interactive panorama for the observer only in conjunction with the PTViewer Java applet, integrated in an HTML file.

6.3.4 REALVIZ Stitcher (multi-row technique)

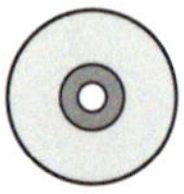

A demo version of REALVIZ Stitcher can be found on the CD at the following paths: \Demo versions\Mac and \Demo versions\PC

REALVIZ Stitcher allows you to edit single-row and multi-row panoramas. Cylindrical, spherical and cubic panoramas can be created. The following explains what steps you need to take to produce a double row cylindrical panorama using REALVIZ Stitcher.

Figure 6.34 shows the program's main window. The first thing you need to do is to create a new project; trace to *File > New* to open a new document. It is now a good idea to save this stitcher project right away by going to *File > Save* as and assigning a specific name. The next step is to import the individual pictures of the panorama via *File > Load Images*. Here, the pictures are merely referenced, which keeps the stitcher project small in size and simplifies correction of the individual pictures later on. Once the pictures are loaded, they appear as thumbnails in the lower part of the editing window. Here, the pictures can be repositioned by clicking on them and rotating them to the correct position via *Edit > Rotate*.

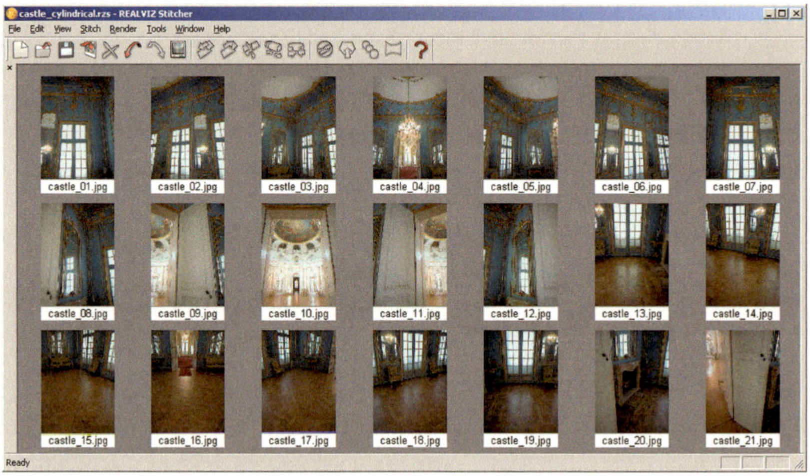

Figure 6.34
Imported pictures prior to starting the stitching process

The software automatically detects the aspect ratio of the pictures, what focal length was used and the type of distortion involved. For the first few tests, it is recommended that you simply apply the preconfigured settings. Values can be individually changed via *Edit > Properties*.

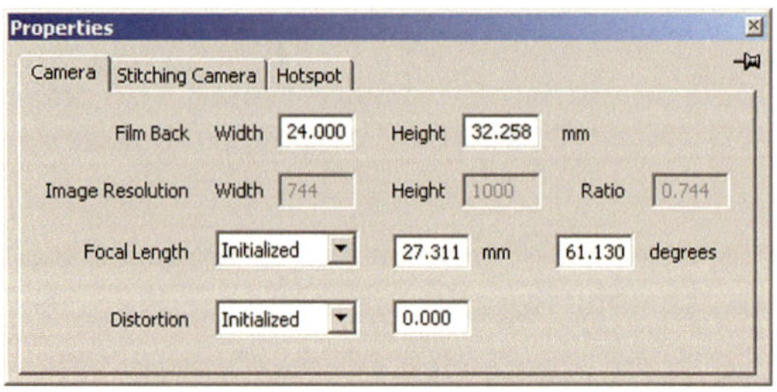

Figure 6.35
Image properties can be set in the *Properties* window

Pictures that were taken with a wide angle lens may reveal distortion toward the edges, which means that additional steps will be required prior to stitching. REALVIZ Stitcher provides options to correct these distortion errors. To this end, the first two pictures are dragged and dropped into the upper editing area and positioned as congruently as possible. The individual pictures now can be rotated for fine positioning. If you are working on a Windows operating system, press the Shift key while moving the picture with the mouse (right button depressed). If you are working on a Macintosh, press the Shift and the Ctrl keys; the picture is rotated with the left mouse button depressed. The pictures should not be stitched just yet, as otherwise it will no longer be possible to correct the distortion. The *Tools > High Distortion > Calibrate* function calculates the distortion present in all pictures included in this project and makes the appropriate corrections (see Figure 6.36). Correction of the distortion can be undone via *Tools > High Distortion > Reset.*

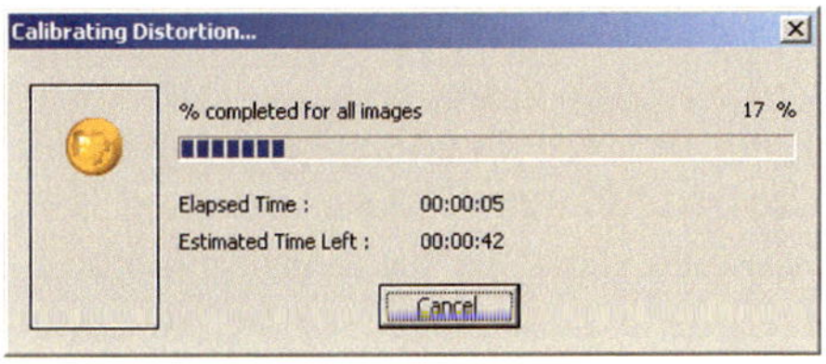

Figure 6.36
Distortion errors can be corrected via the *High Distortion Calibration* function

Before you begin positioning the individual pictures, it is a good idea to exclude any undesired areas. This, for example, can be a passerby at the edge of a picture who should not appear in the subsequent panorama. With the *Tools > Stencil* function, the problematic area of the picture is marked in the shape of a polygon (see Figure 6.37). You now can select whether the marked area or the remaining part of the picture should be excluded by clicking on the respective field by *Stencil Mode*. It is recommended that you only do this in the overlapping area of pictures, as the marked area is supplemented with information from the bordering picture. If no substitute picture information is available, the marked areas in the panorama appear black. Additionally, it is possible to crop the border of the pictures used via the *Crop Border* function. Any vignetting effects can be excluded using the *Vignetting* stencil tool. If desired, these settings can be applied to all pictures associated with this project.

You can undo any setting you have made at any time as well as change the shape of the polygons via *Tools > Stencil.* These settings do not necessarily have to be made prior to stitching; you always have the option of first stitching and visually analyzing the complete panoramic picture, at which time you can go back and work on those areas that need to be improved.

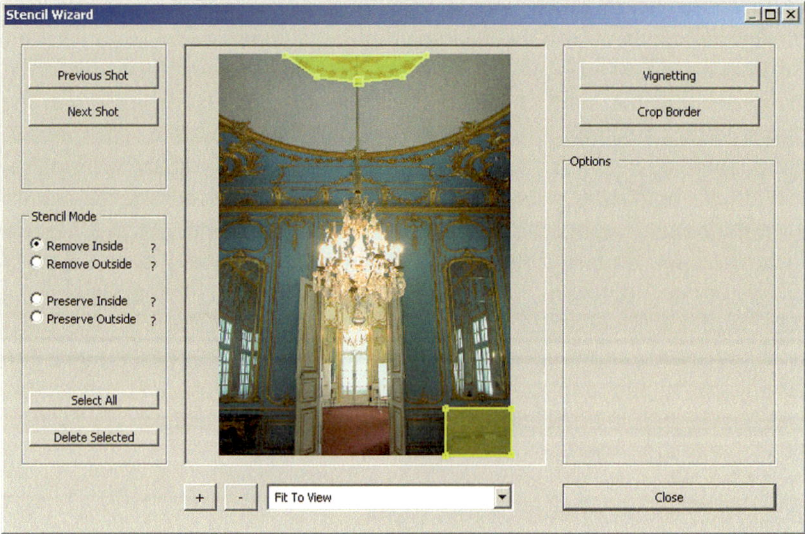

Figure 6.37
The *Stencil* function allows you to exclude undesired areas of a picture

The actual stitching occurs by dragging and dropping the first picture from the thumbnail picture bar up into the editing area. The same is then done for the second picture, which is positioned such that the overlapping areas are as congruent as possible (see Figure 6.38). Approximate, or rough positioning, can be done with a mouse, however it is recommended that you use the arrow keys for fine positioning. For Windows users, each picture can be rotated by pressing the Shift key while moving the image with the mouse (right button depressed). Macintosh users need to press the Shift and Ctrl keys while rotating with the left mouse button depressed. Once the position of the respective picture is okay, stitching can be executed by pressing Enter. After the picture has been stitched, the color bordering the image changes from red (positionable) to green (stitched).

If a particular picture cannot be stitched, a dialog window appears, informing the user accordingly. Here, the *Forced Stitch* function can be used to stitch under any circumstances. The picture then is not automatically positioned by the software; instead, the position in the sequence manually defined is used.

To navigate in a panorama, rotate the view, sweep or zoom, the *View > Pan, Roll* and *Zoom* functions are used. As is the case with the majority of the functions, there is also built-in support for hot keys, which are listed next to the respective functions in the menu. These hot keys can differ from platform to platform, which is why they are not explicitly listed here.

The software is capable of optimizing the values specified at the beginning for focal length and distortion based on the already stitched pictures. This takes place via the *Stitch > Adjust All Images* function. It is recommended that you perform this correction after four or five pictures have been stitched as well as after the complete stitching process is finished.

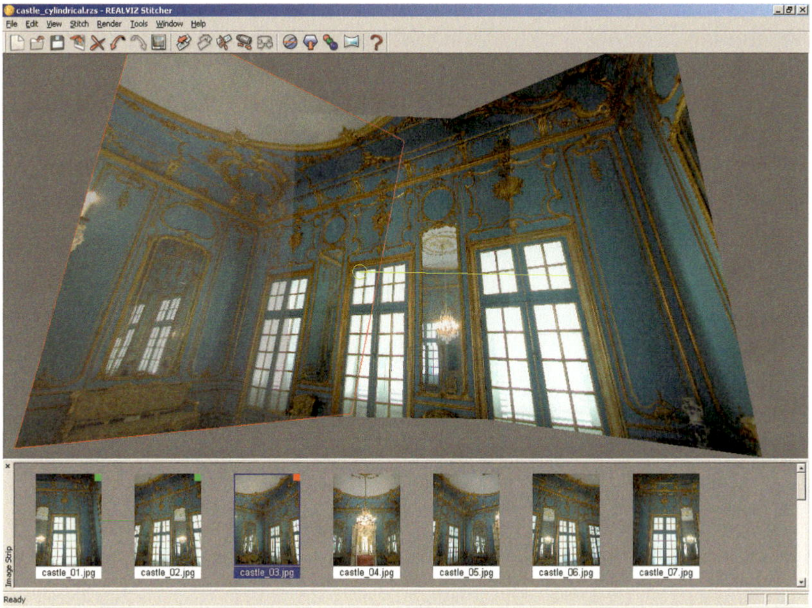

Figure 6.38
Stitching process: Pictures highlighted in red can be positioned; pictures highlighted in green already have been stitched

Once all of the pictures in the first picture sequence have been positioned and stitched, this sequence is closed to form a cylindrical panorama. To do this, select *Close Panorama* from the *Stitch* menu. The background color of the editing window now changes and you can connect the picture stitched last with the first picture in the sequence. These two pictures are then stitched as already described.

At this point, the second picture sequence is added by positioning and stitching the individual pictures. Doing so gives you a double row panoramic picture that, compared to the single row version, has an extended vertical field of view.

If the individual pictures reveal varying degrees of brightness, the *Render > Equalize All Images* function can be used to correct this. Here, all pictures associated with the panorama are adjusted to each other in terms of their brightness. This function is okay to use for smaller differences; however, if the pictures reveal greater fluctuations in color or lighting, it is recommended that you use a targeted color correction technique provided by image editing software.

Before the panorama is rendered for the export, the desired part of the picture should be selected. The panorama is positioned according to that part of the image that currently can be seen in the editing window. The *Tools > Align Panorama* function can be used to define the horizontal plane of the panorama. Horizontal and vertical lines are drawn for alignment purposes. Here, it is useful to activate the grid function by tracing to *Edit > Preferences > Display Grid.* Once the desired position for the initial picture display of the panorama has been found, the panorama is rendered.

There are a number of rendering options available as far as projection and file formats are concerned; REALVIZ Stitcher provides support for cylindrical, spherical and cubic projection.

A cylindrical panorama can be published as a cylindrical QTVR or exported as a filmstrip and displayed as a cylindrical panorama in certain viewers.

In Figure 6.39, you can see which settings are made for the sample panorama shown here in the *Render > Render* mode with regard to rendering and exporting a cylindrical QTVR movie.

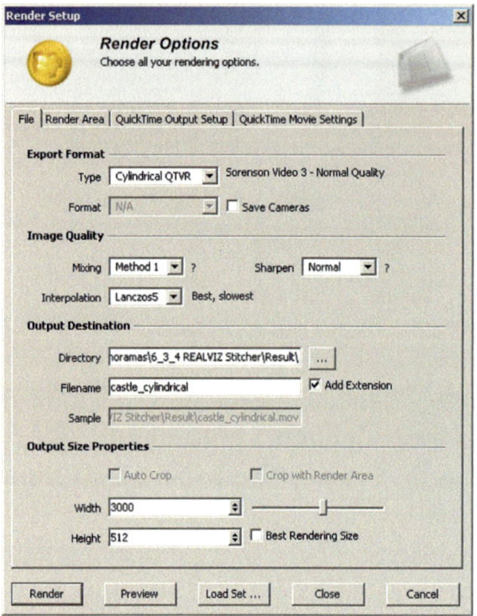

Figure 6.39
File format and resolution for the cylindrical QTVR panorama are defined in the *File* dialog field

The projection format is defined by *File > Export Format > Type* (here: *Cylindrical QTVR*). Factors for image quality such as definition and interpolation are set under *Image Quality.* In *Output Size Properties,* the resolution of the subsequent panoramic picture is defined in pixels. The higher the resolution value selected, the better the image quality, however the file size also increases in proportion to this resolution and image quality. When *Best Rendering Size* is activated, the software calculates the optimum size of the panorama based on raw material (1:1). Starting with an average value, you can estimate the expected image quality and file size.

In the *Render Area* field, the panoramic picture is cropped prior to rendering so that only a specific part of the panorama is used. This function, however, has not been applied in the example.

Additional QTVR-specific settings can be made in the *QuickTime Output Setup* window (see Figure 6.40).

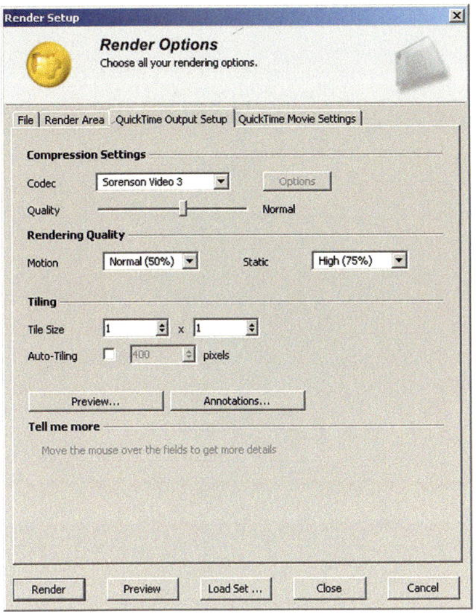

Figure 6.40
Additional QTVR movie properties can be set in the *QuickTime Output Setup* dialog field

The type of compression used is selected by *Compression Settings > Codec* (more information on codecs can be found in chapter 10.1). The desired image quality is set next to *Compression Settings > Quality. Rendering Quality* determines the image quality when the panorama is moving (*Motion*) and not moving (*Static*). In the *Tiling* field, the panoramic picture is subdivided into quadrants (*Tiles*) so that all tiles that already have been downloaded can be played. The tiling function, however, only can be used in REALVIZ Stitcher for cubic QTVR movies. In *Preview,* you can activate "fast start" QuickTime streaming, which allows parts of the panorama to be viewed by the user while continuing to download the QTVR file. It is also possible to create a preview screen for the QTVR movie, which provides the observer a low resolution view of the panorama before the file is completely downloaded from the Internet. In *Annotations,* text information such as the author, copyright and a short description of the content can be added to the QTVR movie.

The *QuickTime Movie Settings* field (see Figure 6.41) is used to define the window size (*Window*) in pixels. *Pan* and *Tilt* allow you to configure the opening picture display of the QTVR movie. The minimum and maximum zoom factors are defined by *FOV.* With the *Optimal Minimum FOV* function, you can specify a maximum zoom range to prevent the panorama from appearing too coarse when the picture is magnified. *Optimal Default FOV* selects an average angle of view as the start position for the QTVR movie in order for the user to be able to pivot up and down.

When all settings have been made, the calculation process is initiated by clicking the *Render* button. The result can be optimized by rendering again with different values.

To learn how cylindrical QTVR panoramas are published, please refer to chapter 10.1. There you will find more information on viewers as well as the source code used to embed panoramas in Web sites.

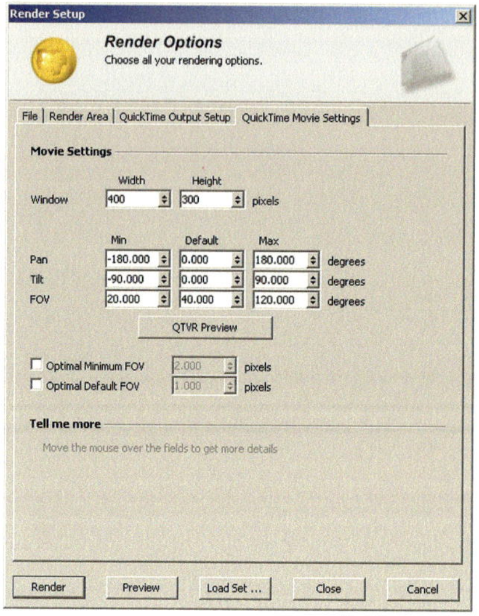

Figure 6.41
The playback properties of the QTVR panorama are defined in the *QuickTime Movie Settings* dialog field

REALVIZ Stitcher allows you to create virtual tours from several QTVR panoramas. The process to follow for defining hot spots and creating a virtual tour is described in detail in chapter 9.3.1.

The second option for publishing cylindrical panoramas is to create a panoramic filmstrip that is cylindrically projected using a viewer. In Figure 6.42, you can see which settings are made for the sample panorama in the *Render > Render* mode with regard to rendering a cylindrical panoramic picture.

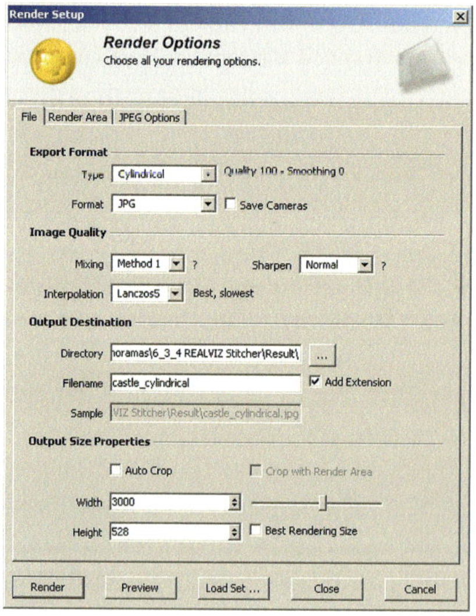

Figure 6.42
File format and resolution for the cylindrical panoramic picture are defined in the *File* dialog field

Cylindrical is selected by *File > Export Format > Type.* Next to *Format,* select the desired file format. For Internet application, the picture typically should be saved as a JPG file. If the panoramic picture needs to be further edited, do not select this option, as the data loss associated with the JPG format is too great due to the level of compression used. Instead, it is better to save the picture in a format (such as TIF) that does not compromise picture data and make any changes to the size or the file format in an image editing program. Factors for image quality such as definition and interpolation are set under *Image Quality.* In *Output Size Properties,* the resolution of the subsequent panoramic picture is defined in pixels. The higher the resolution value selected, the better the image quality, however the file size also increases in proportion to this resolution and image quality. When *Best Rendering Size* is activated, the software calculates the optimum size of the panorama based on raw material (1:1).

In the *Render Area* field, the panoramic picture can be cropped prior to rendering so that only a specific part of the panorama is used. This function, however, has not been applied in the example.

The *JPEG Options/TIFF Options* section is where image compression settings are made.

When all settings have been made, the calculation process is initiated by clicking the Render button, at which point the panoramic picture is created.

Chapter 10.2 provides information on how to publish these cylindrical panoramic pictures. There you will find more information on viewers as well as the source code used to embed panoramas in Web sites. These flat panoramic strips also can be printed out on paper or professionally developed in a photo lab. For more information, refer to chapter 10.6.

You will find the pictures and panoramas shown here on the CD at the following path: \Workshop\ 06 Cylindrical panoramas\ 6_3_4 REALVIZ Stitcher

The sample panorama shown in this chapter is further edited in chapter 7.3.2 by adding additional picture sequences to create a spherical panorama.

Several cylindrical panoramas can be stitched into a virtual tour; for more information on how to produce virtual tours, please refer to chapter 9.

Advantages

- REALVIZ Stitcher supports all common panoramic projection formats.
- The software can be used to import and export a wide variety of file formats.
- Panoramic formats are able to be converted.

Disadvantages

- Only rectilinear lenses may be used. There is no support for fisheye pictures.

7. Spherical and cubic panoramas

7.1 Introduction

Spherical and cubic panoramas only differ in the type of projection used. As far as the actual photography is concerned, the same technique can be applied. Compared to their cylindrical counterpart, spherical and cubic panoramas have an extended vertical angle of view. Vertical travel is not limited here, which makes it possible to view the ground as well as the sky of a scene. When the ground is filmed, parts of the tripod usually are captured as well. If the scene is to be realistically depicted, however, these areas should be edited out.

Spherical panoramas can be photographed using special panoramic cameras. Alternatively, there is the option of taking one or more sequences of individual pictures that overlap each other by a certain percentage. The number of pictures required is a function of the focal length of the lens used (see chapter 2.2.4). The pictures are then stitched into a panoramic picture using special stitching software.

7.2 Photo technology and techniques

7.2.1 Panoramic cameras

Both analog and digital panoramic cameras are available. While analog cameras typically are limited to photographing cylindrical panoramas, digital panoramic cameras are capable of taking cylindrical and spherical panoramic shots. The lens used provides a corresponding vertical field of view. While chapter 6.2.1 presented an analog camera for the production of cylindrical panoramas, this chapter introduces two digital panoramic cameras. Outside of the models that receive mention in this book, there are other panoramic cameras available for purchase. A selection of manufacturers is provided in chapter B.2.4. The digital camera models presented here employ scanning technology. Instead of having a CCD chip typical for digital chip cameras, these cameras are equipped with an RGB line sensor. When a scene is being photographed, the camera rotates about its axis via a motor in order to capture, or scan, the complete environment.

Due to the scanning technology they employ, digital panoramic cameras are not very well suited to filming moving objects. Such objects usually are not depicted realistically, as unwanted distortion frequently crops up (see Figure 7.1). These distortions of course may be used intentionally for effect, e.g. for special artistic panoramas.

Figure 7.1
Moving objects filmed by scanning cameras lead to optical distortion

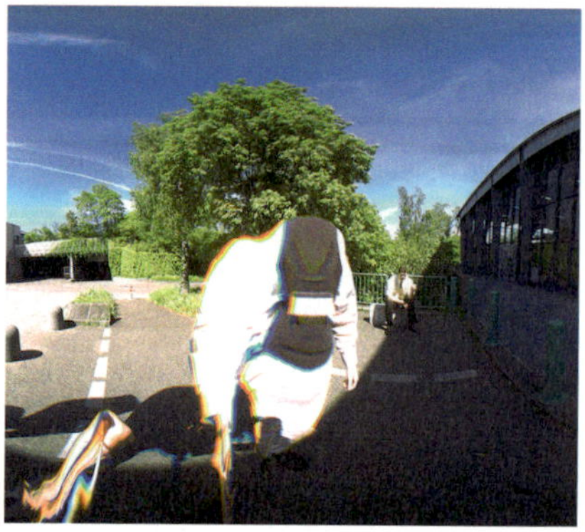

When subjected to direct sunlight, image errors in the form of white stripes are not uncommon (see Figure 7.2). This effect is known as blooming (see chapter 3.4.2). When a short exposure time is selected, this effect is minimized or at least reduced in intensity.

Figure 7.2
When subjected to direct sunlight, scanning cameras can produce a white blooming line

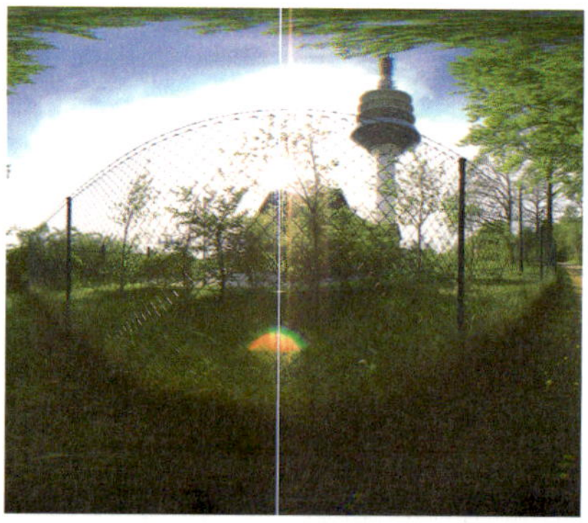

The amount of daylight present influences the rotational speed of the camera as it takes pictures. While the time required to film a panorama with sufficient light is around 1 minute, more darkly lit scenes easily can result in shooting times of 10 minutes and more. It is ineffective to take pictures during the night with such cameras, as the exposure process is extremely long and moving lights lead to distortion in the form of stripes. Although the effects that result can, of course, be intentionally used for special applications, scanning cameras represent the wrong choice if a realistic night scene is to be photographed.

The digital panoramic cameras introduced below only can be used when connected to a notebook. The pictures taken are controlled by the computer and saved on its local hard disk. The software required for this comes with the camera and will function only when the camera is connected. As such, the camera software is not covered in as much detail as the stitching software. More information on the functionality of the respective software products can be obtained from the manufacturers (see chapter B.2.4).

7.2.1.1 Seitz Roundshot Super Digital II

The Roundshot Super Digital II RBG line sensor provides a maximum vertical resolution of 2,700 pixels. Depending on the lens used, this camera can take spherical shots with a vertical field of view of approximately 180 degrees. During the photo shoot, the camera is turned by a step motor; the horizontal angle of rotation ranges from 1 to 400 degrees.

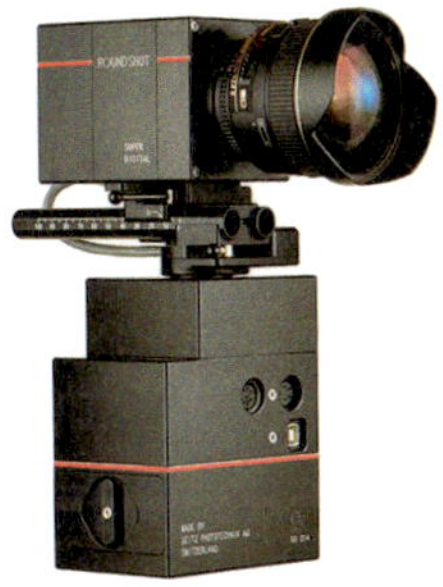

Figure 7.3
Roundshot Super Digital II

Before any pictures are taken, the camera head is positioned in accordance with the respective lens. The camera head can be horizontally moved via an optical bank. This allows the nodal point of the lens to be positioned directly over the pivoting point of the camera head. There is another application for the optical bank, though. If a turntable is set on top of it, the device can be used for the production of object movies.

The Roundshot Super Digital II only can be used in conjunction with a notebook computer. It is from here that the Roundshot software controls the picture taking process and saves the picture information. In order to avoid having yourself being included in the spherical panorama, you will have to move in parallel with the camera while holding the notebook. When the camera is taking pictures, it rotates about the horizontal axis. The field of view captured can be configured by the software. In order to ensure enough overlap when stitching the pictures later on, it is recommended that you film at least 5 percent of the preceding picture.

The camera measures the level of light at the start and end positions of the picture sequence so that there will be no differences in illumination at the overlapping edges. A choice can be made between fixed exposure and automatic exposure. With the latter option, the automatic mechanism controls and changes the exposure time during the shooting sequence via the camera's rotational speed. This way, differences in the level of illumination can be easily balanced out.

Figure 7.4
Roundshot software in action while filming a panoramic scene

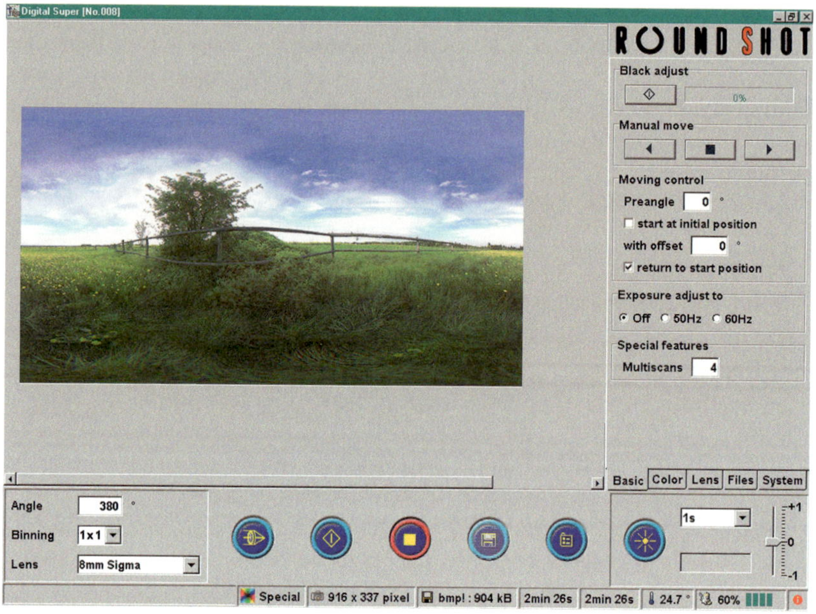

Prior to shooting, it is necessary to set the so-called *Binning* rate in the software application. This value determines the scanning resolution of the scan line and ranges from the highest resolution with 1 x 1 to the lowest resolution with 8 x 8. If 8 x 8 is selected as the *Binning* rate, only every 8th pixel is recorded. The higher the scanning resolution selected, the longer the scanning process takes. The focal length of the lens and the desired panoramic field of view also are specified before shooting begins. In order to achieve the best result, it is important that you use the *Black adjust* function before taking any pictures.

After all relevant settings have been made, the software calculates the expected film time. The fastest rotation time at the optimal level of light is approximately 20 seconds for a full 360 degree spin.

If the light conditions are not ideal (such as is the case in interior rooms), panoramic scanning at the highest available resolution can take 15 minutes or more. For such application scenarios, it is recommended that you use swiveling panel lights from Grigull (or a comparable brand) to achieve better, more uniform lighting of the environment. These lights are attached to the camera by an arm, which allows them to be rotated by the camera motor. The camera software is capable of synchronizing the line read-out frequency with the 50 Hz of the panel lights; this eliminates any light-dark phases during scanning that otherwise would lead to a striping pattern. More information on the Grigull lighting system can be found on the company's Web site at: http://www.grigull.com [status: April 1, 2004].

Figure 7.5 shows the panoramic picture taken using this technique. Refer to chapter 7.3.1 for the additional steps required to produce produce an interactive panorama.

You can find the panoramic picture shown here and the QTVR movie on the CD at the following path: \Workshop\ 07 Spherical panoramas\ 7_3_1 Panoramic picture

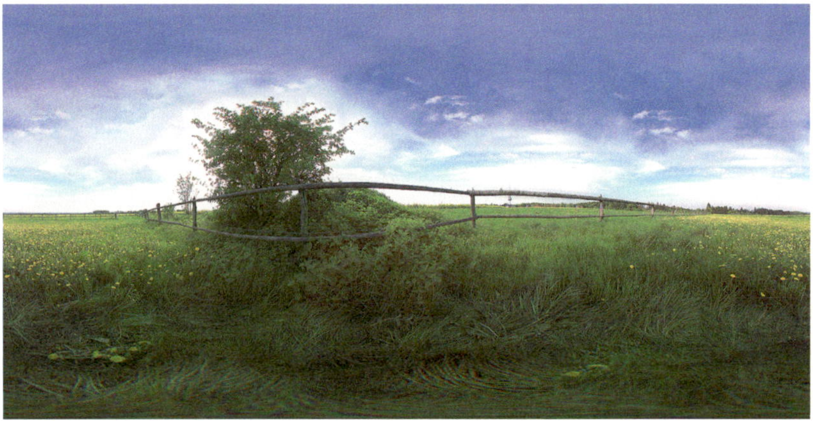

Figure 7.5
Panoramic picture taken using the Roundshot Super Digital II

Advantages

- One shot is all it takes to create a fully spherical view.
- No stitching is required; only the seam edge needs to be edited.
- Given sufficient lighting conditions, a panoramic picture can be taken in a matter of seconds.
- As a notebook is directly connected to the camera, the resulting picture can be visually analyzed right on the set and retaken as required.

Disadvantages

- The camera costs around US $ 6,000 and can only be used for panoramic photography. Traditional shots cannot be taken.
- Due to the scanning technology employed, undesirable distortion errors can arise when filming moving objects. Wide strips of color are photographed to an extent.
- If the available light is not sufficient and cannot be increased using an artificial lighting system, the camera may require 15 minutes or more to take a single picture at the highest resolution.
- Operation is only possible when a notebook is connected, which controls the shooting process. Data are transferred to the notebook as the picture is taken and saved on the local hard disk.
- A white strip can appear in that part of the picture where direct contact with sunlight was made. This phenomenon is known as blooming.

7.2.1.2 Spheron SpheroCam HDR

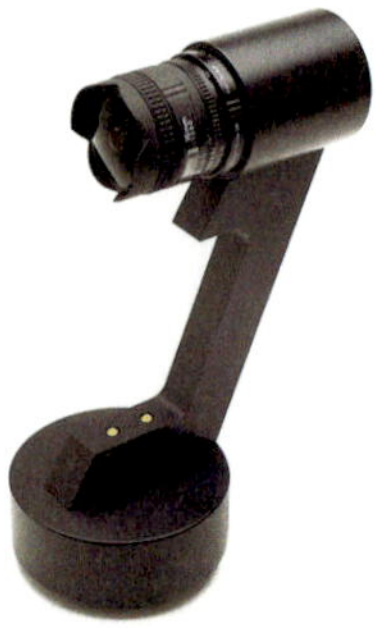

Figure 7.6
SpheroCam HDR

Scanning technology also is employed in the SpheroCam HDR. The RGB line sensor allows for a maximum vertical resolution of 5,300 pixels. This camera is driven by a direct current motor, whereby the scene is scanned in 1,300 intervals at 360 degrees of horizontal rotation. When equipped with a fisheye lens that covers over 180 degrees, fully spherical shots can be taken. The lenses are precisely calibrated by Spheron and fitted according to the position of the nodal point. As the camera and lens represent an optimized, highly integrated complete solution, it is not recommended that you switch to a lens that has not been calibrated. The SpheroCam typically has 12 aperture stops, or f-stops, while the SpheroCam HDR (High Dynamic Range) has up to 26 f-stops. Control of the picture taking process is exercised by a connected notebook running the associated camera software (see Figure 7.7).

Before any pictures are taken, it is a good idea to level the camera. An electronic sensor located in the camera housing makes this task easier. This sensor is triggered by the camera software and helps the photographer to position the camera exactly horizontal.

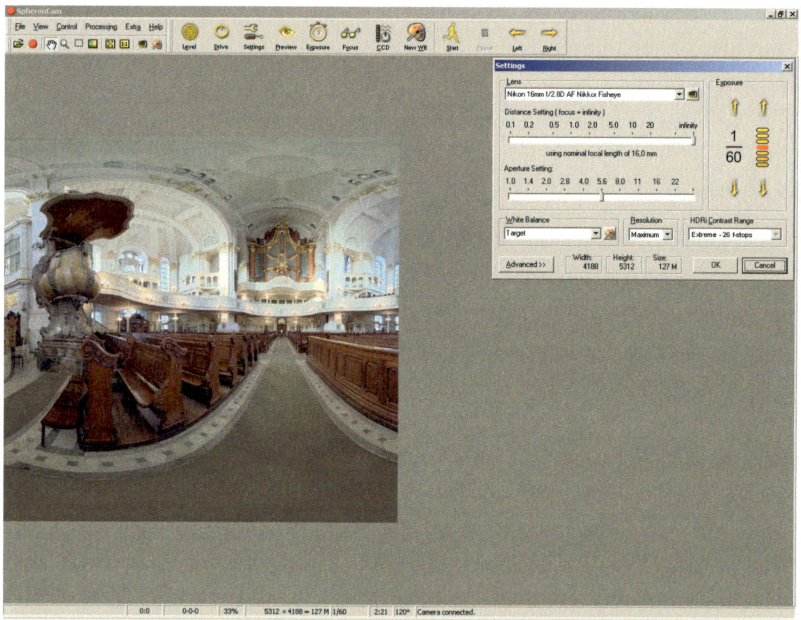

Figure 7.7
SpheronCam software in action while filming a panoramic scene

The lens used is selected by *Settings > Lens;* once this is done, errors such as distortion and chromatic aberration specific to the calibrated lens are automatically corrected by the software. In addition, the desired photographic settings with respect to the horizontal and vertical fields of view are made as well. Here, the horizontal field of view can range from 1 to 1,600 degrees. Light sensitivity is defined based on the *ISO* value. As is the case with every digital photograph, it is recommended that a manual white adjustment be carried out in order to realistically depict the color scheme of a scene. To do this, simply use a white cardboard box or, in the preview picture, define a white spot to focus the camera on for calibration. Exposure settings and the resolution also need to be configured, whereby the number of available f-stops ranges from 12 to 26. The higher the resolution and number of f-stops, the larger the resulting image file. For an HDR picture, *Extreme - 26 f-stops* is selected by *HDRi Contrast Range.* The scanning process is initiated via *Start.* While shooting, the photographer needs to move along with the camera in order to avoid becoming part of the scene.

After the shooting, the seam edge is stitched by the software. As such, it is recommended that you swivel the camera approximately 400 degrees for a 360 degree panorama. Doing this allows the SpheronCam software to blend both image edges into each other in the overlapping area later on. First, a soft transition is created in order to even out any differences in illumination where both pictures meet. For file export, a panoramic picture with a hard edge is created that encompasses exactly 360 degrees in the horizontal plane.

Various different panoramic formats can be selected when saving. The format to select for publication with a spherical Java viewer is the equirectangular format. If a cubic QTVR movie is to be created, it is best to individually export each side of the cube. With the cubic format, it is most convenient to retouch the lower part of the picture if you do not want to have the tripod depicted in the presentation. A cylindrical picture also can be saved and subsequently published in one of several ways.

When an HDR panorama such as the one shown here is shot, the following file formats can be selected: TIFF (8, 16 or 32-bit), JPEG, QuickTime VR, RADIANCE and Open EXR (HDR format).

In addition to be used as high quality interactive panoramas, these special HDR pictures can serve as a basis for illuminating 3-D objects. This technique finds application in the production of science fiction films, for example, where model scenes such as lunar landscapes are photographed with the SpheroCam HDR. The HDR picture obtained in this way can be used as a so-called light map for the realistic illumination, or lighting, of a computer-generated spaceship. This illumination effect based on HDR pictures used for 3-D renderings is known as image-based lighting.

Figure 7.8 shows the panoramic picture taken using this technique. Refer to chapter 7.3.1 for the additional steps required to produce an interactive panorama.

You can find the panoramic picture shown here and the QTVR movie on the CD at the following path:
\Workshop\
07 Spherical panoramas\
7_2_1_2 SpheroCam HDR

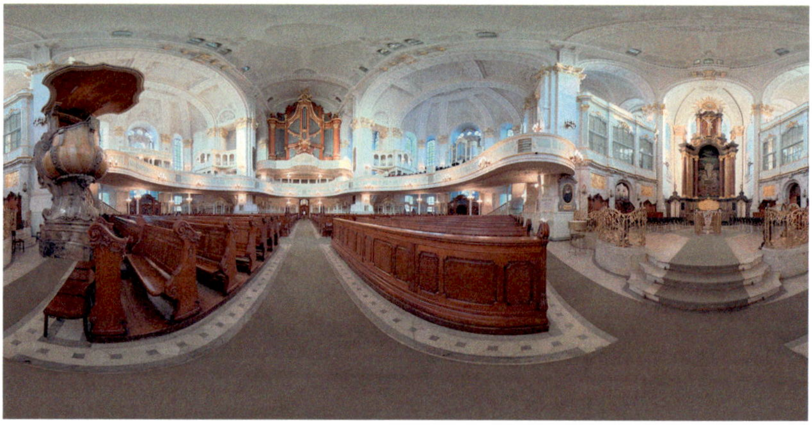

Figure 7.8
HDR panorama taken with the Spheron SpheroCam HDR

Advantages

- One shot is all it takes to create a fully spherical view.
- The camera can be set up relatively quickly and, if light conditions are good, a complete panoramic picture can be taken in just a few minutes.
- No stitching is required.
- Due to the high resolution, the resulting image quality is also sufficient for making printouts.
- The HDR technique allows for a very high range of contrast, which avoids the risk of taking underdeveloped or overdeveloped shots.
- As a notebook is directly connected to the camera, the resulting picture can be visually analyzed right on the set and retaken as required.

Disadvantages

- The price for the SpheroCam is around US $ 22,000, while the SpheroCam HDR costs roughly US $ 60,000.
- The application range of the cameras is focused on panoramic photography. Traditional shots cannot be taken.
- Due to the scanning technology employed, undesirable distortion errors can arise when filming moving objects. Wide strips of color are photographed to an extent.
- If the available light is not sufficient and cannot be increased using an artificial lighting system, the camera may require 15 minutes or more to take a single picture at the highest resolution.
- Operation is only possible when a notebook is connected, which controls the shooting process. Data are transferred to the notebook as the picture is taken and saved on the local hard disk.
- A white strip can appear in that part of the picture where direct contact with sunlight was made. This phenomenon is known as blooming.

7.2.2 Single-row technique

7.2.2.1 Using two fisheye pictures

If you use an 8 mm fisheye lens, for example, the large field of view exceeding 180 degrees allows you to create a spherical panorama from just two fisheye pictures. After the first picture is taken, the camera is swiveled 180 degrees for the next picture. Setup time is relatively short, depending on the tripod head used.

The individual pictures taken using this technique can be made with the iPIX Rotator, the QuickPan III tripod head from Kaidan, the VR-Drive from Roundshot or a monopod with plumb bob (see chapter 7.2.4).

Figure 7.9 shows pictures that were taken using this technique. Refer to chapter 7.3.3 for the additional steps required to produce an interactive panorama.

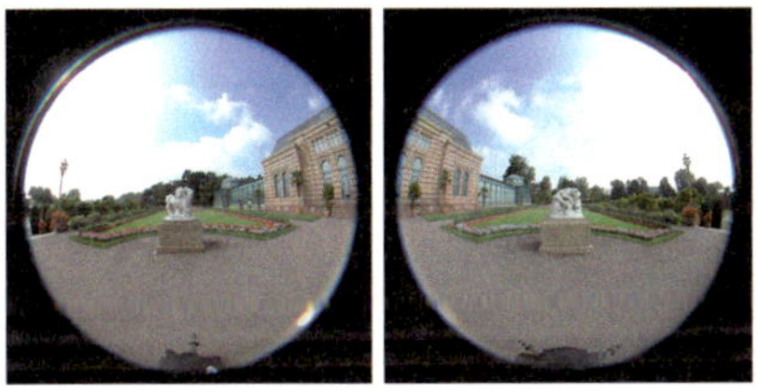

Figure 7.9
Individual pictures of a spherical single-row panorama comprising two fisheye shots

Advantages

- Only two pictures need to be taken, making the time involved with filming a complete spherical panorama relatively short.
- Due to the large field of view associated with fisheye lenses, moving objects represent no problem as long as they are not located toward the edge of the picture.

Disadvantages

- Not all cameras can be equipped with a suitable fisheye lens.
- Fisheye lenses create severe distortion that must be corrected before or during the stitching process.
- As only two pictures are taken, the resolution of the spherical panorama is not very high when compared to other techniques that use more pictures.
- The edges of the individual pictures rarely provide enough overlap for a totally fluid (i.e. unrecognizable) transition. In order to ensure a perfect end result, the seam edge usually needs to be retouched.

7.2.2.2 Using eight fisheye pictures

In place of a circular fisheye lens, a full frame fisheye lens can be used to film an entire scene. Here, more individual pictures are required, which increases the overlap for subsequent stitching and typically improves the image quality of the resulting panorama. The pictures shown in the example below were taken with a 16 mm fisheye lens that has a vertical field of view of approximately 95 degrees. A total of six pictures were taken 60 degrees apart from each other plus zenith and nadir. A special tripod head is recommended in order to precisely pivot the camera about the nodal point of the fisheye lens.

The pictures taken using this technique can be made with the QuickPan III tripod head from Kaidan, for example (see chapter 7.2.4). Figure 7.10 shows pictures that were taken using this technique. Refer to chapter 7.3.4 for the additional steps required to produce an interactive panorama.

Figure 7.10 Individual pictures of a spherical panorama comprising eight fisheye shots

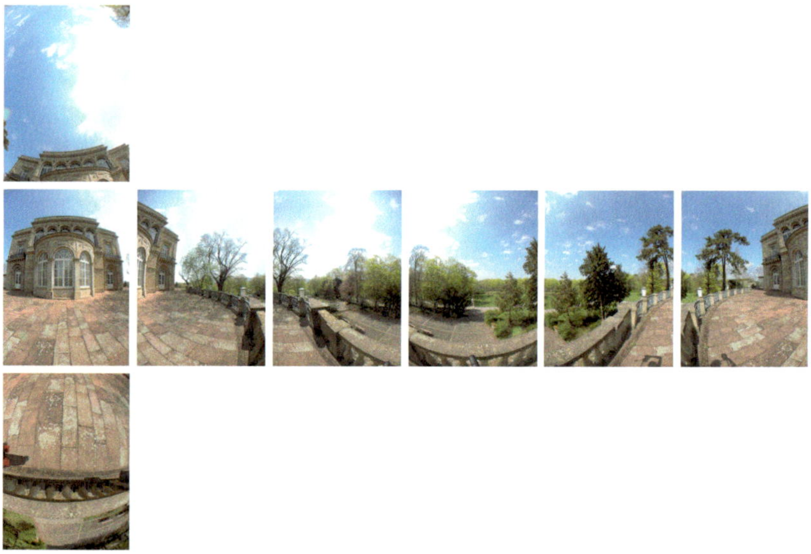

Advantages

- Compared to the multi-row technique, only a few pictures need to be taken.
- Due to the large field of view associated with fisheye lenses, moving objects represent no problem as long as they are not located toward the edge of the picture.

Disadvantages

- Not all cameras can be equipped with a suitable fisheye lens.
- Fisheye lenses create severe distortion that must be corrected before or during the stitching process.

7.2.3 Multi-row technique

The multi-row technique generally requires that a number of pictures be taken, respective of the field of view provided by the lens. Here, several overlapping picture sequences are completed until a sphere is covered. In order to take advantage of the multi-row technique, a tripod head is required that allows the nodal point to be adjusted horizontally and vertically. Such pictures can be made with the QuickPan III Spherical tripod head from Kaidan or the VR-Drive from Roundshot (see chapter 7.2.4).

Figure 7.11 shows several picture sequences of a spherical panorama that were taken using the multi-row technique. Refer to chapter 7.3.2 for the additional steps required to produce an interactive panorama.

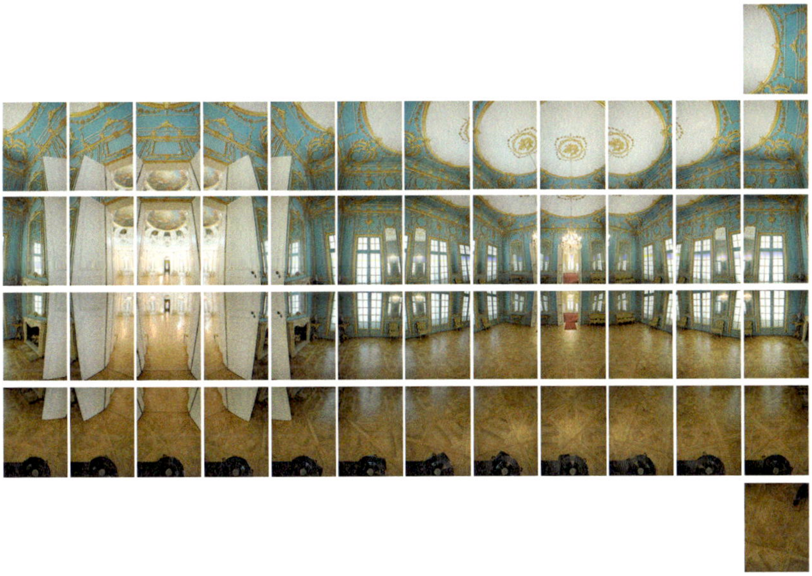

Figure 7.11
Individual pictures of a spherical multi-row panorama

Advantages

- The multi-row technique does not require special camera equipment; practically any camera and lens combination can be used.
- The high number of pictures increases the resolution of the complete panorama.

Disadvantages

- A special panoramic tripod head is recommended in order to exactly align the camera for multi-row shots.
- Depending on the field of view of the lens, anywhere from 15 to 50 pictures need to be taken in order to create a spherical panorama.

- The relatively high number of pictures associated with this technique translates into increased time for shooting and stitching.
- The multi-row technique presents problems when moving objects are introduced. Thus, it cannot be ruled out that such objects will appear incomplete in the panorama.

7.2.4 Tripod heads

In order to pivot the camera exactly about the nodal point, it is recommended that you use a special tripod head. However, there are simpler solutions available for achieving good results. Several tripod heads are introduced in the following text. Other producers of panoramic tripod heads can be found in the list of manufacturers (see chapter B.2.5).

Figure 7.12
Kaidan QuickPan III

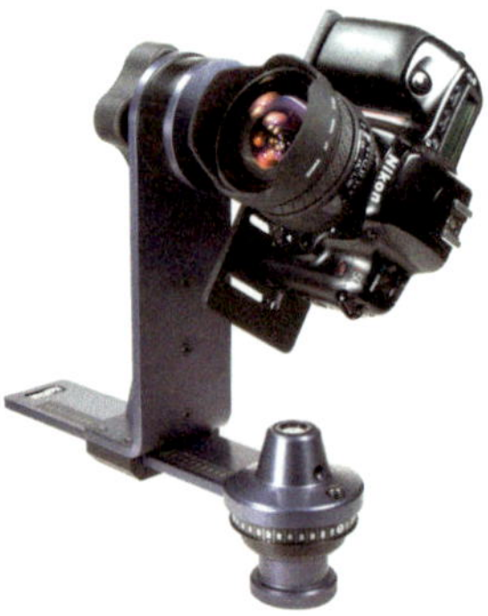

Kaidan QuickPan III Spherical

The QuickPan III tripod head (see Figure 7.12) can be individually adjusted and thus is a viable option for many cameras. With this model, cylindrical and spherical panoramas can be photographed using the single-row or multi-row technique.

Figure 7.13
iPIX Rotator

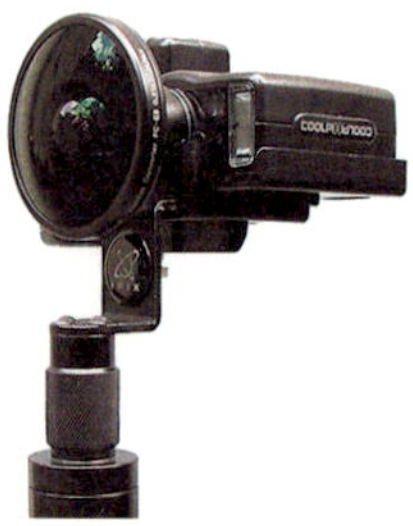

iPIX Rotator

This tripod head (see Figure 7.13) is custom designed for specific camera models with a matching fisheye converter. The Rotator locks up every 180 degrees, which allows you to quickly and easily make adjustments in order to shoot the two fisheye pictures required for the iPIX technique.

Roundshot VR-Drive

The VR-Drive (see Figure 7.14) is a motorized tripod head designed for single-row and multi-row shots. The unit is individually adjustable and can be used to take cylindrical and spherical pictures, depending on the lens fitted. The motor controls not only the rotational movement, but also the release.

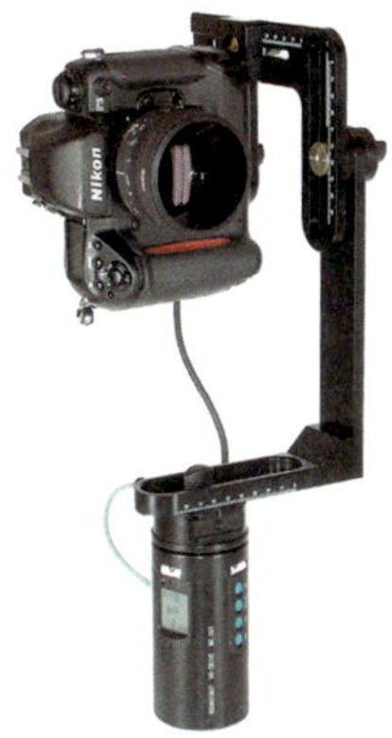

Figure 7.14
Roundshot VR-Drive

Kaidan QuickPan III CS (Camera Specific)

This tripod head (see Figure 7.15) is only designed to be used with specific camera models. With the QuickPan III CS, cylindrical and spherical panoramas can be photographed, depending on the lens used.

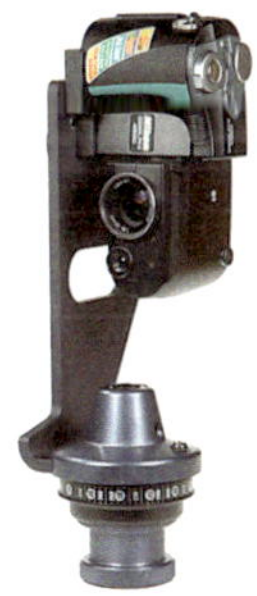

Figure 7.15
Kaidan QuickPan III CS

Monopod with plumb bob

This solution involves a monopod, whereby a plumb bob is connected to the nodal point of the lens (see Figure 7.16). When a mark is made on the ground, the camera can be pivoted exactly about the nodal point using the plumb bob. This setup can be individually adjusted, making it suitable for various camera models. Depending on the lens used, the monopod with plumb bob can be used to photograph cylindrical as well as spherical panoramas. This solution, however, is only good for taking single-row shots and requires exacting work as well as a little experience with this technique.

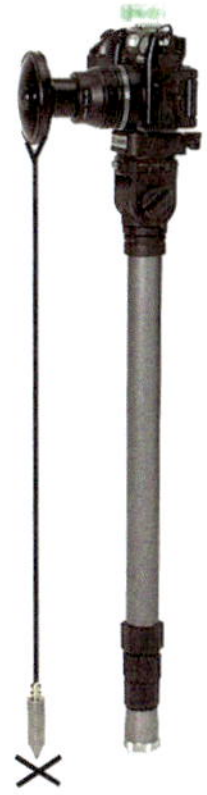

Figure 7.16
Monopod with plumb bob

7.2.5 Additional tips

In order to ensure a realistic depiction of a scene with spherical panoramic shots, it is usually necessary to edit the lower part of the picture. This is where the tripod legs or the feet of the photographer frequently can be seen. The best way to retouch the ground is to convert the spherical panorama into cubic format. This allows you to conveniently edit this specific area (see chapter 7.3.1). If a logo is added here, for example, the ground area does not need to be retouched at all.

7.3 Stitching software

This chapter introduces a number of software products that can be used to produce spherical and cubic panoramas. Additional software producers can be found in the list of manufacturers (see chapter B.10.2). A few of the software products are capable of producing cylindrical, cubic and spherical panoramas. As it would be impossible to list all of the applications and their features here, a comparative overview of the software covered can be found as a table in chapter 12.

7.3.1 REALVIZ Stitcher (panoramic picture)

The following explains the image editing process of spherical shots taken with panoramic cameras. For more information on photographing such panoramas, please refer to chapter 7.2.1. After the photo shooting is finished, additional steps need to be taken in order to acquire a spherical or cubic panorama from a panoramic picture.

A demo version of REALVIZ Stitcher can be found on the CD at the following paths: \Demo versions\Mac and \Demo versions\PC

First, you should make any necessary color and brightness changes. This is best done by working with the complete panoramic picture. After the color correction, the horizontal cut surface is defined. This must be done, for example, when a 380° format is used for overlapping purposes instead of the required 360°. A prominent area in the overlapping region is located and the superfluous parts of the picture are cut out on the right and left sides. Whether the panorama will fit together this way can be determined using REALVIZ Stitcher.

With the *Tools > Panorama Conversion* function, cylindrical, spherical and cubic panoramas can be converted into various other formats. This is how the cropped picture is converted into a *Cubic QTVR,* the required settings for which are shown in the following illustrations.

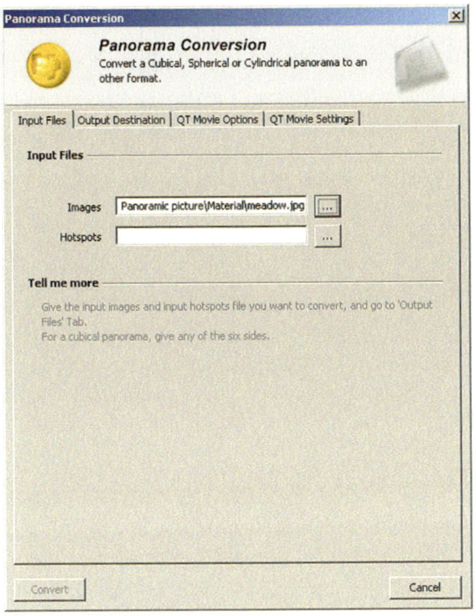

Figure 7.17
Settings in *Input Files*

Under *Input Files > Images,* select the panoramic image to be converted.

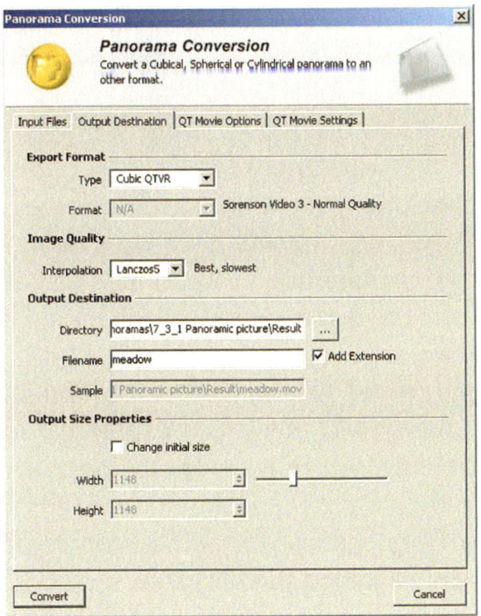

Figure 7.18
Image quality and resolution can be set in the *Output Destination* dialog field

The projection format is defined by *Output Destination > Export Format > Type* (here: *Cubic QTVR*). Factors for image quality and interpolation are set under *Image Quality.* Enter the name and file path of the resulting QTVR file in the *Output Destination* field. In *Output Size Properties,* the resolution of the subsequent QTVR movie is defined in pixels. The higher the resolution value selected, the better the image quality, however the file size also increases in proportion to this resolution and image quality. The software automatically calculates the optimal size of the panorama based on raw material (1:1). This value can be changed by activating *Change initial size.*

By *QuickTime Movie Options* (see Figure 7.19), you can configure additional QTVR-specific settings.

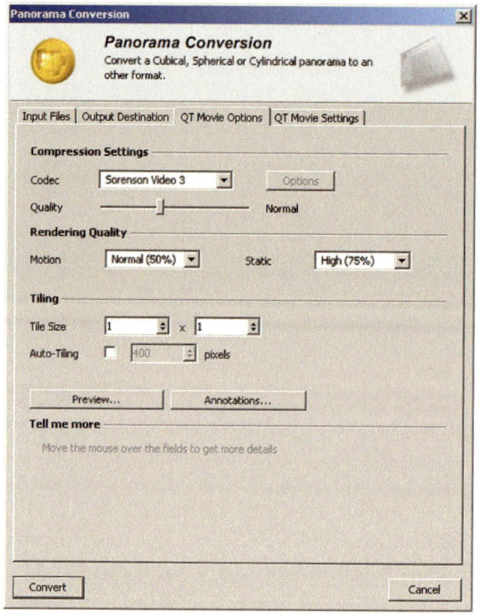

Figure 7.19
Additional QTVR movie properties can be set in the *QuickTime Output Setup* dialog field

The type of compression used is selected by *Compression Settings > Codec* (more information on codecs can be found in chapter 10.1). The desired image quality is set next to *Compression Settings > Quality. Rendering Quality* determines the image quality when the panorama is moving (*Motion*) and not moving (*Static*). In the *Tiling* field, the panoramic picture is subdivided into quadrants (*Tiles*) so that all tiles that already have been downloaded can be played. For large QTVR panoramas, it definitely makes sense to increase the default value. In the present example, however, a tiling setting of 1 x 1 is adequate. In *Preview,* you can activate "fast start" QuickTime streaming, which allows parts of the panorama to be viewed by the user while continuing to download the QTVR file. It is also possible to create a preview screen for the QTVR movie, which provides the observer a low resolution view of the panorama before the file is downloaded from the Internet. In *Annotations,* text information such as the author, copyright and a short description of the content can be added to the QTVR movie.

The *QuickTime Movie Settings* field (see Figure 7.20) is used to define the window size (*Window*) in pixels. *Pan* and *Tilt* allow you to configure the opening picture display of the QTVR movie. The minimum and maximum zoom factors are defined by *FOV.* With the *Optimal Minimum FOV* function, you can specify a maximum zoom range to prevent the panorama from appearing too coarse when the picture is magnified. *Optimal Default FOV* selects an average angle of view as the start position for the QTVR movie in order for the user to be able to pivot up and down.

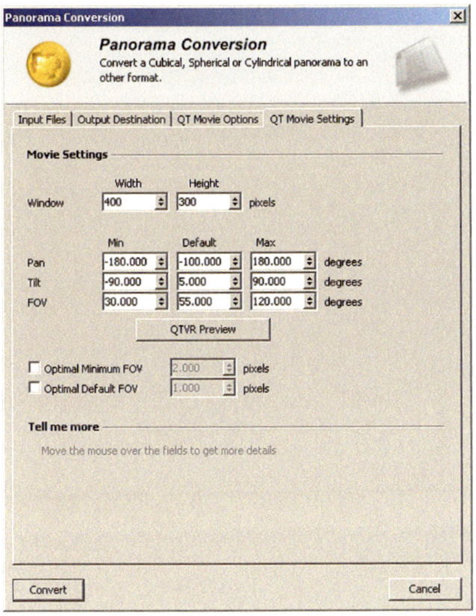

Figure 7.20
The playback properties of the QTVR panorama are defined in the *QuickTime Movie Settings* dialog field

When all settings have been made, the calculation process is initiated by clicking the *Convert* button. Finally, the horizontal interface is checked. If the seam edge is not visible, the cropped picture can be used as is. If this is not the case, the error of course will need to be corrected again in an additional image editing step. When this process is finished, the panoramic picture has the right width.

A few 8 mm fisheye lenses have a field of view that is less than 180 degrees. As such, some vertical picture information inevitably will be missing in a complete spherical presentation. These missing areas are recognized as black circles at the top and bottom of an interactive panorama (see Figure 7.22).

In 2-D spherical panoramic pictures, the upper and lower areas are severely distorted. As a result, it is very difficult to retouch these black parts of the picture, which is why it makes sense to individually save each side of the cubic QTVR as a quadratic image. Figure 7.21 shows the settings required for this.

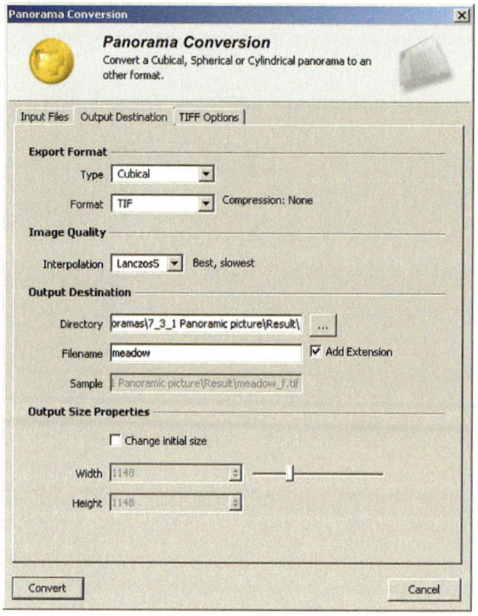

Figure 7.21
Settings for converting a panoramic picture into individual cube sides

When the *Cubical* export format is selected under *Output Destination* in *Tools > Panorama Conversion,* the six sides of the cube are automatically named according to their position. For example: u for up and d for down. Next to *Format,* select the desired file format. For Internet application, the picture typically should be saved as a JPG file. If the panoramic picture needs to be further edited, do not select this option, as the data loss associated with the JPG format is too great due to the level of compression used. Instead, it is better to save the picture in a format (such as TIF) that does not compromise picture data and make any changes to the size or the file format in an image editing program. Factors for image quality and interpolation are set under *Image Quality.* In *Output Size Properties,* the resolution of a cube side is defined in pixels. The higher the resolution value selected, the better the image quality, however the file size also increases in proportion to this resolution and image quality. The software automatically calculates the optimal size of a cube side based on raw material (1:1). This value can be changed by activating *Change initial size.*

The *JPEG Options/TIFF Options* section is where image compression settings are made.

When all settings have been made, the calculation process for the six cube sides is initiated by clicking the *Convert* button.

Image editing begins at this point. In the example, only the upper and lower areas need to be retouched; as such, the up (ending in "_u") and down (ending in "_d") cube sides are selected and the black sections edited in an image editing program. Incidentally, a logo can be inserted in the bottom cubic image in order to cover up the tripod. Doing so saves you the more time-intensive task of retouching this area to make it appear realistic.

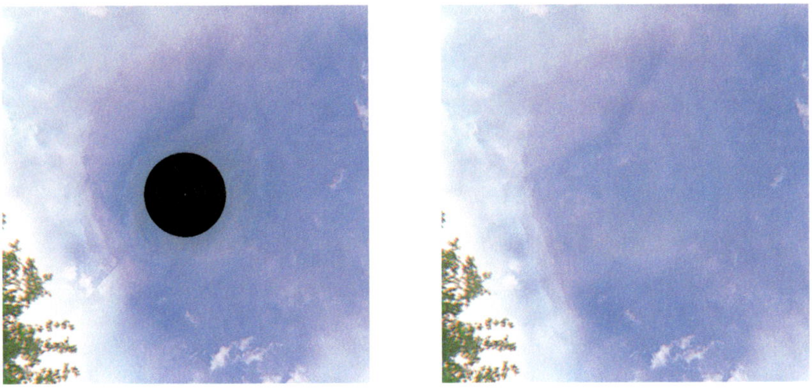

Figure 7.22

Left:
A black circle caused by missing picture information

Right:
Top side of the cube after retouching

When retouching is finished, the individual cube sides are converted into a cubic QTVR by tracing to the *Panorama Conversion* menu. Here, one of the cube sides is selected under *Input Files*. The additional settings for the sample panorama are shown in Figures 7.18 through 7.20.

To learn how cubic QTVR panoramas are published, please refer to chapter 10.1. There you will find more information on viewers as well as the source code used to embed panoramas in HTML files.

If the panorama is not to be published as a cubic QTVR, but as a spherical panorama using a Java viewer, the retouched cube sides are converted into a spherical picture with REALVIZ Stitcher. To this end, the panorama is saved in *JPG* format as *Spherical* with the *Panorama Conversion* function.

Chapter 10.2 provides information on how to publish such spherical panoramic pictures. There you will find more information on viewers as well as the source code used to embed panoramas in HTML files.

Several of these spherical panoramas can be stitched to create a virtual tour. There are a number of different solutions available for such a task, some of which are introduced in chapter 9.3.5.

Another publishing option is that of the VRML format, whereby cubic projection finds application here as well. The panorama is saved in *JPG* format as a *VRML* file with the *Panorama Conversion* function. The result is a VRML file that encompasses six quadratic individual JPG pictures that can be played in a VRML viewer.

To learn how cubic VRML panoramas are published, please refer to chapter 10.5. There you will find more information on viewers as well as the source code used to embed panoramas in Web sites.

You will find the pictures and panoramas shown here on the CD at the following path: Workshop\07 Spherical panoramas\7_3_1 Panoramic picture

Advantages

- REALVIZ Stitcher supports all common projection formats.
- The software can be used to import and export a wide variety of file formats.
- Panoramic formats are able to be converted.

Disadvantages

- Only rectilinear lenses may be used. There is no support for fisheye pictures.

7.3.2 REALVIZ Stitcher (multi-row technique)

A demo version of REALVIZ Stitcher can be found on the CD at the following paths: \Demo versions\Mac and \Demo versions\PC

REALVIZ Stitcher allows you to edit single-row and multi-row panoramas. Cylindrical, spherical and cubic panoramas can be created. The following explains what steps you need to take to produce a quadruple row spherical panorama using REALVIZ Stitcher.

The first thing that is done is to create a new project by tracing to *File > New* and calling up a new document. It is now a good idea to save this stitcher project right away by going to *File > Save as* and assigning a specific name. The next step is to import the individual pictures of the panorama via *File > Load Images*. Here, the pictures are merely referenced, which keeps the stitcher project small in size and simplifies correction of the individual pictures later on. Once the pictures are loaded, they appear as thumbnails in the lower part of the editing window. Here, the pictures can be repositioned by clicking on them and rotating them to the correct position via *Edit > Rotate.*

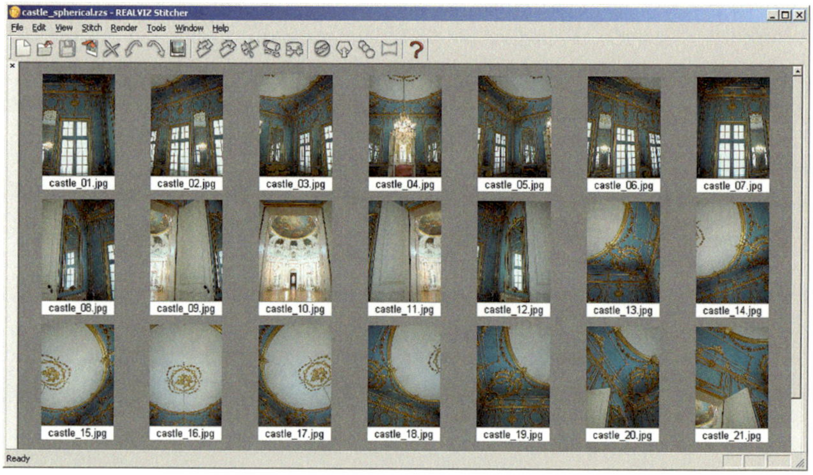

Figure 7.23
Imported pictures prior to starting the stitching process

The software automatically detects the aspect ratio of the pictures, what focal length was used and the type of distortion involved. Values can be individually changed via *Edit > Properties.*

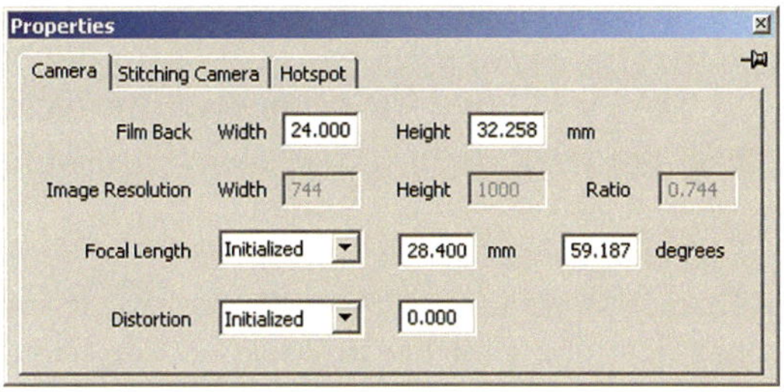

Figure 7.24
Image properties can be set in the *Properties* window

Pictures that were taken with a wide angle lens may reveal distortion toward the edges, which means that additional steps will be required prior to stitching. REALVIZ Stitcher provides options to correct these distortion errors. To this end, the first two pictures are dragged and dropped into the upper editing area and positioned as congruently as possible. The individual pictures now can be rotated for fine positioning. If you are working on a Windows operating system, press the Shift key while moving the picture with the mouse (right button depressed). If you are working on a Macintosh, press the Shift and the Ctrl keys; the picture is rotated with the left mouse button depressed. The pictures should not be stitched just yet, as otherwise it will no longer be possible to correct the distortion. The *Tools > High Distortion > Calibrate* function calculates the distortion present in all pictures included in this project and makes the appropriate corrections. Correction of the distortion can be undone via *Tools > High Distortion > Reset.*

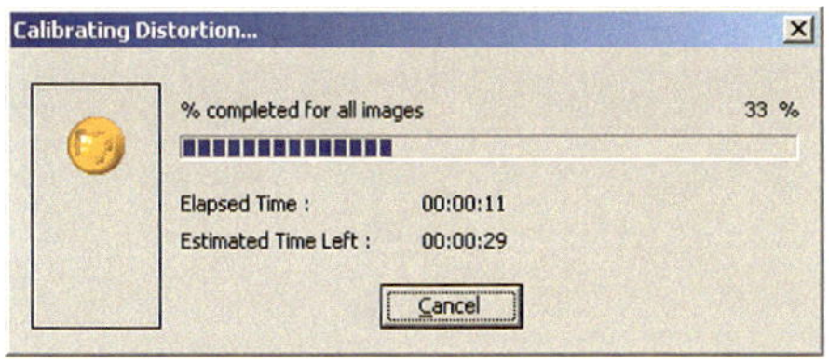

Figure 7.25
Distortion errors can be corrected via the *High Distortion Calibration* function

The actual stitching occurs by dragging and dropping the first picture from the thumbnail picture bar up into the editing area. The same is then done for the second picture, which is positioned such that the overlapping areas are as congruent as possible (see Figure 7.26). Approximate, or rough positioning, can be done with a mouse, however it is recommended that you use the arrow keys for fine positioning. For Windows users, each picture can be rotated by pressing the Shift key while moving the image with the mouse (right button depressed). Macintosh users need to press the Shift and Ctrl keys while rotating with the left mouse button depressed. Once the position of the respective picture is okay, stitching can be executed by pressing Enter. After the picture has been stitched, the color bordering the image changes from red (positionable) to green (stitched).

If a particular picture cannot be stitched, a dialog window appears, informing the user accordingly. Here, the *Forced Stitch* function can be used to stitch under any circumstances. The picture then is not automatically positioned by the software; instead, the position in the sequence manually defined is used.

To navigate in a panorama, rotate the view, sweep or zoom, the *View > Pan, Roll* and *Zoom* functions are used. As is the case with the majority of the functions, there is also built-in support for hot keys, which are listed next to the respective functions in the menu. These hot keys can differ from platform to platform, which is why they are not explicitly listed here.

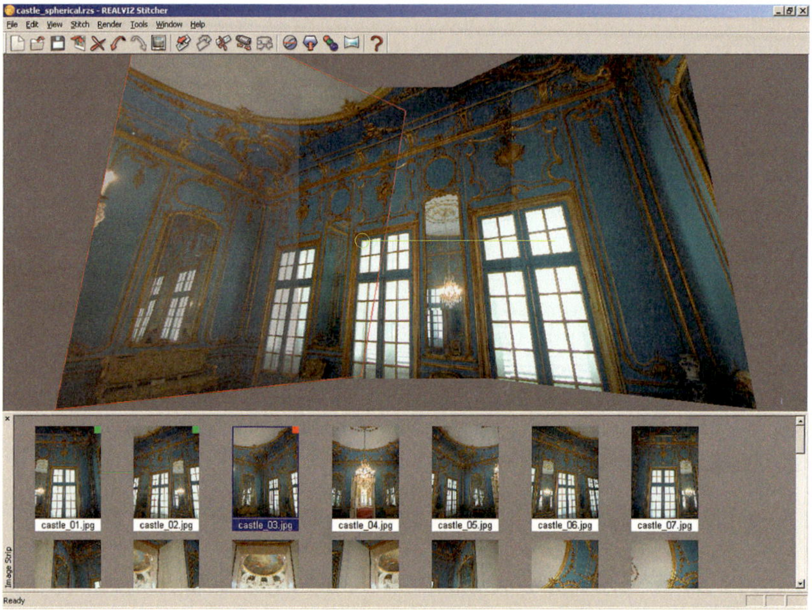

Figure 7.26
Stitching process: Pictures highlighted in red can be positioned; pictures highlighted in green already have been stitched

The software is capable of optimizing the values specified at the beginning for focal length and distortion based on the already stitched pictures. This takes place via the *Stitch > Adjust All Images* function. It is recommended that you perform this correction after four or five pictures have been stitched as well as after the complete stitching process is finished.

Once all of the pictures in the first picture sequence have been positioned and stitched, this sequence is closed to form a cylindrical panorama. To do this, select *Close Panorama* from the *Stitch* menu. The background color of the editing window now changes and you can connect the picture stitched last with the first picture in the sequence. These two pictures are then stitched as already described.

At this point, the subsequent picture sequences are added by positioning and stitching the individual pictures, which is how the total of 50 shots in this example are converged to form a quadruple row panorama.

In the lower picture sequences where the ground is depicted, parts of the tripod usually can be seen as well. This generally undesired effect can be editing out using the *Stencil* function. Another example of undesired objects is passersby located at the edge of a picture, who should not appear in the subsequent panorama. With the *Tools > Stencil* function, the problematic area of the picture is marked in the shape of a polygon (see Figure 7.27). You now can select whether the marked area or the remaining part of the picture should be excluded by clicking on the respective field by *Stencil Mode.* It is recommended that you only do this in the overlapping area of pictures, as the marked area is supplemented with information from the bordering picture. If no substitute picture information is available, the marked areas in the panorama appear black.

Additionally, it is possible to crop the border of the pictures used via the *Crop Border* function. Any vignetting effects can be excluded using the *Vignetting* stencil tool. If desired, these settings can be applied to all pictures associated with this project. You can undo any setting you have made at any time as well as change the shape of the polygons via *Tools > Stencil.* These settings do not necessarily have to be made prior to stitching; you always have the option of first stitching and visually analyzing the complete panoramic picture, at which time you can go back and work on those areas that need to be improved.

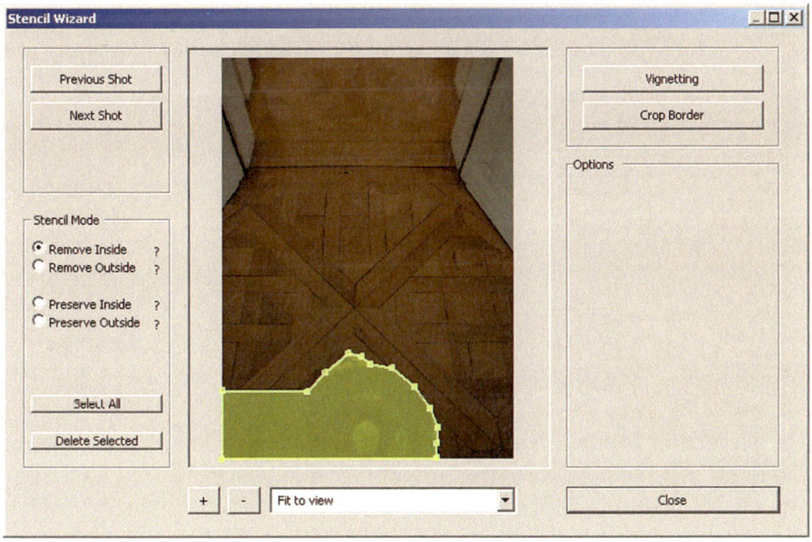

Figure 7.27
The *Stencil* function allows you to exclude undesired areas of a picture (here, the tripod)

If the individual pictures reveal varying degrees of brightness, the *Render > Equalize All Images* function can be used to correct this. Here, all pictures associated with the panorama are adjusted to each other in terms of their brightness. This function is okay to use for smaller differences; however, if the pictures reveal greater fluctuations in color or lighting, it is recommended that you use a targeted color correction technique provided by suitable image editing software.

Before the panorama is rendered for the export, the desired part of the picture should be selected. The panorama is positioned according to that part of the image that currently can be seen in the editing window. The *Tools > Align Panorama* function is used to define the horizontal plane of the panorama. Horizontal and vertical lines are drawn for alignment purposes. Here, it is useful to activate the grid function by tracing to *Edit > Preferences > Display Grid.* Once the desired position for the initial picture display of the panorama has been found, the panorama is rendered.

There are a number of rendering options available as far as projection and file formats are concerned; REALVIZ Stitcher provides support for cylindrical, spherical and cubic projection.

A cubic panorama can be published as a cubic QTVR or as a VRML file. Another solution is to export a spherical panoramic picture and present it using a spherical panoramic viewer.

In Figure 7.38, you can see which settings are made for the sample panorama shown here in the *Render > Render* mode with regard to rendering and exporting a cubic QTVR movie.

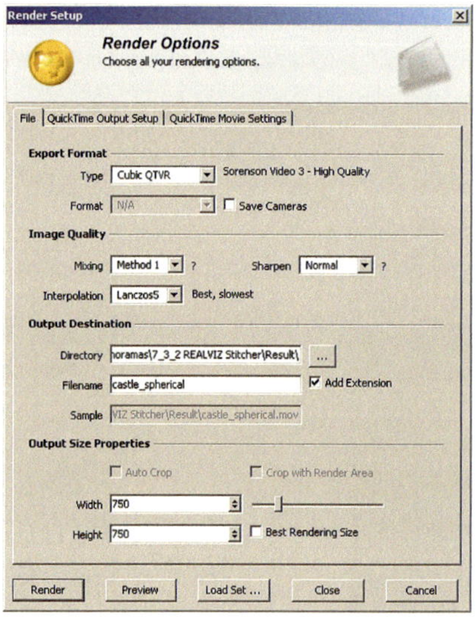

Figure 7.28
File format, compression and resolution for the cubic QTVR panorama are defined in the *File* dialog field

The projection format is defined by *File > Export Format > Type* (here: *Cubic QTVR*). Factors for image quality such as sharpness and interpolation are set under *Image Quality.* In *Output Size Properties,* the resolution of the subsequent panoramic picture is defined in pixels. The higher the resolution value selected, the better the image quality, however the file size also increases in proportion to this resolution and image quality. When *Best Rendering Size* is activated, the software calculates the optimum size of the panorama based on raw material (1:1). Starting with an average value, you can estimate the expected image quality and file size.

In the *Render Area* field, the panoramic picture is cropped prior to rendering so that only a specific part of the panorama is used. This function, however, has not been applied in the example.

Additional QTVR-specific settings can be made in the *QuickTime Output Setup* window (see Figure 7.29).

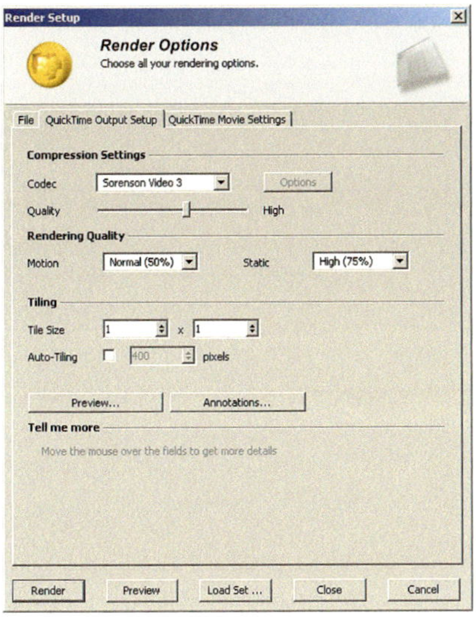

Figure 7.29
Additional QTVR movie properties can be set in the *QuickTime Output Setup* dialog field

The type of compression used is selected by *Compression Settings > Codec* (more information on codecs can be found in chapter 10.1). The desired image quality is set next to *Compression Settings > Quality. Rendering Quality* determines the image quality when the panorama is moving (*Motion*) and not moving (*Static*). In the *Tiling* field, the panoramic picture is subdivided into quadrants (*Tiles*) so that all tiles that already have been downloaded can be played. For large QTVR panoramas, it definitely makes sense to increase the default value. In the present example, however, a tiling setting of 1 x 1 is adequate. In *Preview,* you can activate "fast start" Quick-Time streaming, which allows parts of the panorama to be viewed by the user while continuing to download the QTVR file. It is also possible to create a preview screen for the QTVR movie, which provides the observer a low resolution view of the panorama before the file is completely downloaded from the Internet. In *Annotations,* text information such as the author, copyright and a short description of the content can be added to the QTVR movie.

The QuickTime *Movie Settings* field (see Figure 7.30) is used to define the window size (*Window*) in pixels. *Pan* and *Tilt* allow you to configure the opening picture display of the QTVR movie. The minimum and maximum zoom factors are defined by *FOV.* With the *Optimal Minimum FOV* function, you can specify a maximum zoom range to prevent the panorama from appearing too coarse when the picture is magnified. *Optimal Default FOV* selects an average angle of view as the start position for the QTVR movie in order for the user to be able to pivot up and down.

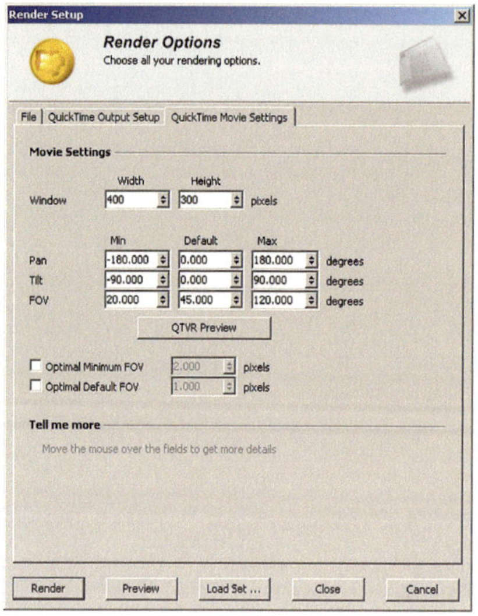

Figure 7.30
The playback properties of the QTVR panorama are defined in the *QuickTime Movie Settings* dialog field

When all settings have been made, the calculation process is initiated by clicking the *Render* button. The result can be optimized by rendering again with different values.

To learn how cubic QTVR panoramas are published, please refer to chapter 10.1. There you will find more information on viewers as well as the source code used to embed panoramas in Web sites.

REALVIZ Stitcher allows you to create virtual tours from several QTVR panoramas. The process to follow for defining hot spots and creating a virtual tour is described in detail in chapter 9.3.1.

The second option for publishing cubic panoramas is provided by the VRML format. Here, a VRML file is created that encompasses six quadratic individual JPG pictures that can be played in a VRML viewer. In Figure 7.31, you can see which settings are made for the sample panorama in the *Render > Render* mode with regard to rendering a cubic VRML panorama.

VRML is selected by *File > Export Format > Type.* Next to *Format,* select the desired file format. For Internet application, the picture typically should be saved as a *JPG* file, however you also can select the *PNG* format. Factors for image quality such as definition and interpolation are set under *Image Quality.* In *Output Size Properties,* the resolution of the subsequent panoramic picture is defined in pixels. The higher the resolution value selected, the better the image quality, however the file size also increases in proportion to this resolution and image quality. When *Best Rendering Size* is activated, the software calculates the optimum size of the panorama based on raw material (1:1).

The *JPEG Options/PNG Options* section is where image compression settings are made.

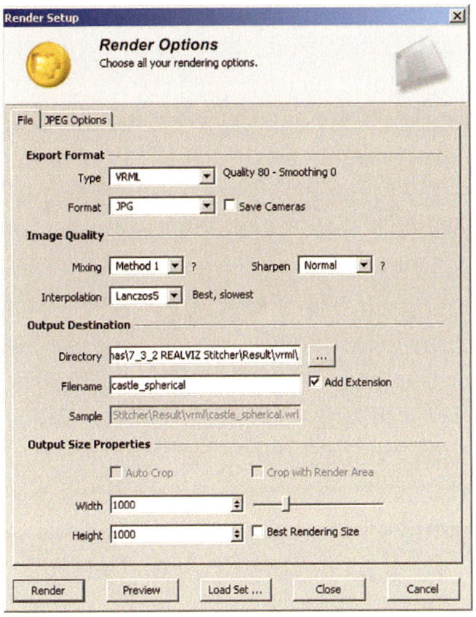

Figure 7.31
File format and resolution for the VRML panorama are defined in the *File* dialog field

When all settings have been made, the calculation process is initiated by clicking the *Render* button, at which point the VRML file is created.

To learn how cubic VRML panoramas are published, please refer to chapter 10.5. There you will find more information on viewers as well as the source code used to embed panoramas in Web sites.

Another option for publishing such a panorama is to create a spherical panoramic filmstrip that is spherically projected using a viewer. In Figure 7.32, you can see which settings are made for the sample panorama in the *Render* > *Render* mode with regard to rendering a spherical panoramic picture.

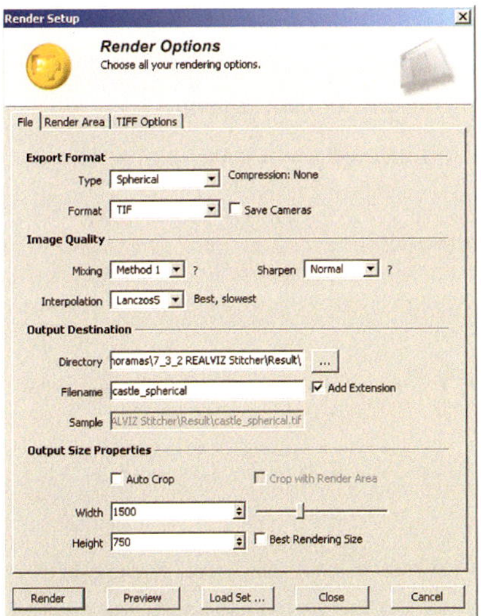

Figure 7.32
File format and resolution for the spherical panoramic picture are defined in the *Render Setup* dialog field

You will find the pictures, projects and panoramas shown here on the CD at the following path: \Workshop\ 07 Spherical panoramas\ 7_3_2 REALVIZ Stitcher

Spherical is selected by *File > Export Format > Type*. Next to *Format,* select the desired file format. For Internet application, the picture typically should be saved as a JPG file. If the panoramic picture needs to be further edited, do not select this option, as the data loss associated with the JPG format is too great due to the level of compression used. Instead, it is better to save the picture in a format (such as TIF) that does not compromise picture data and make any changes to the size or the file format in an image editing program. Factors for image quality such as definition and interpolation are set under *Image Quality*. In *Output Size Properties,* the resolution of the subsequent panoramic picture is defined in pixels. The higher the resolution value selected, the better the image quality, however the file size also increases in proportion to this resolution and image quality. When *Best Rendering Size* is activated, the software calculates the optimum size of the panorama based on raw material (1:1).

In the *Render Area* field, the panoramic picture can be cropped prior to rendering so that only a specific part of the panorama is used. This function, however, has not been applied in the example.

The *JPEG Options / TIFF Options* section is where image compression settings are made.

When all settings have been made, the calculation process is initiated by clicking the *Render* button, at which point the panoramic picture is created.

Chapter 10.2 provides information on how to publish these spherical panoramic pictures. There you will find more information on viewers as well as the source code used to embed panoramas in Web sites.

Several spherical panoramas can be stitched to create a virtual tour. There are a number of different solutions available for such a task, some of which are introduced in chapter 9.3.5.

Advantages

- REALVIZ Stitcher supports all common projection formats.
- The software can be used to import and export a wide variety of file formats.
- Panoramic formats are able to be converted.

Disadvantages

- Only rectilinear lenses may be used. There is no support for fisheye pictures.

7.3.3 iPIX Interactive Studio (two fisheye pictures)

iPIX Interactive Studio is a software application that can be used to edit fisheye pictures with a field of view of 180°. The following explains what steps you need to take to produce a spherical panorama using two fisheye pictures.

First, both hemispheres are imported via *File > Open.* In order to edit two fisheye pictures, *Fisheye* is selected by *Scene Category* and *2-Shot-Fisheye* by *Scene Type* (see Figure 7.33).

You will find a demo version of iPIX Interactive Studio on the CD at the following paths:
\Demo versions\Mac and
\Demo versions\PC

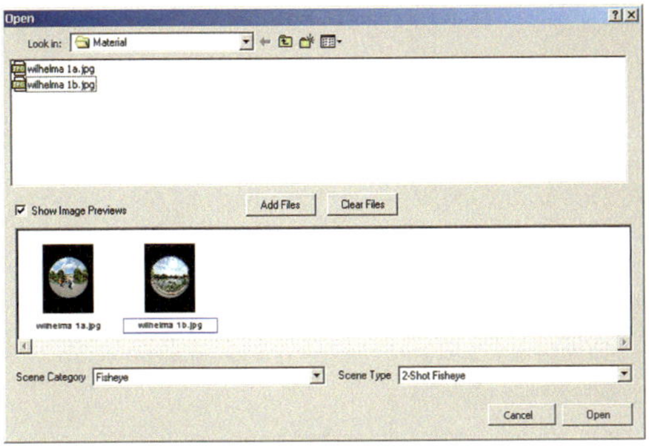

Figure 7.33
Both fisheye pictures are imported

After the individual pictures have been imported, the software automatically generates a stitched view of the panorama (see Figure 7.34).

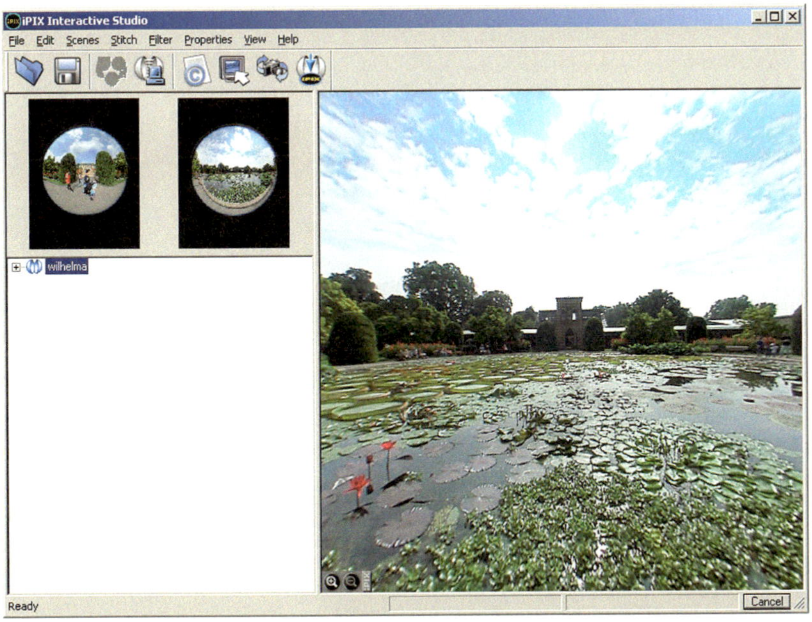

Figure 7.34
Editing window of iPIX Interactive Studio

The right window of Figure 7.34 shows a preview of the spherical panorama in the iPIX viewer. This preview is identical to the subsequent presentation via the plug-in. The panorama can be rotated and zoomed to check all areas of the picture.

Should this auto stitch function not reveal the desired result, the corresponding settings can be changed via *Stitch > Auto Stitch.* Here, changes are made in the *Stitch Parameters* editing window (see Figure 7.35).

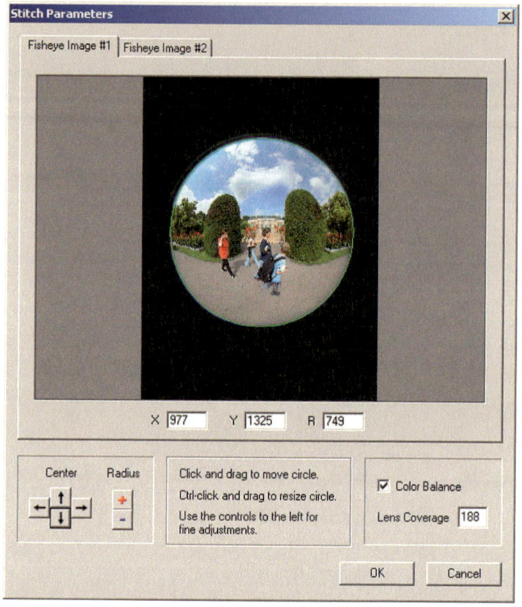

Figure 7.35
The auto stitch function parameters can be changed in the *Stitch Parameters* window

First, the green designated circle radii should be aligned with the fisheye picture. If necessary, the size and position of the radii can be altered. The changes you make will be applied to all pictures associated with this scene. Press the *OK* button to restitch the pictures into a panorama.

If there are still areas at the overlapping edge that are not visibly perfect, they can be immediately retouched within the software application. The onboard image editing tools can be used to copy square/rectangular chunks of the image and paste them elsewhere. A stamp tool also is available for targeting specific areas of an image (see Figure 7.36).

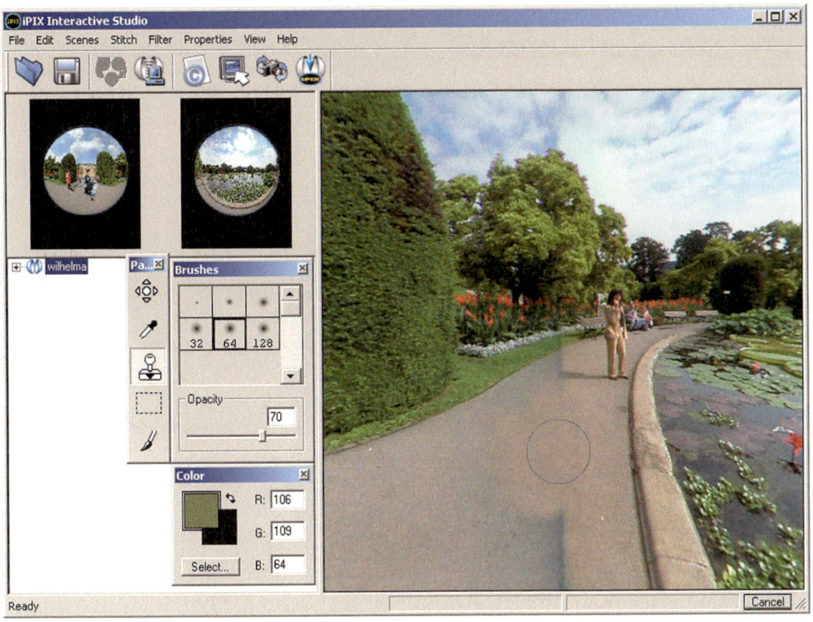

Figure 7.36
Image editing tools can be used to retouch imperfect overlapping edges

The software includes an integrated High Dynamic Range (HDR) function that allows you to generate a panorama with increased dynamic range from a series of pictures of the same motif. Simply import all of the associated pictures into the software in pairs and select Combine Selected in the Scenes menu. This allows you to convert up to six pictures of a picture series into an HDR panorama.

You can define the playback properties of the respective panorama as well as add text information prior to saving. To access the editing area for these settings, trace to the *Properties* menu. By *Properties > Copyright Info*, you can include information such as the title of the panorama, name of the photographer and a short description of the scene. The initial viewpoint can be changed via the *Properties > Initial Viewpoint* function. The original horizontal plane of the panorama can be manipulated as needed (i.e. marginally shifted up or down) by configuring settings in *Properties > Reference Viewpoint*. If you do not want to retouch the bottom part of the panorama (where the tripod usually is depicted), but instead cover it up with a graphic, the *Properties > Tripod Cap* function is quite useful. Here, you can select from already made iPIX graphics, however custom graphics also can be added.

Finally, the panorama is saved; trace to *File > Save* to access the *Save as* dialog field (see Figure 7.37). One of a number of output formats can be chosen: *Bubble, Cube Strip, Equirectangular Projections, Flat Images, iPIX Images, iPIX Proof Images, QuickTime Cubic Panoramas* and *Thumbnails*. If you would like to retouch the panorama in an external image editing program, the two best formats are *Bubble* and *Cube*. Retouched files can be reimported after editing and converted into an iPIX panorama. To create a spherical iPIX panorama, select the *iPIX Image* file format.

You will find the pictures and the panorama shown here on the CD at the following path: \Workshop\07 Spherical panoramas\7_3_3 iPIX Interactive Studio

Figure 7.37
Various output formats are available

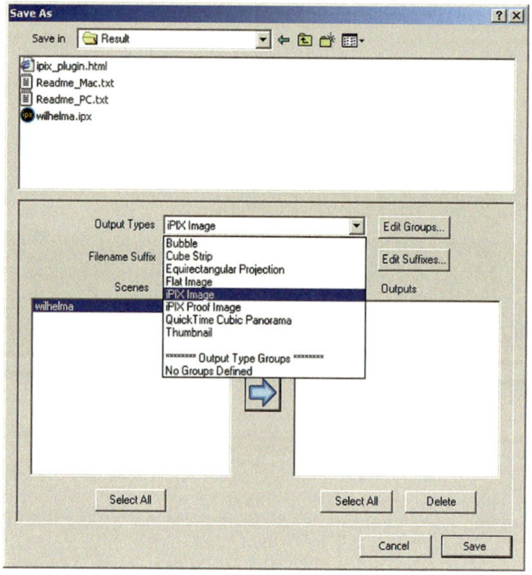

Virtual tours can be produced by combining several iPIX panoramas. Special software products that have this capacity include iLinker (see chapter 9.3.4) and HotMedia (see chapter 9.3.3).

To learn how spherical iPIX panoramas are published, please refer to chapter 10.3. There you will find more information on viewers as well as the source code used to embed panoramas in Web sites.

Advantages

- Only two pictures need to be taken, making the time involved with filming a complete panorama relatively short.
- Due to the large field of view associated with fisheye pictures, moving objects represent no problem as long as they are not located toward the edge of the picture.
- The software is relatively easy to use.

Disadvantages

- As only two pictures are taken, the resolution of the spherical panorama is not very high when compared to other techniques that use more pictures. Alternatively, there is the option of using three fisheye pictures with iPIX Interactive Studio.
- In order to ensure a perfect end result, the seam edge usually needs to be retouched.
- iPIX panoramas appear distorted in some areas. Some observers like this spherical impression, while others find it too distorted.

7.3.4 PanoTools – PTGui (eight fisheye pictures)

Panorama Tools (PanoTools) consists of several components and is designed to be used for the production of cylindrical, spherical and cubic panoramas. In addition, PanoTools is capable of correcting image distortion caused by camera lenses as well as creating object filmstrips for the production of object movies.

PanoTools can be found on the CD at the following paths: \Demo versions\Mac and \Demo versions\PC

The PanoTools suite comprises the following applications:

- *PTEditor* – a graphical panoramic editor
- *PTStitcher* – used to stitch panoramas
- *PTPicker* – graphically depicts the arrangement of pictures
- *PTStereo* – computes 3-D data from image pairs with different angles of view
- *PTInterpolate* – gives two pictures from the same scene with different angles of view a common angle of view
- *PTMorpher* – morphing software
- *PTAverage* – reduces "noise" in digital pictures and increases the range of contrast (density) of a picture by averaging several images
- *PTStripe* – combines a sequence of object pictures to create a filmstrip for viewing in an object viewer (see chapter 8.3.1)
- *Panorama Tools for Photoshop* – plug-ins for editing and converting panoramas as well as correcting image distortion errors (see chapter 4)

As PanoTools is not very user-friendly, it is recommended that an add-on program such as PTGui or PTMac is used. This software integrates all of the PanoTools functions in a well organized, easy to understand graphic interface. PTGui runs on Windows, with a comparable product available for the Mac appropriately termed PTMac.

Demo versions of PTGui and PTMac can be found on the CD at the following paths:
\Demo versions\Mac and
\Demo versions\PC

In the following example, a spherical panorama is produced that consists of 8 individual pictures. Here, 6 photos were taken in sequence at an interval of 60 degrees, plus zenith and nadir for the top and bottom of the panorama.

In the following example, a cylindrical panorama is produced that consists of 12 individual pictures. The 12 pictures were taken in sequence at an interval of 30 degrees. Creating a panorama using PTGui software requires use of the following editing tabs: *Source Images, Lens Settings, Panorama Settings, Crop, Image Parameters, Control Points, Optimizer, Preview* and *Create Panorama.*

The first step is to import the individual pictures in the *Source Images* tab (see Figure 7.38) by clicking the *Add* button. Here, the *Correct* PanoTools application can be called up as required in order to correct any lens-related image distortion errors. Please note that when this function is used from PTGui, the original pictures will be overwritten; as such, it is wise to make a backup of the respective pictures beforehand. Please refer to chapter 4 for more information on the correction possibilities offered by the *Correct* PanoTools function.

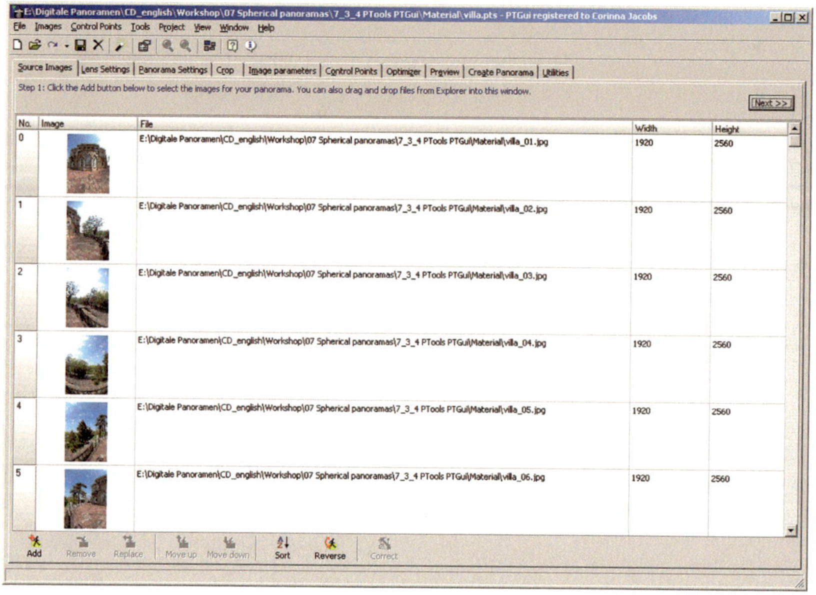

Figure 7.38 Individual pictures are loaded in the *Source Images* tab

In the *Lens Settings* tab (see Figure 6.39), select your lens type in the pull-down menu by *Lens type*. By *Hor. Field of View,* enter the horizontal field of view of the pictures or, alternatively, select a value for the focal length. The software then automatically calculates the corresponding parameter value based on one of these two values. If a digital single lens reflex is used, you can directly enter the focal length multiplier value in the *Focal length multiplier* field. Picture data can be integrated under *EXIF,* provided that your camera is supported by the software. In the *Advanced* section, correction values for the lens used can be numerically entered and saved via *Restore defaults.* If you are not aware of the correction values for your lens, simply ignore these fields.

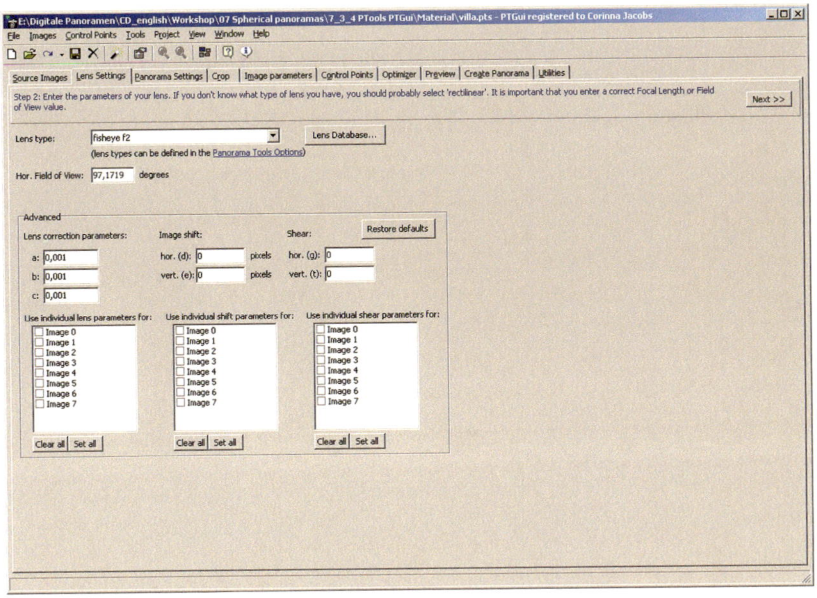

Figure 7.39
Exposure parameters are entered in the *Lens Settings* tab

Settings for the resulting panoramic file are configured in the *Panorama Settings* window (see Figure 7.40). Select the desired file format in the drop-down menu by *File format*. Some of possible formats include *Photoshop with masks* (ideal for retouching later on), *BMP, JPG and TIF.* If the *JPG* format is selected, the degree of compression can be set by *JPEG quality. Projection* specifies the form of projection; here, the possible settings are *Rectilinear* (for planar pictures), *Cylindrical* (for cylindrical 360° panoramas) and *Equirectangular* (for spherical 360° panoramas). The horizontal and vertical fields of view of the resulting panorama are defined by *Field of View.* In the *Advanced* section, the overlap width between the individual pictures can be set under *Feather width.* A large value leads to a softer transition, while a small value effects a hard edge. The tonal value range of the panoramic picture can be influenced under *Gamma,* whereby a value of 1 leaves the gamma curve unchanged. *Interpolator* specifies the interpolation method used to converge the individual pictures. The default method - *Poly 3* - brings about good results, without placing an overly large load on computer resources (which in turn leads to long processing times). The *Color correction* function is used to correct differences in color and lighting between the individual pictures. Correction is activated in the *Apply color correction* dialog box, at which time you can select a reference picture (via *Anchor image*) to which all other pictures in the sequence are adapted. This function is okay to use for smaller differences; however, if the pictures reveal greater fluctuations in color or lighting, it is recommended that you use a targeted color correction technique provided by image editing software.

Figure 7.40
Panorama properties are defined in the *Panorama Settings* tab

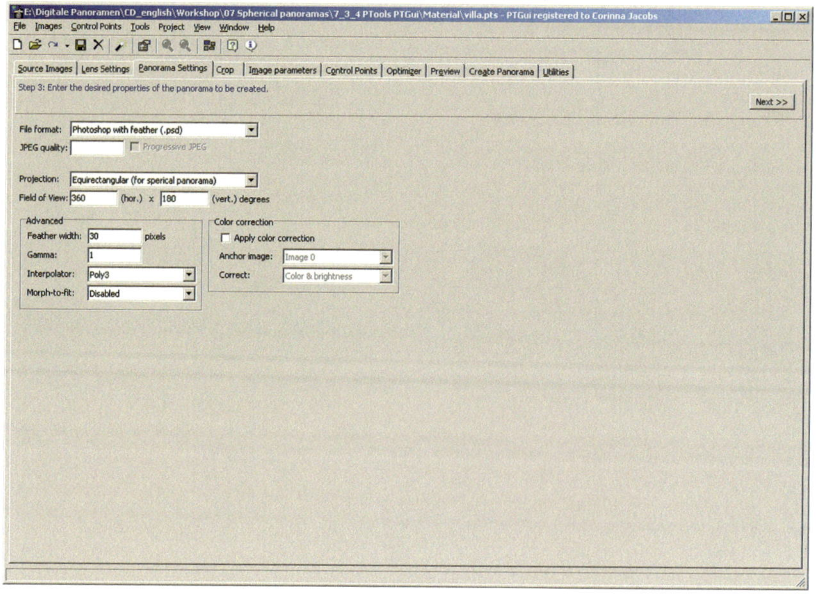

Individual pictures can be cut, or cropped as required in the *Crop* tab (see Figure 7.41). This function is helpful when using scanned or circular fisheye pictures, as the black perimeter can be factored out to further edit the panorama. The size of the original pictures does not change after this function has been applied. If cropping is to be identical for each picture in a panoramic sequence, press the *Apply to all images* button.

Figure 7.41
Pictures can be cropped in the *Crop* tab

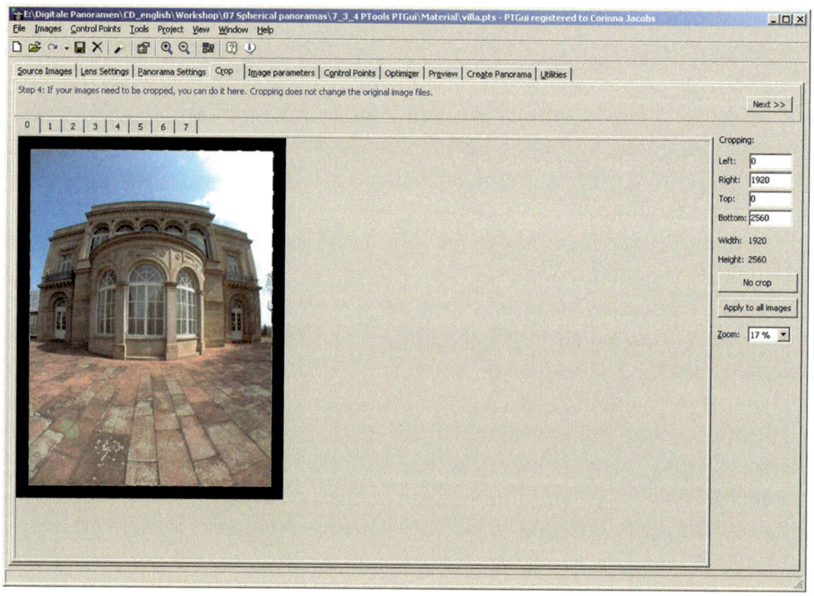

The arrangement of the individual pictures in the panoramic strip is defined in the *Image parameters* tab (see Figure 7.42). You can enter the numerical values for each picture in the table or use the *Panorama Editor* (see Figure 7.43).

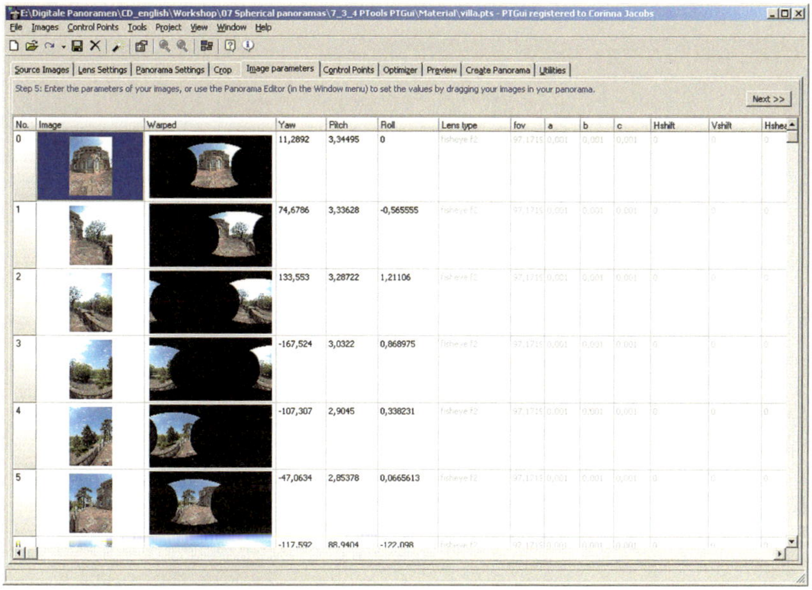

Figure 7.42
Individual pictures are positioned in the *Image Parameters* tab

The table shows the pictures scaled down; in *Warped,* the pictures appear according to their arrangement in the panoramic strip. The type of distortion (*warp*) depends on the form of projection (*Rectilinear, Cylindrical* or *Equirectangular*) selected. *Yaw* (horizontal), *Pitch* (vertical) and *Roll* (rotation) define the position coordinates of each individual picture. Instead of numerically entering the coordinates, it is recommended that you use the *Panorama Editor* (see Figure 7.43), which is called up via *Window > Panorama Editor.*

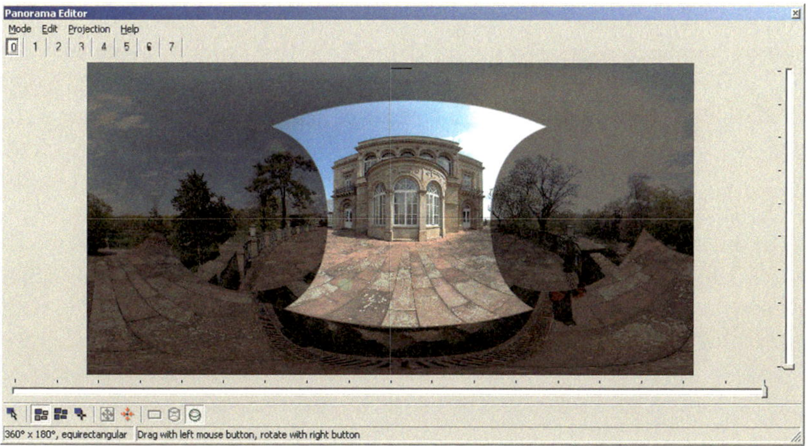

Figure 7.43
In *Panorama Editor,* pictures can be positioned using a mouse

In *Panorama Editor,* the individual pictures in the panoramic strip can be positioned with the mouse. For better positioning, the pictures are displayed in distorted format analogous to the form of projection selected. The settings configured here are applied as position coordinates in the table of the *Image parameters* window (see Figure 7.42).

Figure 7.44
In the *Control Points* tab, stitching points are defined in the overlapping area of the individual pictures

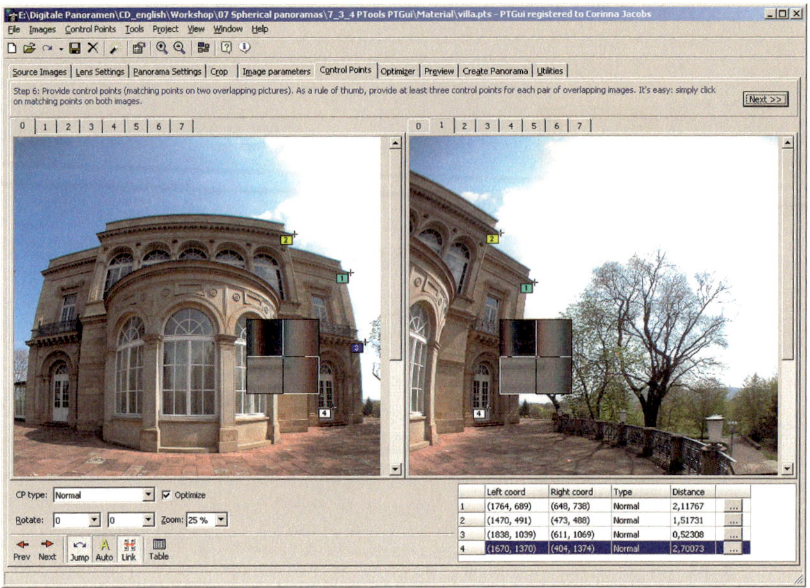

The *Control Points* tab (see Figure 7.44) is used to specify individual points in the overlapping area of the individual pictures that are to coincide in the panorama. These points should be distributed as equally as possible in the overlapping area. The more control points are defined, the greater the fitting accuracy. When selecting points, it is advantageous to focus on areas of the picture that are rich in contrast. In the editing window, two neighboring pictures are placed next to each other. The stitching points are set using the left mouse button and appear in the table in the lower right corner of the window. The *Auto* function simplifies the process of setting control points; as soon as you have defined the first point of a control point pair in the left picture, the software automatically jumps to a similar point in the right picture. Once all of the required control points have been defined, the *Next* or *Prev* button is pressed to go to the next overlapping area. When all of the points for all of the pictures have been set, it is time to click on the *Optimizer* tab.

In this tab (see Figure 7.45), the previously defined parameters such as focal length, field of view, position and distortion of the individual pictures are optimized such that the stitching points selected coincide with each other as much as possible. For most application scenarios, the *Simple interface* is sufficient. *Anchor Image* is used to define the reference picture to which all other pictures in the panoramic sequence are adapted.

When the *Optimize lens Field of View* checkbox is activated, the values already defined for the focal length and the field of view in the *Lens Settings* tab (see Figure 7.39) are optimized based on the existing pictures. The *Minimize lens distortion* function is used to correct distortion errors. The optimization process is started by clicking the *Run Optimizer* button.

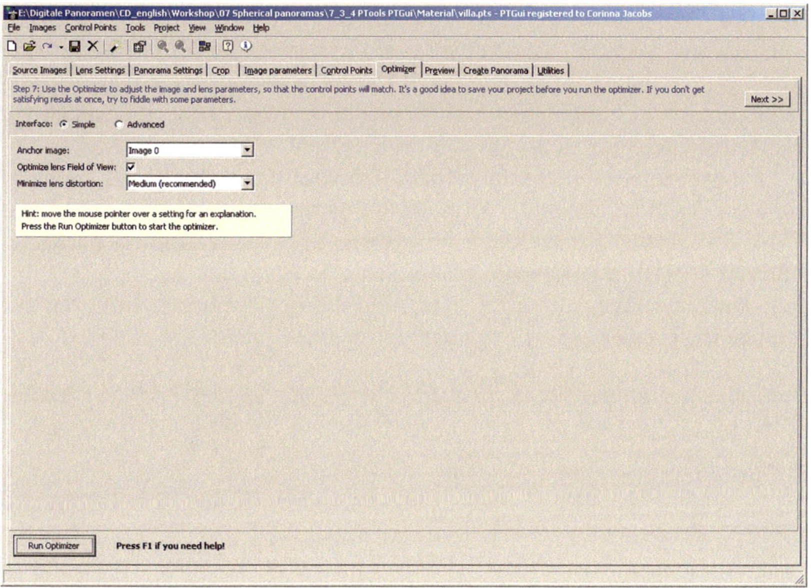

Figure 7.45
In the *Optimizer* tab, parameters are optimized based on the control points

While the optimization process is running, an additional window opens that allows you to track the progress. *Optimizer* shows the average distance between the control points (average control point distance). The smaller the number, the better the chance of obtaining a good result. After optimization has concluded, a message window is displayed that informs you of the expected result (see Figure 7.46).

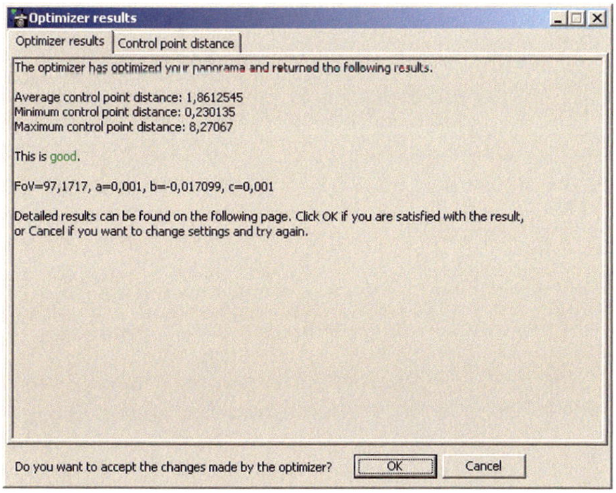

Figure 7.46
The expected result is notified in the *Optimizer results* window

If you are okay with the optimization result, confirm the changes by clicking the *OK* button. If the optimizer does not expect a good result, it is recommended that you delete the control points with a greater difference and redefine them. To do this, refer to the control point list to determine the stitching points in question. The respective points are then changed in the preceding tab, *Control Points* (see Figure 7.44). If you have made any changes, the optimization process should be run through again.

After this, you can see a preview of the panoramic picture in the *Preview* tab (see Figure 7.47). *Width* and *Height* determine the size of the preview picture. If certain pictures should be left out, simply uncheck the respective checkbox in the *Include images* field.

In the example the eighth picture, showing the ground, was taken by hand (i.e. without a tripod). As such, the picture cannot be integrated into the overall panorama without a little work. Because the control points reveal too great of a distance, it makes sense to leave this last picture of the sequence out of the panorama calculation for the time being. How you can retouch the ground area is explained towards the end of this chapter.

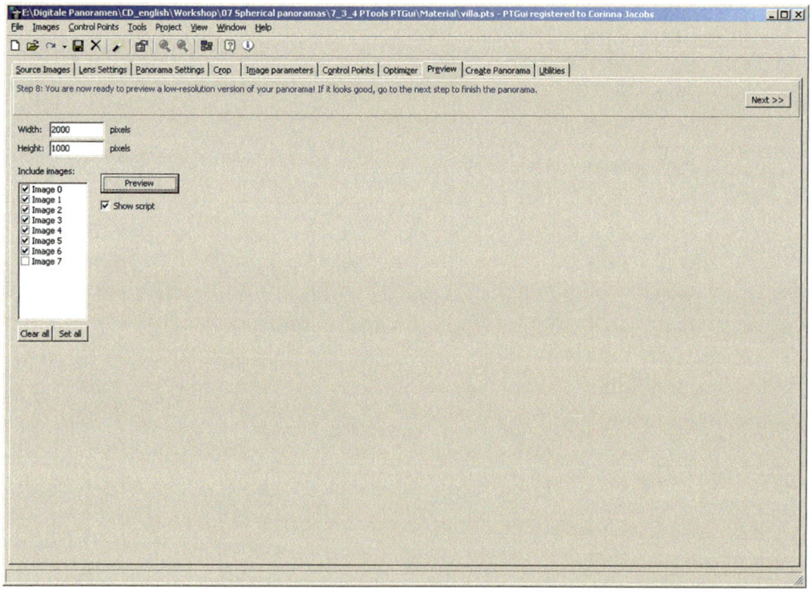

Figure 7.47
You can see a preview of the panoramic picture in the *Preview* tab

The software stitches the individual pictures using a script that can be viewed at any time. This script is displayed by activating the *Show script* dialog box (see Figure 7.48).

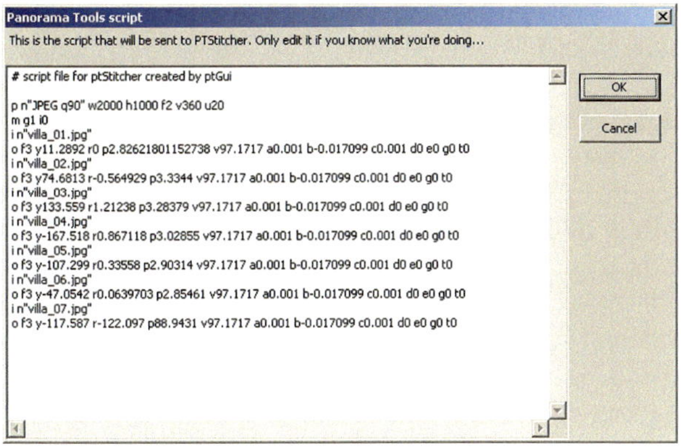

Figure 7.48
Script used by PTStitcher (PanoTools application) to process the pictures

Only advanced users should make changes to the PanoTools script. The preview is started by clicking the *Preview* button. If no preview picture is displayed, it is possible that the path information for the PTStitcher application and the viewers is missing. Without this information, PTGui cannot call up the respective PanoTools functions. Proper configuration can be made via *Tools > Options > Directories & files.*

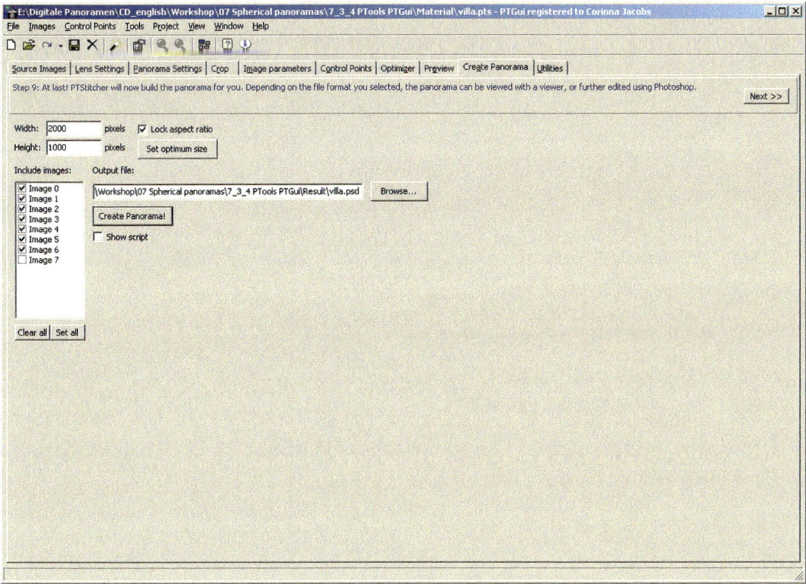

Figure 7.49
The final panoramic file is created in the *Create Panorama* tab

The panoramic picture is created in the *Create Panorama* field (see Figure 7.49). The size of the picture is specified in pixels by *Width* and *Height*. If you have activated *Lock aspect ratio,* the aspect ratio of the panoramic picture remains consistent, even when one of the two values is changed. The *Set optimum size* function triggers the software to calculate the optimum size of the panorama based on raw material (1:1). Under *Include images,* you can include or exclude certain pictures from the calculation process. *Show script* shows the script that is sent to PTStitcher. Clicking the *Create*

Panorama button initiates the final stitching process and saves the resulting panoramic picture.

An additional editing step is required to retouch the ground area. First, you should convert the spherical panoramic picture into a cubic display consisting of six sides. The "psphere2cube" script template is ideal for this and can be easily used from the PTGui software to convert an equirectangular picture into separate cube sides. More information can be found at: http://www.path.uni-melb.edu.au/~bernardk/tutorials/360/readme/scripts.html [status: April 15, 2004]. Now, the bottom area of the picture can be conveniently edited with external software such as Adobe Photoshop. Once retouching is finished, the cube sides are converted back into equirectangular format via the "cube2pshere" script, which also can be found at the above link. After this, you will need to save the panoramic picture. For Web publication, it is best to save in JPG format.

You will find the pictures and the panorama shown here on the CD at the following path: \Workshop\07 Spherical panoramas\7_3_4 PanoTools PTGui

Chapter 10.2 provides information on how to publish these spherical panoramic pictures. There you will find more information on viewers as well as the source code used to embed panoramas in Web sites. These flat panoramic strips also can be printed out on paper or professionally developed in a photo lab. For more information, refer to chapter 10.6.

Several of these spherical panoramas can be stitched to create a virtual tour. There are a number of different solutions available for such a task, some of which are introduced in chapter 9.3.5.

Advantages

- The software is free of charge (freeware).
- PanoTools runs on Linux, Mac and PC platforms.
- The software supports all lens types. Fisheye and rectilinear pictures can be used for stitching.
- PanoTools supports a large number of file formats.
- The software not only can be used for stitching; PanoTools is capable of correcting optical distortions.
- The script, which can be viewed in any text editor, makes the algorithms used very transparent.

Disadvantages

- Large monochrome areas (e.g. the night sky) are difficult to stitch with this software. The overlapping points defined should reveal a high range contrast, as otherwise they cannot be identified as reference pixels for stitching.
- PanoTools is not intuitive for beginners, however add-on programs such as PTGui and PTMac make operating the software easier.
- The filmstrip appears as an interactive panorama for the observer only in conjunction with the PTViewer Java applet, integrated in an HTML file.

8. Object movies

8.1 Introduction

As the term implies, object movies are a type of movie, whereby various vantage points of the object are played back in succession. Depending on the position of the observer's mouse, the images move in a forward or backward direction. The individual pictures are saved as a filmstrip such that the next respective angle of view of the object is displayed. This gives the observer the impression that they are rotating the object themselves. In multi-row object movies, the pictures can be tilted as well.

Typically, the objects are photographed on a turntable with a neutral background; the camera remains in a fixed position while the object rotates. When larger objects that do not fit on a turntable are involved, it is the object that remains fixed, while the camera circles it.

8.2 Photo technology and techniques

8.2.1 Single-row technique

With a single-row object movie, the respective object can be rotated about a certain point by the observer. On the horizontal plane, it is possible to rotate a full 360 degrees. Upward and downward pivoting of the object, however, is not possible with the single-row technique; this is where the multi-row technique comes in (see chapter 8.2.2).

Photographing is done by placing the object at the center of a turntable, which is turned by a certain number of degrees for each successive shot. In the process, the camera remains in the same position (static) for the entire sequence. For example, the object can be rotated at intervals of 10 degrees, whereby a total of 36 pictures are taken per picture sequence. It is, of course, possible to take a greater or lesser number of pictures per sequence.

It is recommended that a special turntable be used to photograph single-row movies (see chapter 8.2.3).

Figure 8.1 shows pictures that were taken using this technique. Refer to chapter 8.3 for the additional steps required to produce an object movie.

Figure 8.1
Picture sequence of a single-row object movie

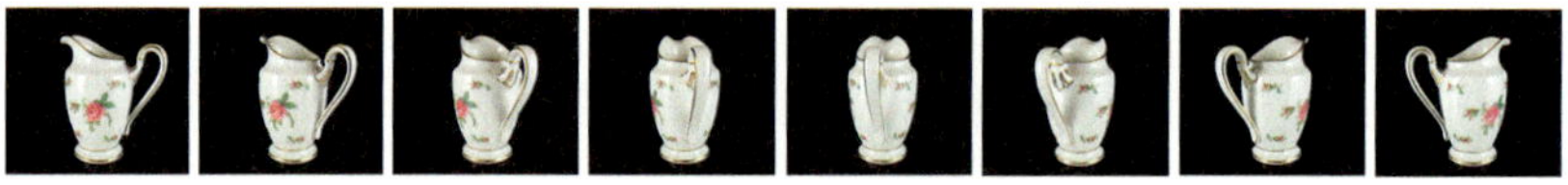

Advantages

- Quick and easy production of an object movie.

Disadvantages

- The object only can be rotated in the horizontal plane by the user.

8.2.2 Multi-row technique

With a multi-row object movie, the object can be vertically pivoted by the observer in addition to rotating on the horizontal plane. Depending on the number of pictures taken and the position of the picture sequences, it is possible to completely rotate the object in all directions.

The photo shooting process required to produce such multi-row object movies is quite a bit more complex and involved than that associated with the single-row technique. Here, only the middle, or center row is filmed using the single-row approach. For the additional rows, a device is required that allows the camera to be swiveled around the object always equidistant to the object's midpoint. After the first row of pictures has been taken (usually at 0 vertical degrees), the camera is swiveled e.g. 30 degrees vertically upwards. Once the camera is positioned, the individual pictures of the second row are taken. If a complete multi-row object movie is desired, a total of 7 rows at 36 pictures each must be taken at a vertical distance of 30 degrees, respectively.

For multi-row object movies, it is recommended that you use a turntable as well as a special camera rig for swiveling the camera (see chapter 8.2.3). As an alternative to photography, the pictures for an object movie can be created using a 3-D computer program. Chapter 8.2.5 provides more information on the process of creating computer generated pictures for the production of object movies.

Figure 8.2 shows pictures that were taken using this technique. Refer to chapter 8.3.3 for the additional steps required to produce an object movie.

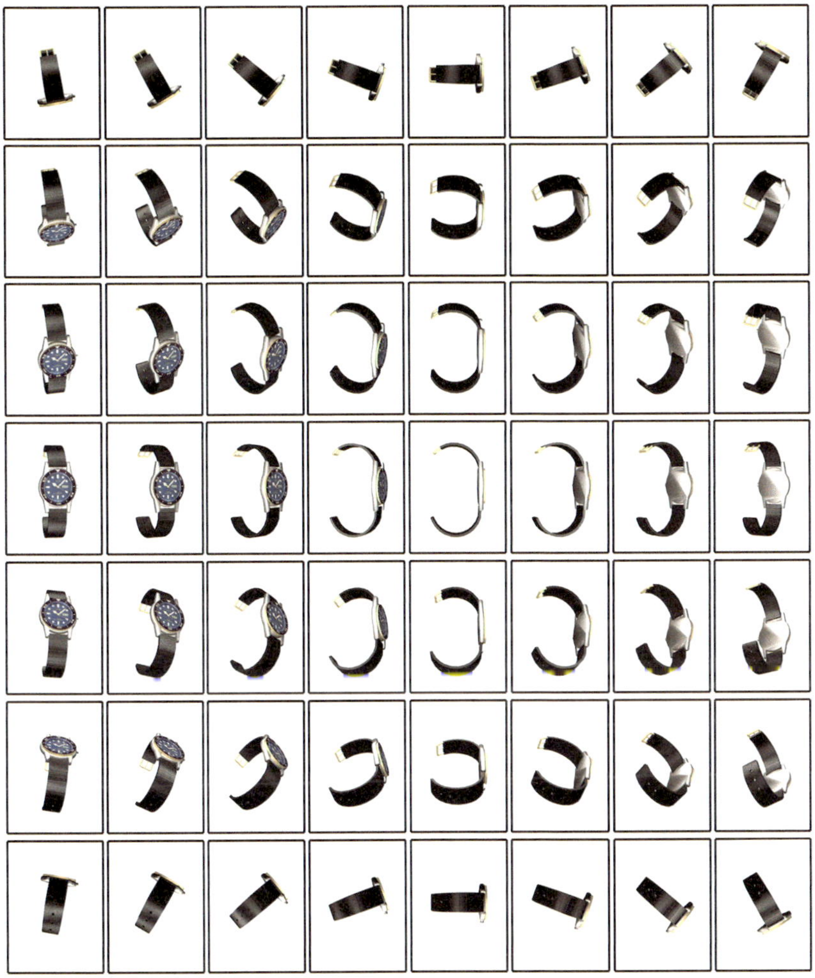

Figure 8.2
Picture sequences of a multi-row object movie

The picture sequences are arranged as follows:

Row 1: +90°
Row 2: +60°
Row 3: +30°
Row 4: +/-0°
Row 5: -30°
Row 6: -60°
Row 7: -90°

Advantages

- Full rotation gives the observer a very realistic impression of the object.

Disadvantages

- The production of a multi-row object movie is much more complex and time-consuming than that of a single-row object movie.
- A camera rig (see Figure 8.7) is required for the arched camera movement around the object.

8.2.3 Turntables

A special turntable is recommended for rotating the object exactly around its center point. However, there are simpler solutions available for achieving good results. A few turntables and alternative solutions are presented in the text that follows. For additional manufacturers of turntables, please refer to chapter B.2.6.

Kaidan Pixi Manual Turntable

The manual Pixi turntable features click stops every 10 degrees and a number scale at 5 degree intervals to aid adjustment. A pedestal set is available as an accessory, on which smaller objects can be positioned. With the pedestal set, objects can be photographed from above or below, without the turntable itself appearing in the shots.

Figure 8.3
Kaidan Pixi Manual Turntable with adjustable pedestal set

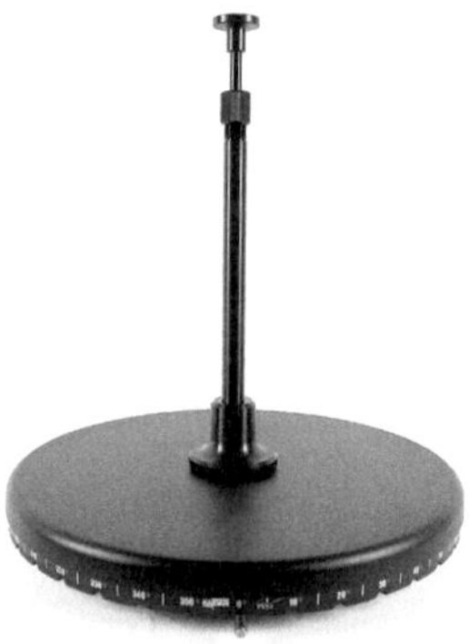

Tripod as turntable

The object can be placed on a tripod and exactly positioned and rotated using a spirit level and a grade scale. The downside to this method is that the size of the object is limited. For initial testing, however, this is a very practical solution.

Figure 8.4
A tripod can be used as a turntable for initial testing

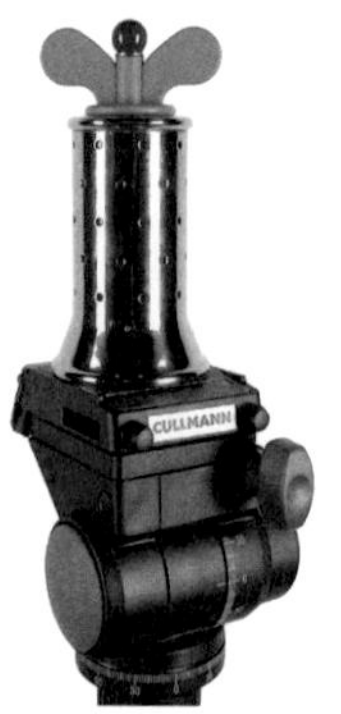

Roundshot VR-Drive

The VR-Drive is a motorized tripod head that is used to take shots of panoramas and objects. The turntable can be purchased as an accessory. Objects are rotated on the turntable via the motor, while the connected camera automatically takes all of the required shots.

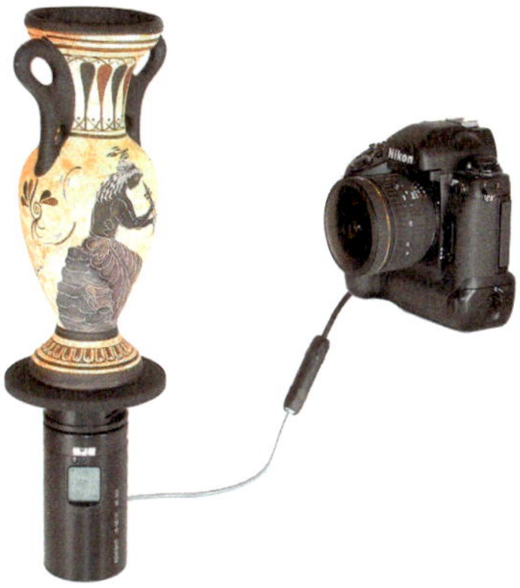

Figure 8.5
Roundshot VR-Drive with turntable attachment

Walk Around

The following method can be used for objects that are not able to be set in motion: Circle the camera around the object, thereby fulfilling the rotational movement required. It is important to note that you need to move in precise, circular fashion about the object's center point. To accomplish this, it is recommended that you use a tripod with a built-in water level that is exactly positioned at all filming locations. In order to ensure proper circular movement, a cable should be used that allows you to walk around the object much like a mathematical compass is used. Here, it is best to mark the degree intervals on the ground using chalk, adhesive tape or sticks (depending on the composition of the ground).

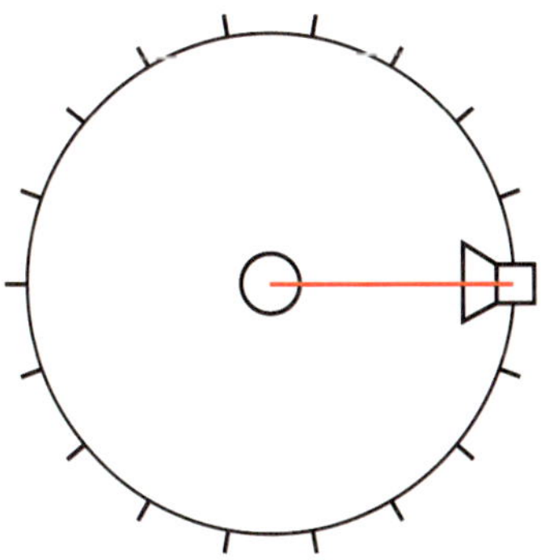

Figure 8.6
Schematic display of the walk around method

Kaidan Magellan 2500 Object Rig

In order to vertically move the camera around the object in an exact circle for multi-row shots, special camera rigs can be used that permit the corresponding adjustments. A turntable is integrated for rotation of the object. Kaidan offers these rigs in both manual and motorized versions.

Figure 8.7
Kaidan Magellan 2500 Object Rig

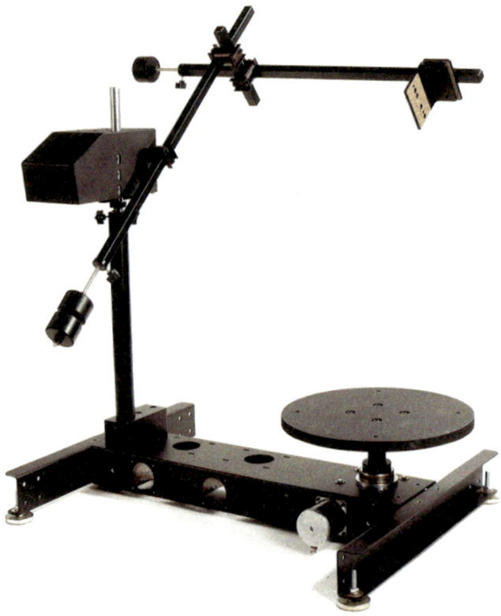

8.2.4 Tips for taking pictures of objects

In panoramic production, the individual pictures are stitched to create a panoramic picture by means of overlapping. As such, it is not absolutely necessary to keep an exact distance between the shots; good results also can be achieved with varying distances. This is not the case with object movies. As the name implies, object movies are a type of movie, whereby various vantage points of the object are played back in succession with respect to the position of the observer's mouse. Here, the individual pictures are not stitched, which is why varying distances between the individual shots are more likely to be noticed in that the object does not evenly rotate. For this reason, you should ensure that the distance between the pictures is exact during the production stage. As a general rule, the more pictures that are taken, the more natural movement appears in the movie. However, including an increased number of pictures also increases the file size.

Usually, it is not required to photograph more than 36 pictures per row. Here, the object is rotated at intervals of 10 degrees, with one picture taken per position of rotation. With an interval of 20 degrees, a total of 18 pictures need to be taken to capture a complete rotation. This also is a sufficient number that will provide for soft rotational movement. If only a few pictures are taken per row, the object movie visibly jerks during rotation. You also can present the user an object in various file sizes and image qualities. This doesn't affect the shooting process; 36 pictures are taken at an interval of 10 degrees. Later on, three object movies can be created, for example, whereby the first movie contains 36 pictures per row, while the other two contain 18 and 12 pictures, respectively. For the reduced quality versions, the superfluous pictures are removed from the picture sequence prior to creating the movie.

Number of individual pictures

Exactly congruent positioning of the object in all individual pictures is critical in order to obtain a perfect object movie. As analog cameras can lead to tolerances during film transport and slight differences in position when scanning, it is recommended that you use a digital or a video camera here.

The object movie should be positioned at the center of all pictures

When a sequence of pictures is being taken, the camera should not be moved; to this end, it is recommended that you use the camera's self-timer function or a remote control triggering device. The batteries also should be charged to avoid having to change them during the photo shoot. If the camera's position is altered just slightly, this will have negative consequences on the subsequent object movie.

The turntable and the camera both should be positioned exactly horizontal. This can best be achieved by using a water level. The more exacting you work when taking pictures, the less correction work you will have later. Although the position of the object can be corrected in the editing stage, this usually requires more time than simply taking the pictures properly.

Especially when shooting asymmetrical objects is it recommended that you carry out a trial rotation using the desired settings after you are finished positioning the object. This allows you to verify whether the object is seen by the camera in every position of rotation or not.

If larger objects are to be photographed using the walk around technique, the object may suffer slight displacement in position in the individual pictures, even if you are working conscientiously. This, then, can considerably reduce the overall quality of the object movie. Therefore, it is a good idea to position these pictures as congruently as possible using an image editing program.

Homogenous illumination of the object is essential if you want your object movie to make a uniform, realistic impression. If the illumination or color values deviate from picture to picture, the visual result in the object movie is flickering. As such, it is recommended that you take the pictures for interactive object presentations in a studio with good lighting and a neutral background. Illumination also is a factor to consider when taking outdoor shots using the walk around method. Here, it is best to photograph in sunlit or overcast conditions.

Ensure a uniform level of light in each picture

The lower part of the picture should be retouched

In order to give the observer the illusion of a "floating" object, it is recommended that you retouch the lower part of the picture, where the turntable usually can be seen. Many turntables can be used in conjunction with an accessory pedestal, which is positioned in the center of the turntable (see chapter 8.2.3). Smaller objects can be placed on these pedestals (which rise above the turntable) and photographed, leading to only a small part of the ground area becoming visible. As a result, less retouching work is involved than if the object were to be shot resting on the complete turntable.

It is a good idea to affix objects prior to photographing them

For objects that will not stand in an upright position on their own, it is recommended that you use adhesive tape or modeling clay to affix them to the turntable or pedestal. Actually, it is a good ideal to do this no matter what, as even stable objects are subject to moving around a little when rotated.

8.2.5 Alternatives

As an alternative, the individual pictures can be created using 3-D software

Object movies can be created from computer-generated images as well as from photos. The pictures required for this, or so-called 3-D renderings, are put together using 3-D software. Due to the almost unlimited possibilities associated with 3-D programs, various production paths can be taken here easier than in reality. Either the camera remains in a static position and the object rotates around its center point, or the object remains static and the camera swivels around the perimeter in exact circle formation. Whereas in reality, it can be difficult to exercise the precise movement required, this can be accomplished with very professional results using 3-D software. Even multi-row object movies can be produced with much less effort than in reality when a 3-D program is involved. Here, the object can be precisely rotated in all directions, with the top and bottom views not posing the slightest problem. In order to obtain such images using photographic means, a special device is needed that allows the camera to sweep around the object in an arched pattern.

With the 3-D version, on the other hand, the respective objects must be modeled using appropriate software, which requires some experience to create a realistic impression. A list of professional 3-D software can be found in the list of manufacturers (see chapter B.1.8).

If the presentation is to be made in a VRML viewer, the VRML file format usually can be selected as an export option directly within the 3-D software. If a QTVR object movie is to be created, an extra plug-in typically is required that allows you to select the QuickTime properties. Rendering and the QTVR export then take place via this plug-in. An additional option is to save the object views as separate files. In this way, the individual pictures can be converted into an object movie using special software. Chapter 8.3.3 explains how to produce a multi-row object movie based on such computer-generated pictures.

8.2.6 Specials

Object movies in which the object additionally moves while being rotated

In addition to static object movies, there are object displays, whereby the object executes additional movements while rotating. For example, a notebook computer that opens and closes. This animation effect is created by photographing the object in different positions. As pictures are being taken throughout a complete object rotation sequence, the object is additionally moved. For a single-row object movie comprising 36 individual pictures, the object can be positioned as follows: In picture 1, the notebook is closed. Picture 2 shows the notebook slightly opened, while the object is opened even further in picture 3. In picture 18, the notebook is fully opened. This is the halfway point. Starting with picture 19, the notebook is gradually closed all the way to picture 36. In order to create a homogeneous impression of the resulting object movie, the object's additional movement should be very uniform and in direct relation to its rotation on the turntable. Chapter 8.3.2 deals with the production of an object movie in which the object executes movements in addition to its rotation.

8.3 Software for creating object movies

The following introduces a number of software products for the production of object movies. Additional software manufacturers can be found in the list of manufacturers (see chapter B.1.3). A few of the software products are capable of producing panoramas as well as object movies. As it would be impossible to list all of the applications and their features here, a comparative overview of the software covered can be found as a table in chapter 12.

Before the individual pictures are edited with the software, it is wise to verify that the images are labeled in the correct sequence. Here, it is important to note that most programs import picture files in alphanumeric order. As such, you should add zeros to numbers under ten, i.e. 001, 002, 003. If the picture files are labeled as 1, 2, 3, the playback sequence in the subsequent object movie will be incorrect. The pictures then would be loaded and edited as follows: 1, 11, 12 followed by 2, 21, 22, etc. With multi-row shots, you begin with the topmost row - the bird's eye view of the object (see table in chapter 8.3.3).

8.3.1 PanoTools – PTStripe

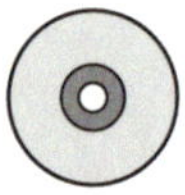

PanoTools can be found on the CD at the following paths: \Demo versions\Mac and \Demo versions\PC

PTStripe is one of the components of the Panorama Tools (PanoTools) software. From a sequence of object views, PTStripe creates an object filmstrip that, in conjunction with the PTViewer Java applet, appears as an object movie to the observer. The following illustrates the production of a single-row object movie consisting of 36 individual pictures.

To create an image filmstrip, drag the folder that contains the picture onto the PTStripe icon (see Figure 8.8).

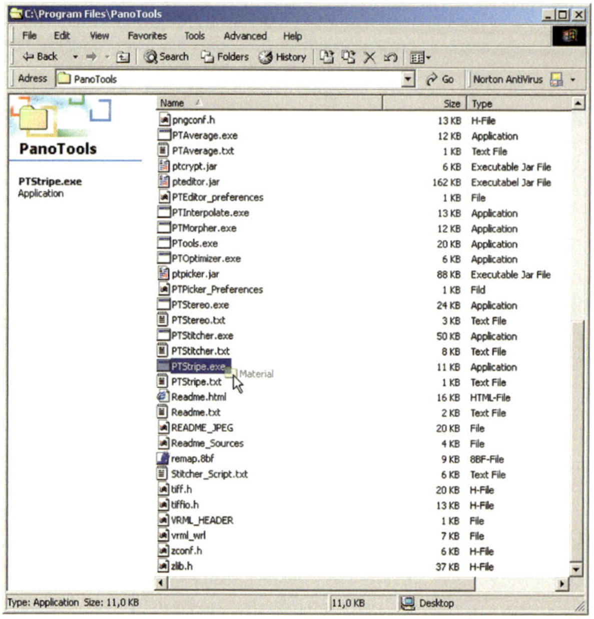

Figure 8.8
Individual pictures are dragged onto the PTStripe icon for editing

A dialog window then appears in which you specify where the resulting image should be saved (see Figure 8.9).

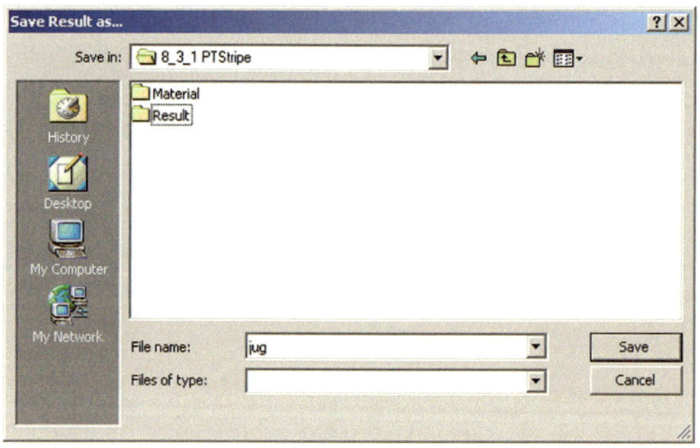

Figure 8.9
The destination path for the resulting file is specified before editing begins

The editing time required to create the filmstrip is a function of the file size of the individual pictures and of your computer's processing power. Figure 8.10 shows part of an object filmstrip created with PTStripe.

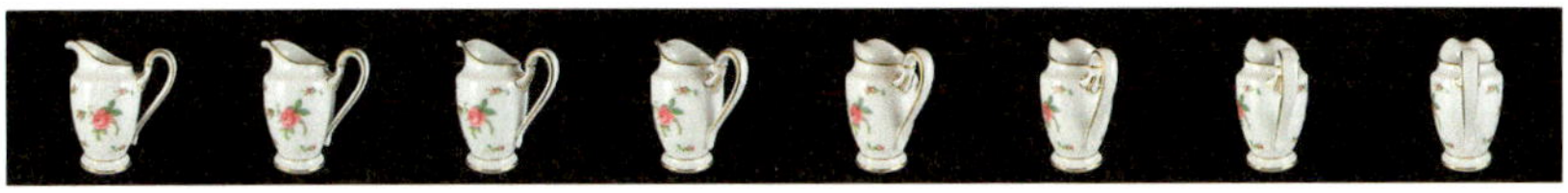

Figure 8.10
Part of the image filmstrip created using PTStripe

This type of filmstrip can, of course, also be assembled using traditional image editing software. Exact positioning of the images to create a filmstrip, however, typically takes longer than if the PTStripe PanoTools application is used for this step.

To learn how object filmstrips are published as object movies, refer to chapter 10.2.1.3. There you will find more information on viewers as well as the source code used to embed object movies in Web sites.

You will find the pictures and the object movie shown here on the CD at the following path: \Workshop\ 08 Object movies\ 8_3_1 PTStripe

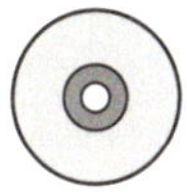

Advantages

- Quick and easy production of an object filmstrip.
- The software is free of charge (freeware).
- PanoTools runs on Linux, Mac and PC platforms.

Disadvantages

- No correction options available in PTStripe. Image correction must be performed using external image editing software.
- The filmstrip appears as an object movie for the observer only in conjunction with the PTViewer Java applet, integrated in an HTML file.

8.3.2 QTVR Edit Object

With QTVR Edit Object, it is possible to convert a normal QuickTime movie into a QTVR object movie. Prior to using this tool, a QuickTime movie is created from the individual pictures of an object display. This can be done in one step with the professional version of the QuickTime player (QuickTime Pro). The following shows how a QuickTime movie is created and then converted into a QTVR object movie.

Chapter B.1.3 tells you where you can purchase QuickTime Pro and QTVR Edit Object

First, the pictures are transformed into a movie using QuickTime Pro. This is done by opening the QuickTime player and calling up the object displays by tracing to *File > Open Image Sequence.* Before the images are loaded, the *Image Sequence Settings* dialog window appears, in which the number of pictures per second (*frame rate*) are defined for the movie (see Figure 8.11). For this particular application scenario, *1 frame per second* must be selected in the pull-down menu.

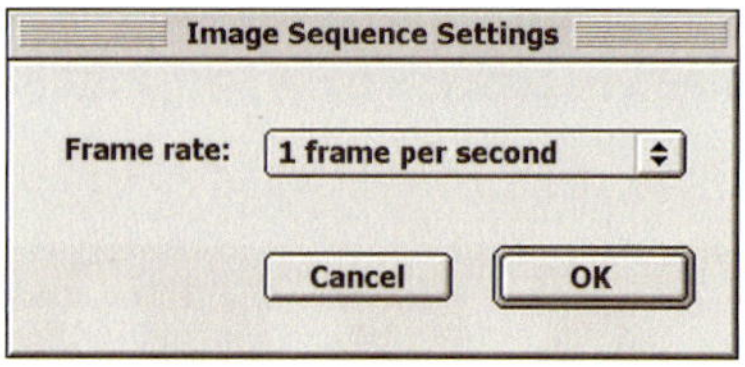

Figure 8.11
In the Image sequence settings dialog window, select *1 frame per second*

The individual pictures are imported and can be played back as a movie in the player window (see Figure 8.12).

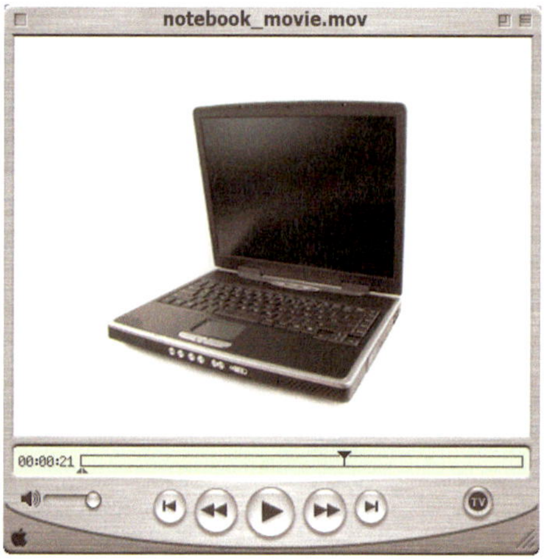

Figure 8.12
The individual pictures were converted into a QTVR movie

In order to convert this movie into an object movie using QTVR Edit Object, it must be saved as a self-contained movie (*Make movie self-contained*) by tracing to *File > Save as.*

In the next step, the movie is further edited using QTVR Edit Object. To this end, the QuickTime movie is loaded via *File > Open.* In the program, a preview of the object movie is displayed next to the editing window. Inside the editing window (see Figure 8.13), the playback properties of the subsequent QTVR movie can be defined as follows:

The number of individual pictures is entered in the *Columns* section. Under *Pan,* the start and end angles for object rotation are defined. Looping of the object in the horizontal plane is activated via the *Wrap* dialog box. If *Wrap* is deactivated, rotation stops when the first or last image of the movie is reached. The *Reverse Control* function allows the object to be rotated in the direction opposite to that of the mouse.

Under *Rows,* you can enter the total number of picture sequences shot. The example here only involves one row, as this is a single-row production. For multi-row object movies, enter the maximum angle from above (e.g. 90 degrees) by *Tilt > Start* and the maximum angle from below (e.g. -90 degrees) by *Tilt > End. Wrap* refers to looping of the object in the vertical direction. Mouse and object movements can be reversed via *Reverse Controls. Swap Pan & Tilt Controls* reverse assigns the pan and tilt controls.

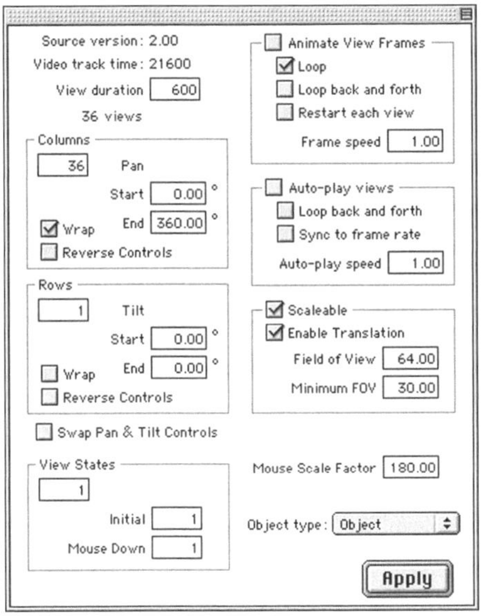

Figure 8.13
The QTVR Edit Object image editing window

The number of interactions that can be additionally controlled by the mouse during playback is specified in the *View States* section. A normal object movie shows only one state of the object and therefore has just one view state. Additional interactivity during playback usually involves displaying an alternative state of the object via the mouse functions. This can be a car door, for example, that automatically opens and closes when touched by the mouse pointer. The individual images of the alternative state of course need to be integrated into the image sequence of the movie so that they can be controlled.

In *Animate View Frames,* you can set the playback properties of this additional animation effect. When the *Loop* checkbox is activated, the animation is played back in loop format. Selecting *Loop back and forth* makes the animation loop forwards and backwards in alternating fashion, while *Restart* each view resets the animation. Playback speed of the animation is set by *Frame speed,* whereby a value of 1 translates into 1 image per second.

In the *Auto-play views* field, you specify whether the object automatically should rotate when the movie is started. When the *Loop back and forth* dialog box is activated, the object is rotated forwards and backwards in alternating fashion; when this function is deactivated, the object is continually rotated forwards. Activating *Sync to frame rate* synchronizes the playback speed to the image rate of the movie (1.00 = one image per second). In *Auto-play speed,* the rotational speed can be changed by entering a number.

By *Scalable,* you determine whether or not the object can be increased in size in the QTVR movie. Checking *Enable Translation* allows the user to drag the zoomed object in the movie window when the QTVR controller bar's drag button is pressed. Leaving the box unchecked disables the drag function. If *Scalable* is activated, the *Field of View* determines the opening picture display of the movie, while *Minimum FOV* specifies the maximum zoom factor.

The *Mouse Scale Factor* stipulates how many degrees the object can be displaced from the left to the right edge of the playback window when the mouse is moved.

By *Object type,* you can select how the object movie will be controlled in a drop-down menu. Your selection options are *Object, Scene, Drag-only* and *Absolute.* When *Object* is selected, the observer can move the object with the mouse hand icon as well as by using the arrows on the left and right sides of the window. With *Scene,* a pound sign appears in place of the mouse hand icon that turns into arrows as it is moved toward the edge of the window. If *Drag-only* is selected, the object only can be rotated via the mouse hand icon; no arrows appear for playback of the movie. *Absolute* displays the mouse hand icon as a pointer and also does not include arrows at the edge of the window. The differences between the way in which a QTVR object movie is controlled are best grasped by doing a test run.

Once all settings have been made, the properties go into effect for the object movie when the *Apply* button is clicked and can then be tested in the preview window. If the object movie creates the desired impression, save the QTVR under a new name via *File > Save As;* this way, you will have both movies (QuickTime and QTVR) at your disposal.

The file size of the resulting object movie may be too large for Internet publication following this step. At this point, the QTVR movie is not compressed and the size of the file is determined by the total number of individual pictures. If you want to compress the QTVR file, open the object movie with QuickTime Pro. Now select the *Interframe Compressed QTVR Object Movie* format by tracing to *File > Export.* Via *Options,* a dialog window is accessed in which you can specify the target file size as well as select a compression code. For additional information on QuickTime codecs, please refer to chapter 10.1. This chapter also tells you how to publish QTVR movies. There you will find more information on viewers as well as the source code used to embed QTVR movies in Web sites.

You will find the pictures and object movies shown here on the CD at the following path: \Workshop\08 Object movies\8_3_2 QTVR Edit Object

Advantages

- Quick and easy production of object movies.
- The software is free of charge (freeware).

Disadvantages

- Few options for making corrections.
- The software only runs on a Mac OS.

8.3.3 VR Worx – VR ObjectWorx

VR Worx can be used to create single-row as well as multi-row object movies. The following focuses on how a multi-row object movie is produced. Here, the naming convention used for the individual pictures is critical, as this determines the display sequence in the subsequent movie. For the example, 7 vertical rows at 36 pictures each were taken (or rendered in a 3-D program), whereby each row is 30 degrees apart from the next. The table that follows shows the naming convention used for the 252 pictures in total.

A demo version of VR Worx can be found on the CD at the following paths: \Demo versions\Mac and \Demo versions\PC

Naming convention for a multi-row object movie

Row	Position	File names
1	+ 90°	001 - 036
2	+ 60°	037 - 072
3	+ 30°	073 - 108
4	+/- 0°	109 - 144
5	- 30°	145 - 180
6	- 60°	181 - 216
7	- 90°	217 - 252

In VR Worx, the VR ObjectWorx program module is called up via the *Create New Project > Create an Object* function in *File > New*. To create an object movie using VR ObjectWorx, the six editing tabs *Setup, Acquire, Hot Spots, Effects Compose* and *Preview* are run through.

Figure 8.14
The properties of the individual pictures are defined in the *Setup* tab

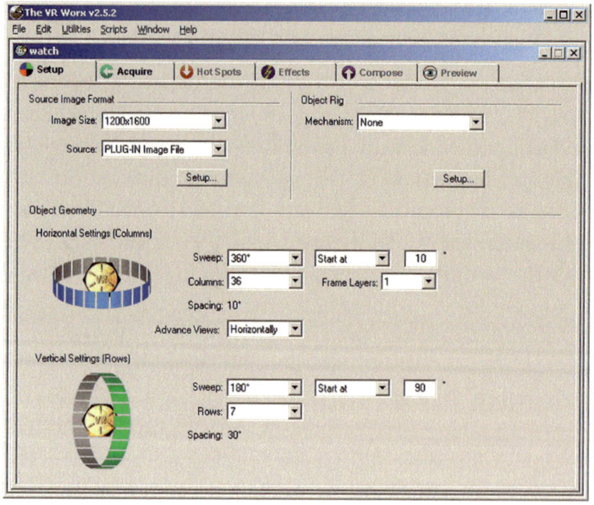

First, the exact size of an individual picture is given in pixels under *Source Image Format* in the *Setup* tab (see Figure 8.14). If the corresponding size cannot be found in the popup menu, custom values are entered by selecting the *Custom* option. By *Source,* image sources such as scanners or video cards can be selected. If the required images already are on your computer's hard disk, select *Source > PLUG-IN Image File.* A motorized turntable can be controlled in the *Object Rig* section. If you took the pictures using a manual turntable, select *Mechanism > None.* Information on the number of horizontal and vertical picture sequences is entered by *Object Geometry.* In *Horizontal Settings > Sweep,* you define whether or not the object completes a full 360 degree turn. *Horizontal Settings > Columns* determines how many images are in a picture sequence. The *Spacing* between the images is calculated by the software based on this information. The position of the images is specified by *Advance Views,* whereby *Horizontally* means that all images first will be shown in a horizontal plane before the next picture sequence is displayed vertically offset. When *Vertically* is selected, the opposite occurs. *Vertical Settings > Sweep* defines the vertical sweep of a picture sequence in degrees. With a single-row production, sweep is set to 0°. In the multi-row example, however, *Sweep* is at 180°, which means that the object is completely depicted in the vertical plane. The number of picture sequences is entered by *Vertical Settings > Rows.* The Spacing between the images is calculated by the software based on this information. When you have made all of your selections, switch to the *Acquire* tab.

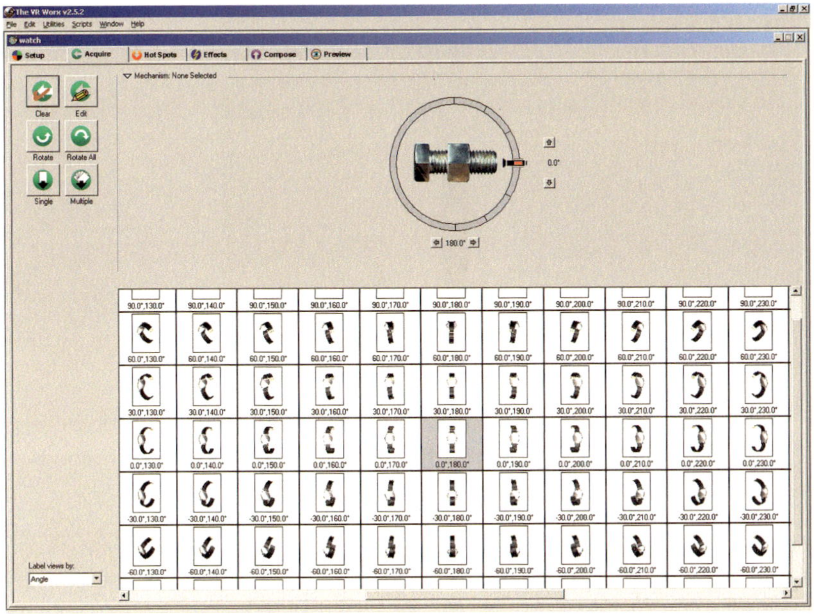

Figure 8.15
Individual pictures are imported in the *Acquire* tab

The *Acquire* tab (see Figure 8.15) includes placeholders for the individual pictures respective of the information you entered in the *Setup* tab. Pictures are imported via *Image > Multiple.* If some pictures need to be exchanged for others, the *Tools > Clear* function can be used to remove the pictures from the window, with replacement pictures imported via *Image > Single.* Pictures can be rotated using the *Rotate* function. If individual pictures need to be edited, you can switch to an external image editing program such as Adobe Photoshop via *Edit.* The software integrates all of the individual pictures into the existing VR Worx document, which is why VR Worx files are quite large when compared to the project files created by other programs.

In the *Hot Spots* editing tab, hot spots can be defined in any desired form using the *Tools* function. Hot spots can be assigned various functions. For more information, refer to chapter 9.3.2.

In the *Effects* window, the position and picture display area of the object movie can be changed with the *Center, Crop* and *De-wobble* functions. Effects can be added to the object movie via *Matte* and *Sound.* The following provides information on the individual effects; in the sample multi-row object movie, however, none of these effects are used.

Figure 8.16
The center point of rotation can be corrected in *Effects > Center*

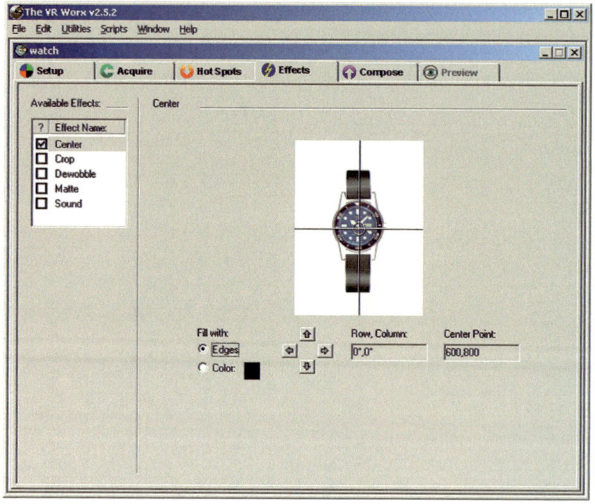

A new center point can be defined for all pictures in an object movie via the *Center* function (see Figure 8.16). This effect is especially beneficial if the object was rotated from the center of the turntable, yet is not positioned in the middle of the picture. The *Center* effect is activated by clicking the corresponding dialog box.

Figure 8.17
The picture display area of the object movie is set via *Effects > Crop*

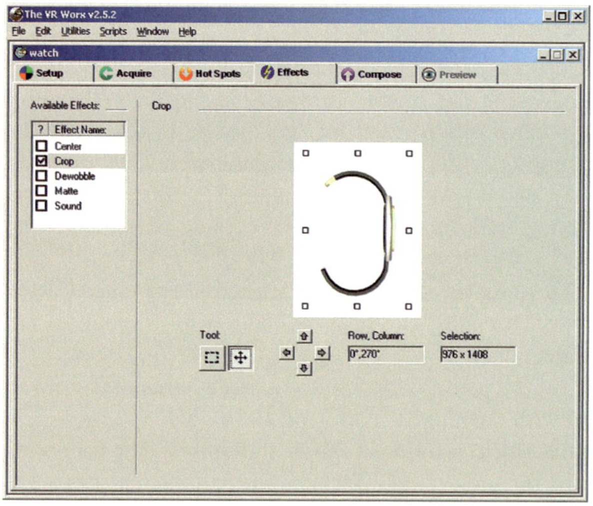

The *Crop* function (see Figure 8.17) trims the picture display area of the subsequent object movie. This can be useful when too much of the background scene is visible around the object. To activate the effect, make the respective selection in the *Crop* dialog box. The object can be lassoed to the desired size in order to define the visible area of the object movie.

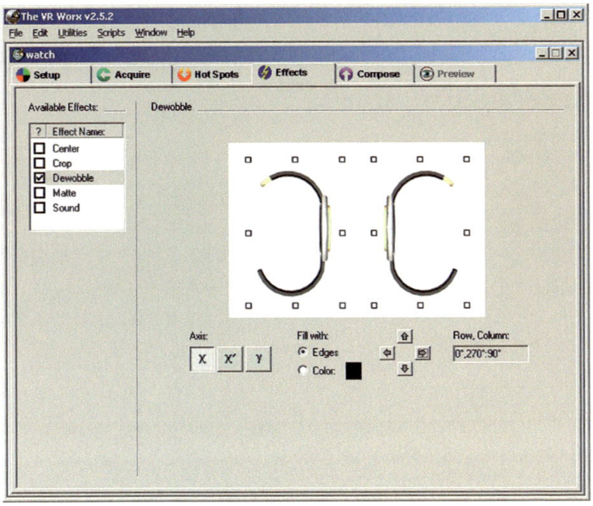

Figure 8.18
The position of an object can be corrected via *Effects > De-wobble*

The *De-wobble* function (see Figure 8.18) allows you to recenter an object not positioned exactly correct in a picture. Here, correction can be made in three axes: X, X' and Y. Adjustments can be made in the X and X' axes for object movies that cover a 360 range. The Y axis only can be influenced for multi-row shots. In order to position the center axis, opposing pictures are displayed. The *De-wobble* effect is activated by clicking the respective checkbox.

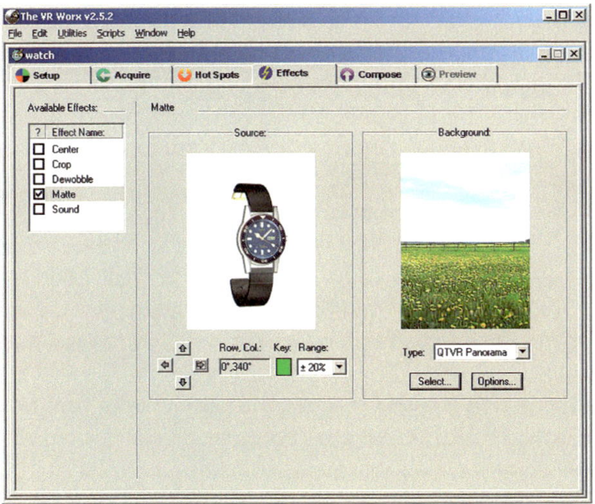

Figure 8.19
Effects > Matte allows you to separate the object from its original background and place it in front of another background

The *Matte* function (see Figure 8.19) is capable of separating objects from their original background. If the object was shot in front of a blue screen, for example, it can be masked and placed in front of another background. This new background could be a colored area, an image or a QTVR panorama. Although the *Matte* function can be applied to various background colors, the color selected must not also be in the object if errors are to be avoided. This effect is activated in the *Matte* dialog box.

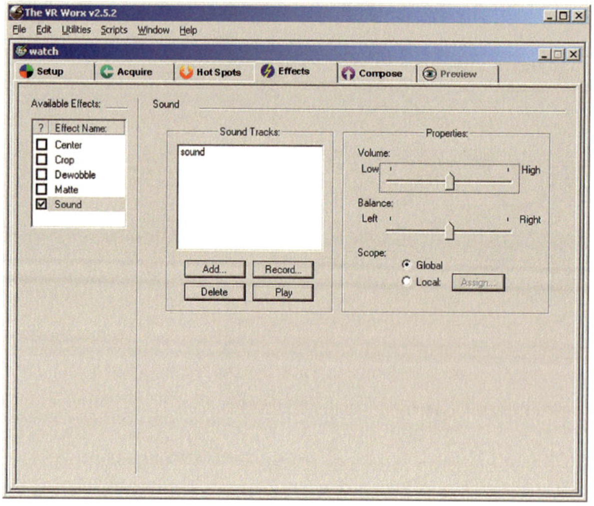

Figure 8.20
Soundtracks can be added to the QTVR movie via *Effects > Sound*

The *Sound* function (see Figure 8.20) is capable of integrating one or more soundtracks. Existing sound files in various formats can be included via *Sound Tracks > Add.* Likewise, new sounds can be recorded with *Sound Tracks > Record* when a microphone is connected. *Volume, Balance* and *Scope* properties can be defined for each soundtrack. The output of the respective sound file is controlled by *Volume.* The distribution of sound (left/right) can be set via *Balance. Scope* allows you to determine whether the sound will be able to be heard throughout the entire object movie or only at certain points. If the sound should be continuously heard, select *Scope > Global.* With *Scope > Local,* certain areas of the object movie can be selected at which the sound will be heard.

In *Compose* (see Figure 8.21), the compression codec used can be specified via *Compression > Codec > Set.* The default setting is *Photo-JPEG Quality Medium,* however other compression settings also provide good results. Chapter 10.1 provides more information on QuickTime codecs. *Color Depth* is used to specify the depth of color. Here, it is recommended that you apply the preselected *24 bits (millions).* You can specify a file size by activating the *Target Size* dialog box and entering the numerical figure. The software then will create a QTVR file that does not exceed your desired file size. The size of the window for the subsequent QuickTime movie can be set via *Frame Size.* If you are publishing for the Web, the *Optimize for Web Delivery* field should be selected so that "fast start" QuickTime streaming is activated. When "fast start" is activated, parts of the object movie are able to be viewed by the user while the QTVR file is being downloaded. Once all of the settings have been properly configured, the object movie is rendered via *Actions > Build.*

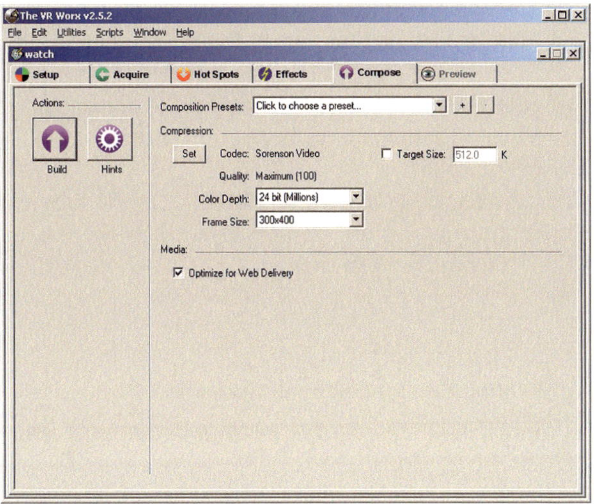

Figure 8.21
The QTVR movie is created and compressed using the selected codec in the *Compose* tab

The finished movie then can be viewed and tested in the *Preview* window (see Figure 8.22).

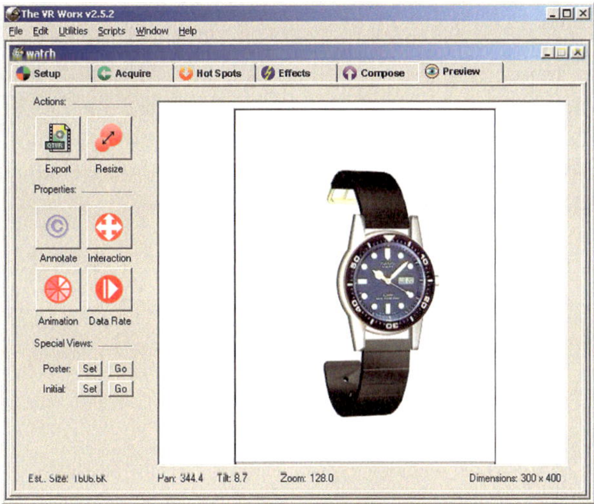

Figure 8.22
The object movie is analyzed in *Preview* and saved after defining additional properties

The final size of the window is defined via *Actions > Resize.* Under *Properties > Annotate,* information such as name, copyright and a short description of the content can be added to the object movie. *Properties > Interaction* sets the mouse and key functions used by the observer to navigate the object movie in the QuickTime player. *Properties > Animation* influences the motion of the object movie, e.g. the movie starts from the beginning to achieve a perfect loop. This gives the user the impression of an infinitely rotating object. In the *Properties > Data Rate* field, the download speed for various connections can be calculated. With the *Special Views > Poster* function, a specific individual image is selected to represent, or iden-

You will find the pictures and the object movie shown here on the CD at the following path: \Workshop\08 Object movies\8_3_3 VR Worx

tify the object movie. This image is displayed in the file dialogs and is used in thumbnail format. The *Initial View* is that part of the object that the observer first sees when the movie is opened. It is recommended that you use the same image for the *Poster View* and *Initial View* so that the object movie can be better identified. When all settings have been configured, the object movie is saved via *Actions > Export.*

Chapter 10.1 provides information on how to publish QTVR movies. There you will find more information on viewers as well as the source code used to embed QTVR movies in Web sites.

Advantages

- Easy to use and the individual functions are intuitive in scope.
- VR Worx offers a comprehensive range of correction and effects functions.
- Additional functions such as the adding of sound are available.
- The software provides support for importing numerous file formats and scanned pictures can be directly loaded via the TWAIN interface.

Disadvantages

- As the picture and sound data are not referenced, but integrated, VR Worx documents are comparatively large (depending on the number of imported files). This is why the book CD only includes the pictures and the finished object movie for the example shown and not the associated VR Worx document.

9. Virtual tours

9.1 Introduction

In the simplest application scenario, several individual panoramas are linked to each other using hot spots. When a hot spot is clicked in the panorama, the viewer is brought to the next area of the tour. In more complex virtual tours, panoramas, object movies, videos, sound and graphics can be linked to each other. The most frequent form of use, however, is the linking of individual panoramas to create a virtual tour. As such, the focus of the next chapter is on this type of application.

9.2 Photo technology and techniques

In theory, all of the panoramic forms introduced can be used to create virtual tours. Cylindrical, spherical and cubic tours can be produced. Linking to object movies is also possible. Individual panoramas and object movies are put together according to the form of projection selected as described in chapters 6, 7 and 8. At this point, the presentations can be linked to form virtual tours using the software products introduced here.

9.2.1 Tips for picture taking

In order not to confuse the visitor of the virtual tour, it is recommended that you select the hot spots such that the individual panoramas can be seen in relation to each other. This makes it easier for the user to jump from one panorama to the next. A floor plan can be included that is linked to the panorama to indicate the current position and to improve orientation. In this way, the observer has the option of accessing the next panorama by clicking the hot spots or navigating using the floor plan. In addition, the vertical position of the camera should be more or less the same for all panoramas associated with a tour. A realistic impression is best achieved when the camera is positioned at eye level.

9.3 Software for virtual tours

The following introduces a number of software products for the production of virtual tours. Additional software manufacturers can be found in the list of manufacturers (see chapter B.1.4). A few of the software products are capable of producing panoramas and object movies as well as linking them to create virtual tours. As it would be impossible to list all of the applications and their features here, a comparative overview of the software covered can be found as a table in chapter 12.

9.3.1 REALVIZ Stitcher

A demo version of REALVIZ Stitcher can be found on the CD at the following paths: \Demo versions\Mac and \Demo versions\PC

REALVIZ Stitcher allows you to stitch panoramas and link them to create a tour. The following shows how a virtual tour is produced from cubic panoramas.

With REALVIZ Stitcher, you can define hot spots that are linked to a URL or another panorama. These hot spots are defined in Hotspot mode in the editing window after stitching is finished. Hot spots only can be defined and exported for QTVR movies; with all other export formats offered by REALVIZ Stitcher, the hot spot function is not supported.

The hot spots are defined in an existing stitcher project in *Hotspot Creation Mode*. It is recommended that you position hot spots in a panorama only once it has been completely stitched together. How panoramas are stitched using REALVIZ Stitcher was learned in chapters 6.3.4 and 7.3.2. *Hotspot Creation Mode* is activated via *Tools > Hotspots*. In the panoramic picture that is open in the editing window, the desired part of the image is made visible via the *Pan* and *Zoom* functions.

The first point of the hot spot polygon is defined by double clicking with your mouse. The subsequent points of the polygon are set with a single mouse click. To close the polygon, double click once again (see Figure 9.1).

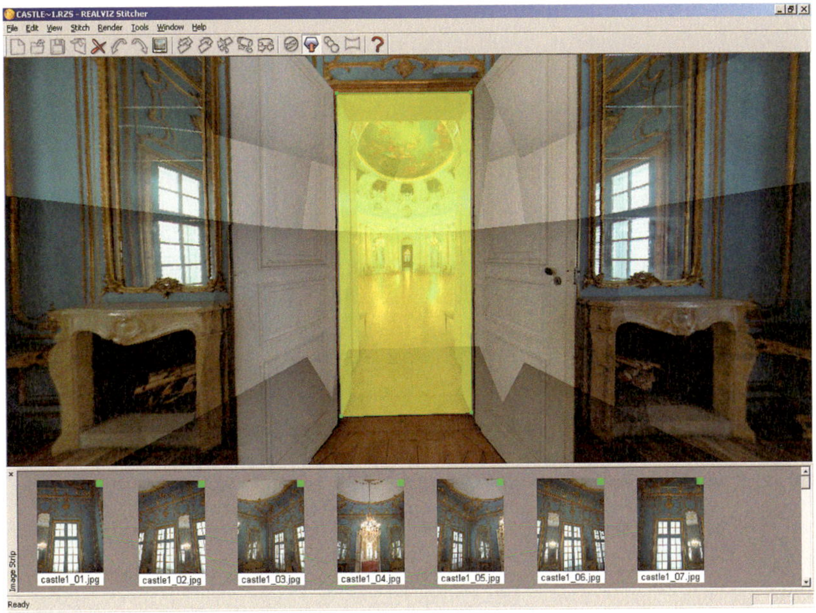

Figure 9.1
Hot spot polygons can be plotted in *Hotspot creation mode*

In order to link the hot spot, the respective polygon must be selected. This is done by clicking on the polygon; a selected polygon is demarcated with a green border. The *Hotspot* submenu is accessed via *Edit > Properties* (see Figure 9.2).

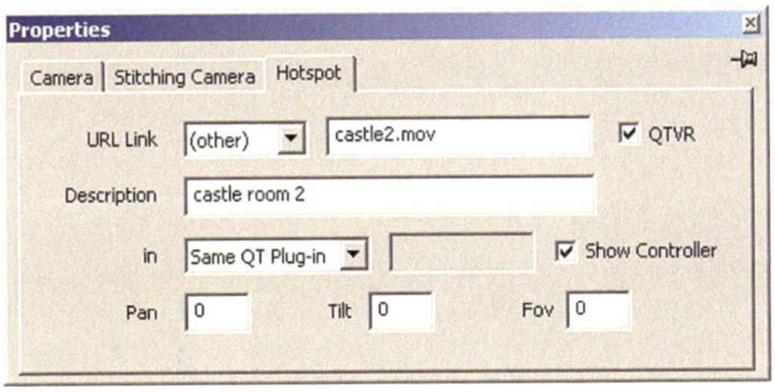

Figure 9.2
The properties of the hot spots are defined in the *Properties* window

The required link settings can be made here. In *URL Link,* you can select *http://, ftp://, mailto:* or *(other)* in the pull-down menu. If you would like to link the panorama to another Web site, select *http://* and enter the address of the site in the following line. If the panorama to which you want to link is located on the same Web server, choose *(other).* The relative path of the panoramic file is entered in the address line.

In the *Description* field, a name for this hot spot can be assigned that is displayed in the navigation bar of the QuickTime player while the QTVR movie is being played.

In a drop-down menu by *in,* you can select *Same Window, New Window* or *Named Frame,* whereby *Same Window* means that the target Web site will be displayed in the same browser window as the first panorama. *New Window* opens a new browser window in which the linked panorama is displayed, while the *Named Frame* option presents the linked panorama in a defined frame on the respective Web site. The name of the target frame is entered in the adjacent text field.

If the target of the hot spot link is another QTVR panorama (as is the case with the example), QTVR settings can be made for the target panorama. To do this, activate the *QTVR* dialog box. The following additional selection options then appear in the in pull-down menu: *Same QT Plug-in* and *New QT Player. Same QT Plug-in* loads the new panorama in the same movie window. If *New QT Player* is selected, the subsequent panorama is loaded in a new player window. *Pan, Tilt* and *Fov* define the part of the picture that is to be seen when the linked QTVR movie is started. If you want to apply the properties of the target movie, select "0" for *Pan, Tilt* and *Fov.*

Virtual tours may not be able to be directly viewed in the QuickTime player, depending on the settings made in the *Properties* menu. These tours only reach their full functionality when they are embedded in a Web site and are viewed via the browser plug-in. As the *Same QT Plug-in* setting was selected in the sample panorama (see Figure 9.2), however, it is possible to jump from one hot spot to the next in the QuickTime player.

When all desired hot spots have been defined, the QTVR movie is rendered and saved via *Render > Render.* Figures 9.3 to 9.5 show the settings for the sample panorama.

Figure 9.3
File format and resolution for the cubic QTVR panorama are defined in the *File* dialog field

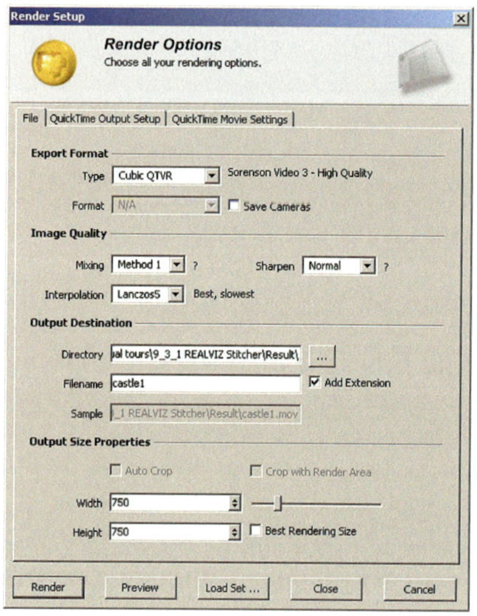

The projection format is defined by *File > Export Format > Type* (here: *Cubic QTVR*). Factors for image quality such as sharpness and interpolation are set under *Image Quality.* In *Output Size Properties,* the resolution of the subsequent panoramic picture is defined in pixels. The higher the resolution value selected, the better the image quality, however the file size also increases in proportion to this resolution and image quality. When *Best Rendering Size* is activated, the software calculates the optimum size of the panorama based on raw material (1:1). Starting with an average value, you can estimate the expected image quality and file size.

Additional QTVR-specific settings can be made in the *QuickTime Output Setup* window (see Figure 9.4).

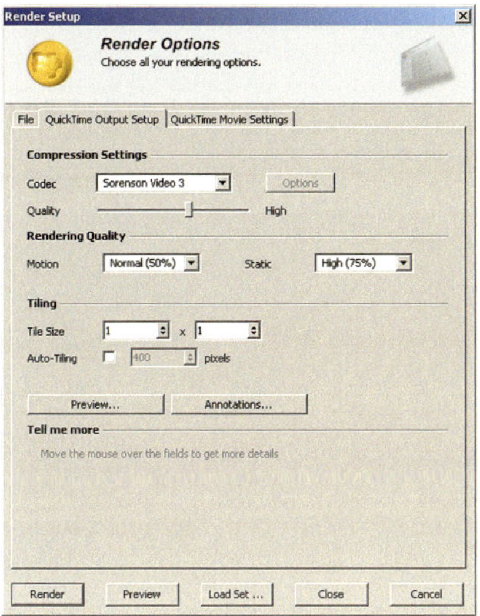

Figure 9.4
Additional QTVR movie properties can be set in the *QuickTime Output Setup* dialog field

The type of compression used is selected by *Compression Settings > Codec* (more information on codecs can be found in chapter 10.1). The desired image quality is set next to *Compression Settings > Quality. Rendering Quality* determines the image quality when the panorama is moving (*Motion*) and not moving (*Static*). In the *Tiling* field, the panoramic picture is subdivided into quadrants (*Tiles*) so that all tiles that already have been downloaded can be played. For large QTVR panoramas, it definitely makes sense to increase the default value. In the present example, however, a tiling setting of 1 x 1 is adequate. In *Preview,* you can activate "fast start" QuickTime streaming, which allows parts of the panorama to be viewed by the user while continuing to download the QTVR file. It is also possible to create a preview screen for the QTVR movie, which provides the observer a low resolution view of the panorama before the file is completely downloaded from the Internet. In *Annotations,* text information such as the author, copyright and a short description of the content can be added to the QTVR movie.

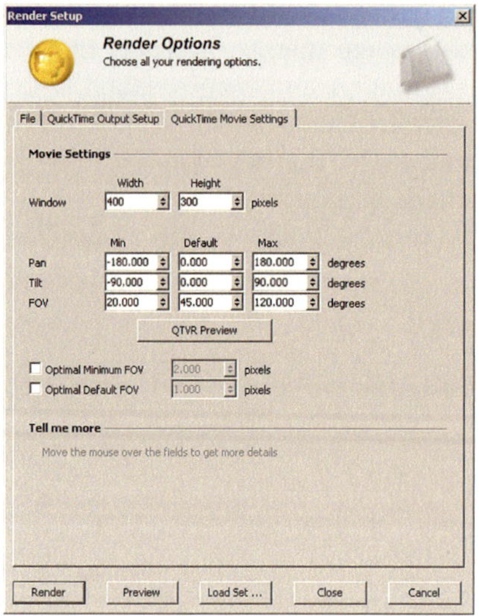

Figure 9.5
Additional QTVR movie properties can be set in the *QuickTime Output Setup* dialog field

The *QuickTime Movie Settings* field (see Figure 9.5) is used to define the window size (*Window*) in pixels. *Pan* and *Tilt* allow you to configure the opening picture display of the QTVR movie. The minimum and maximum zoom factors are defined by *FOV*. With the *Optimal Minimum FOV* function, you can specify a maximum zoom range to prevent the panorama from appearing too coarse when the picture is magnified. *Optimal Default FOV* selects an average angle of view as the start position for the QTVR movie in order for the user to be able to pivot up and down.

You will find the pictures, panoramas and the virtual tour shown here on the CD at the following path: \Workshop\ 09 Virtual tours\ 9_3_1 REALVIZ Stitcher

When all settings have been made, the calculation process is initiated by clicking the *Render* button. The result can be optimized by rendering again with different values.

Chapter 10.1 provides information on how to publish QTVR tours. There you will find more information on viewers as well as the source code used to embed panoramas in Web sites.

Advantages

- Quick and easy definition of hot spot polygons and properties of the respective hot spots.
- Although the QTVR movies are linked, they can be saved separately. As such, each panorama is only loaded as needed and the observer does not need to wait until the complete tour has been transferred.

Disadvantages

- REALVIZ Stitcher only allows you to link QTVR movies into virtual tours.

- Virtual tours whose hot spots are linked to URLs can only be tested embedded in HTML files by the browser plug-in. Tours in which the QTVR movies are directly linked to each other can be tested by the QuickTime player without an HTML file.

9.3.2 VR Worx – VR SceneWorx

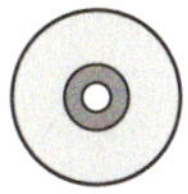

A demo version of VR Worx can be found on the CD at the following paths: \Demo versions\Mac and \Demo versions\PC

VR Worx software is capable of editing panoramas and object movies as well as creating virtual tours. With VR SceneWorx, hot spots can be defined not only in QTVR panoramas, but also in QTVR object movies. How panoramas are stitched using VR Worx was learned in chapter 6.3.2. More information on producing object movies with VR Worx can be found in chapter 8.3.3. The following chapter shows how cylindrical panoramas are linked to create a virtual tour.

In VR Worx, the VR SceneWorx program module is called up via the *Create New Project > Create a Scene* function in *File > New.* To create a virtual tour in VR SceneWorx, the five editing tabs *Setup, Background, Nodes, Compose* and *Preview* must be run through.

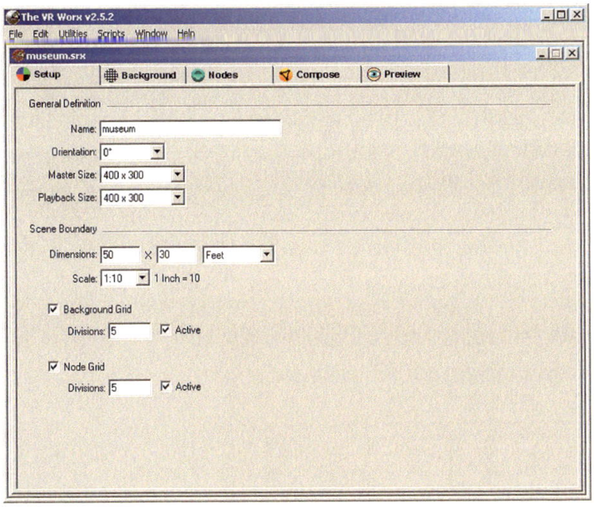

Figure 9.6
The properties of the scene are defined in the *Setup* tab

First, a name is entered for the scene under *General Definition* in the *Setup* tab (see Figure 9.6). The view of the panoramas that is to be seen when loaded is selected in the *Orientation* pull-down menu. If *Initial View* is selected here, the picture display area that was previously defined for the respective QTVR movie is used. *Master Size* specifies the size of the movie in the editing window, whereas *Playback Size* defines the size of the resulting QTVR movie. The size of the area covered by the entire scene is entered in the *Scene Boundary > Dimensions* field, whereby *Scale* gives the graduation. A grid can be displayed via *Background Grid* and *Node Grid.* Here, it is best to assume the default settings.

When all of the basic settings have been made, it is time to switch to the *Background* tab (see Figure 9.7).

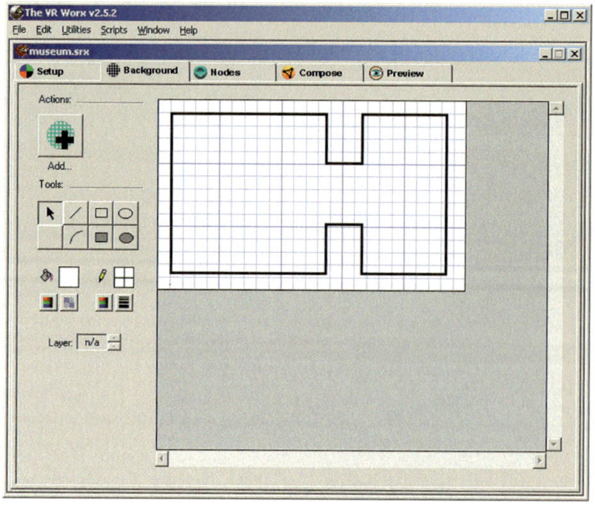

Figure 9.7
Floor plans can be used as background images

Here, it is possible to define floor plans as background images, which facilitate positioning of the panoramas in the scene. These floor plan sketches can be imported as image files via *Actions > Add* or created using the drawing tools.

In the *Nodes* tab (see Figure 9.8), panoramas and objects are imported and positioned; their properties can be modified as well. Individual panoramas and object movies are loaded via *Actions > Add. Actions > Clear* removes imported files. The respective movie can be tested via *Actions > Edit.* The easiest way to link the panoramas is to use the arrow icons in the *Tools* field.

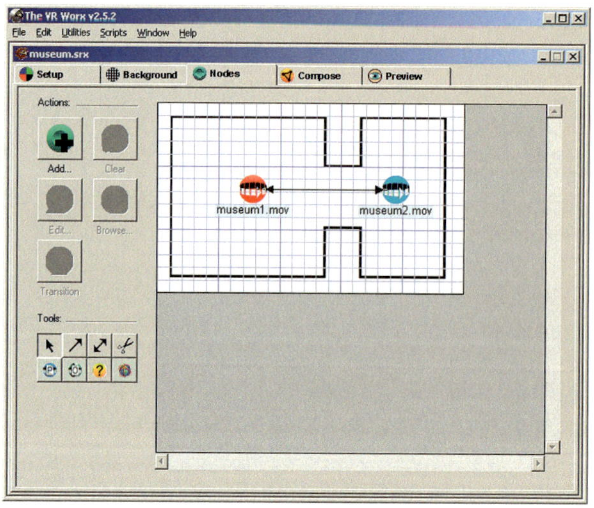

Figure 9.8
Panoramas and objects are positioned in the scene in the *Nodes* tab

When the *Actions > Browse* button is pressed, the *Node Browser* window (see Figure 9.9) is opened for the marked panorama. In this dialog window, the interaction properties of the movie can be defined and altered.

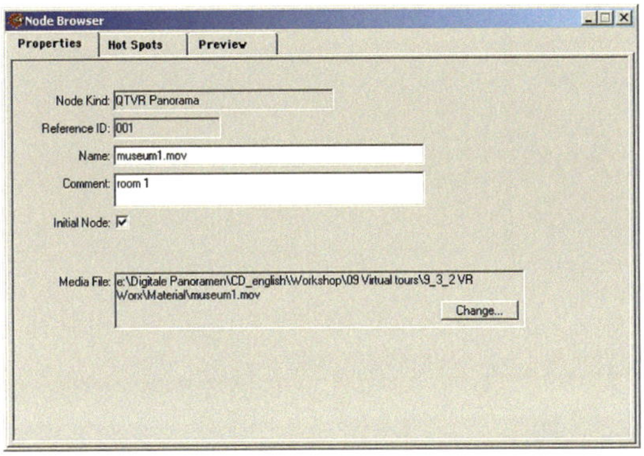

Figure 9.9
The properties of a movie are defined in the *Node Browser* window

Node Browser contains three tabs: *Properties, Hot Spots* and *Preview.* In the *Properties* tab (see Figure 9.9), elements such as *Name* and *Comments* can be entered for the respective panorama or object movie. If the QTVR movie will be the first movie in the virtual tour, the *Initial Node* dialog box is activated. Now the next tab is clicked.

In the *Hot Spots* tab (see Figure 9.10), the drawing tools can be used to select various shapes for the hot spots. Once a hot spot polygon has been defined, the corresponding colored area is double clicked to access the *Hot Spot Properties* submenu.

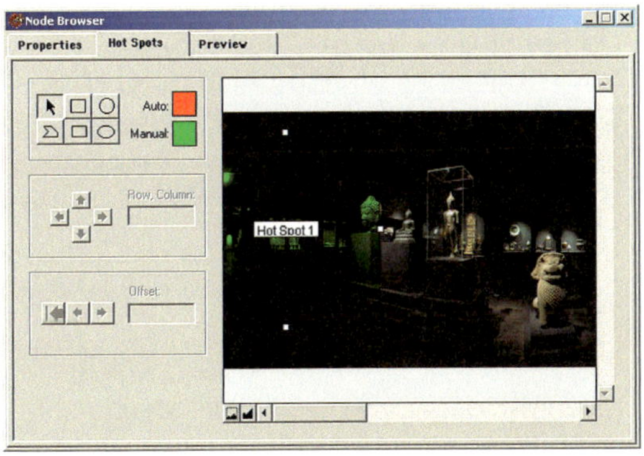

Figure 9.10
Colored hot sopts can be drawn in the *Hot Spots* tab

The *Hot Spot Properties* dialog window comprises four tabs: *General, Cursors, Link* and *URL.* In the *General* tab (see Figure 9.11), the type of link is selected in the pull-down menu by *Kind.* Here, *Link* is selected in order to establish a simple link between several panoramas. In the *Name* field, a name can be assigned that is displayed in the navigation bar of the QuickTime player while the QTVR movie is being played. Other remarks that pertain to this hot spot can be entered in the *Comment* field.

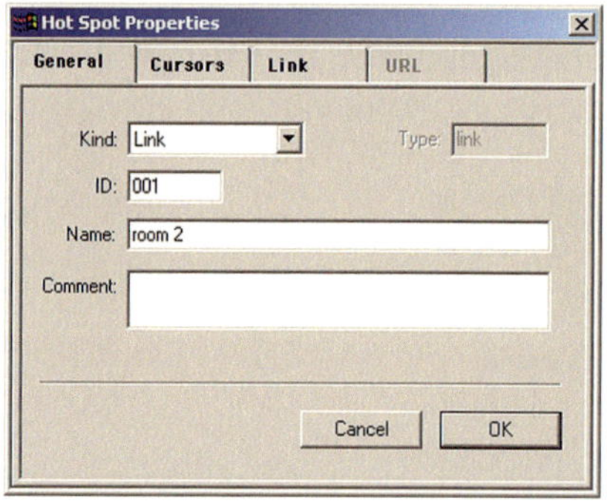

Figure 9.11
The properties of a hot spot are defined in the *General* tab

In the *Cursors* tab (see Figure 9.12), additional functions and visual properties can be allocated to the mouse pointer as required.

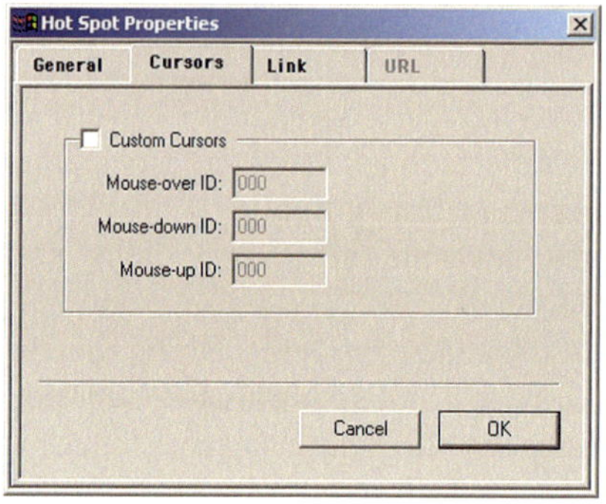

Figure 9.12
The properties of the mouse pointer can be changed in the *Cursors* tab

The "Virtual Reality Programming with QuickTime VR" manual provides more information on the exact meaning and significance of these so-called IDs. This manual can be obtained online as a PDF file at: http://developer.apple.com/referencelibrary/API_Fundamentals/QuickTime-api-date.html [status: May 20, 2004].

Various attributes of the target panorama can be set in the *Link* tab (see Figure 9.13).

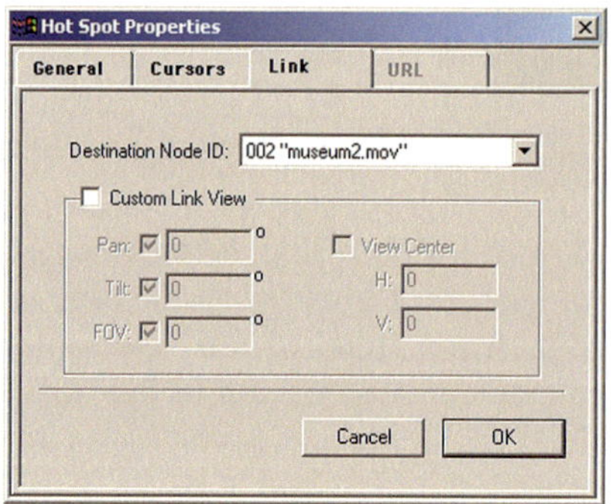

Figure 9.13
Various attributes of the target panorama can be set in the *Link* tab

The desired target file is selected in the pull-down menu by *Destination Node ID*. In the *Custom Link View* section, the opening picture area of the movie is defined via the *Pan, Tilt* and *FOV* functions. These settings, however, are made more effectively in the *Node Browser* window, as you can see the picture area configured. If the checkboxes are not activated, the values defined for the respective movie are applied.

The *URL* tab (see Figure 9.14) is only active if *URL* was selected in place of *Link* in the *General* tab. Here, the Internet address of the Web site that is to be called up when the hot spot is clicked is entered by *URL*.

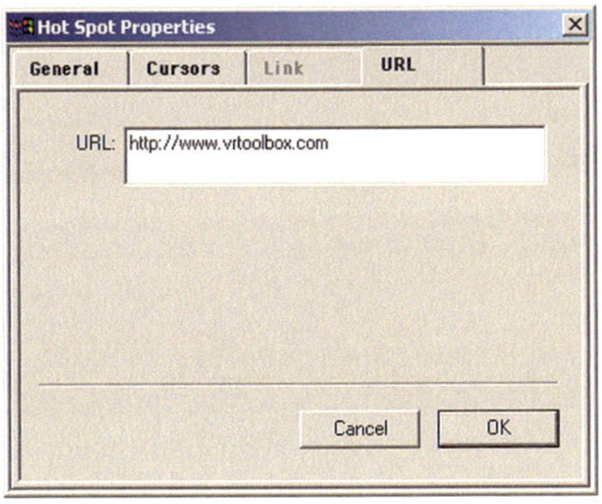

Figure 9.14
Web adresses that are to be called up when the respective hot spots are clicked are entered in the *URL* tab

After all relevant properties have been defined, click *OK* to exit the *Hot Spot Properties* dialog window.

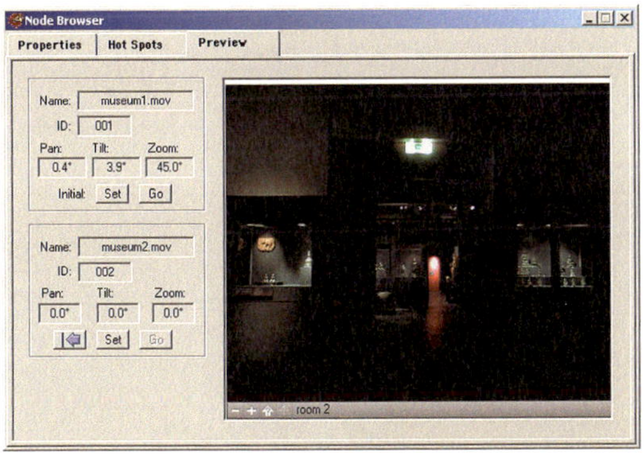

Figure 9.15
The picture areas to be displayed when the QTVR movie is started are defined in the *Preview* tab in *Node Browser*

Now switch to the *Node Browser* window (see Figure 9.15) again to test the virtual tour in the *Preview* tab. The picture area of the visible panorama can be changed via the *Pan, Tilt* and *Zoom* functions available here. When all of the settings have been made in *Node Browser,* the main editing window of VR SceneWorx is reaccessed. Now click on the next editing tab, *Compose*.

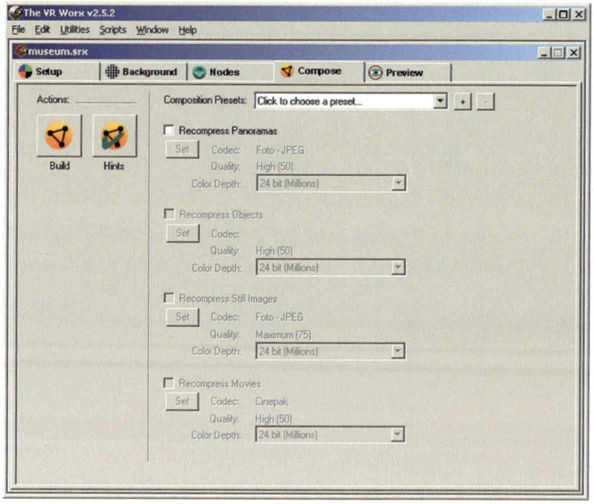

Figure 9.16
The virtual tour is created in the *Compose* editing tab

In the *Compose* tab (see Figure 9.16), the virtual tour is calculated by executing the *Actions > Build* function. If necessary, panoramas and object movies can be compressed using an alternative codec. The changes you make are applied via the *Recompress Panoramas* function. Chapter 10.1 provides more information on QuickTime codecs. The finished tour is viewed and tested in the *Preview* tab.

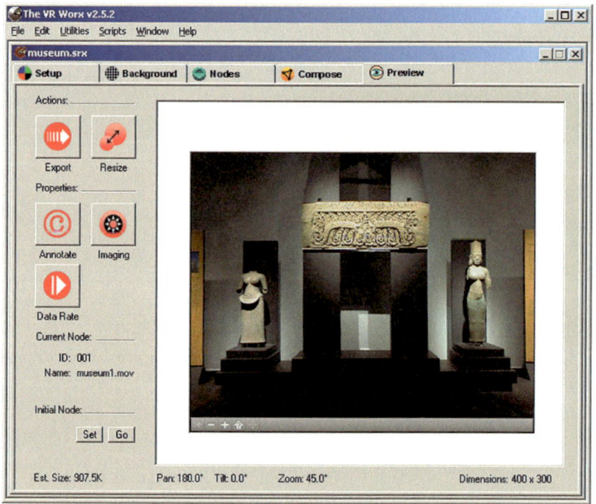

Figure 9.17
The tour is tested in the *Preview* tab and saved after defining additional properties

The final window size is defined via *Resize* in the *Preview* tab (see Figure 9.17). Under *Properties > Annotate,* information such as name, copyright and a short description of the content can be added to the movie. *Properties > Imaging* is used to influence the picture quality when moving (*Motion*) and not moving (*Static*). With the *Properties > Data Rate* function, the download speed for various connections can be calculated. When all settings have been made, the virtual tour is saved via *Actions > Export*. You can choose between a number of options when saving. If no additional settings are made, the virtual tour (including all of its constituent files) is saved as a complete movie. The resulting QTVR file is relatively large and therefore not very well suited for Web application. Alternatively, you can save the QTVR movies with all of your defined hot spots as separate files. To do this, select the additional *Split into separate nodes* function in the *Export* dialog box.

Chapter 10.1 provides information on how to publish QTVR movies. There you will find more information on viewers as well as the source code used to embed panoramas in Web sites.

You will find the panoramas shown here on the CD at the following path: \Workshop\09 Virtual tours\9_3_2_ VR Worx

Advantages

- The software provides support for importing numerous file formats and scanned pictures can be loaded via the TWAIN interface.

Disadvantages

- Only QTVR movies can be created; other file formats are not supported.
- As the picture data are not referenced, but integrated, VR Worx documents are comparatively large (depending on the number of imported files). This is why the book CD only includes the individual panoramas and the finished QTVR tour for the example shown and not the associated VR Worx document.

9.3.3 HotMedia

HotMedia is a so-called rich media application developed by IBM that was specially designed for Web use in the form of a Java applet. Panoramas, object movies, graphics, video and sound can be linked using the HotMedia applet. The following chapter shows how cylindrical panoramic pictures are linked to create a virtual tour. Spherical iPIX panoramas also can be merged into a virtual walk.

More information on the HotMedia software an be found online at: http://www-3.ibm.com/software/awdtools/hotmedia/

HotMedia allows you to define hot spots in the panoramic pictures; these hot spots are able to be combined with text information and sound. Subsequently, the panoramas (.jpg, .bmp, .tif) are converted into HotMedia files (.mvr), at which point they can be played back via the HotMedia applet.

First, a panoramic picture is imported from the main menu *Workspace > Panorama > Add* (see Figure 9.18).

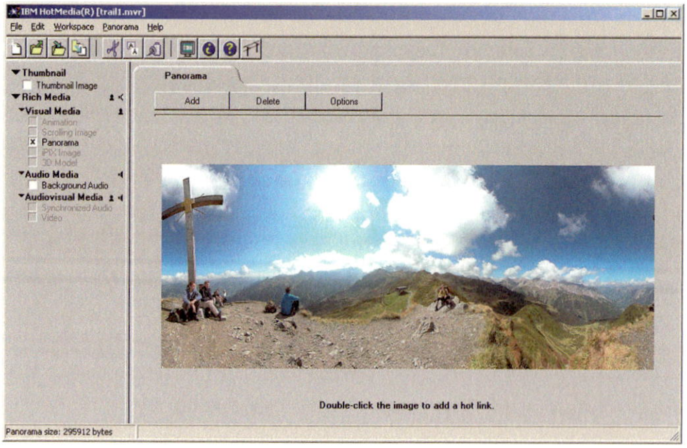

Figure 9.18
The panoramic picture is imported in HotMedia

Double click on the picture to access the hot spots editing area (see Figure 9.19).

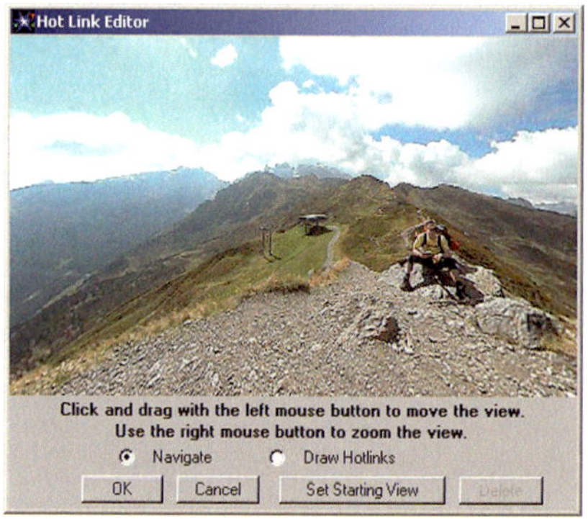

Figure 9.19
You can navigate in the panorama as you normally would in the *Hot Link Editor* window

Here, in the first editing window, you can navigate in the panorama as usual via the *Navigate* function. When the area of the picture reserved for the hot spot appears in the viewer, the *Draw Hotlinks* function is used to draw in a red border for the hot spot (see Figure 9.20).

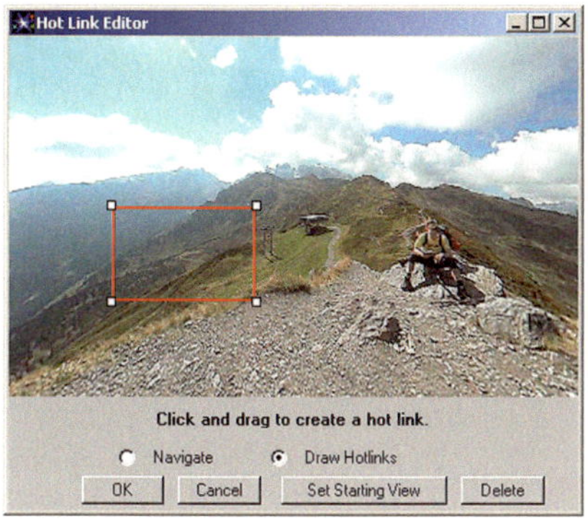

Figure 9.20
Hot spots are lassoed in red

Once a red hot spot border has been defined, the *Hot Link Triggers* dialog window opens (see Figure 9.21). This is where various attributes are assigned to the hot spot.

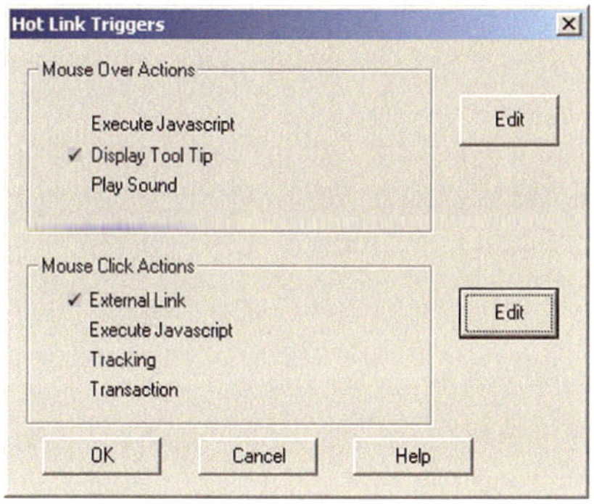

Figure 9.21
Hot spot properties are defined in the *Hot Link Triggers* winwdow

For example, when *Display Tool Tip* is activated under *Mouse Over Actions,* you can enter an info text that is displayed in the viewer when the hot spot is traveled over (see Figure 9.22).

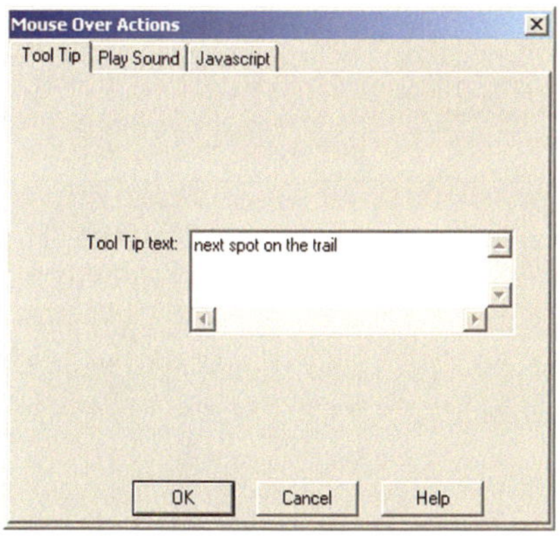

Figure 9.22
An info text can be entered for the hot spot via *Tool Tip* in the *Mouse Over Actions* window

Panoramas can be linked to each other in a number of ways in the *External link* tab in the *Mouse Click Actions* window (see Figure 9.23). Activate the *Replace file* checkbox if you would like to interlink HotMedia files. A sound file is linked to the hot spot via *Play audio.* The *Link to HTML* option establishes a link to HTML files and URLs.

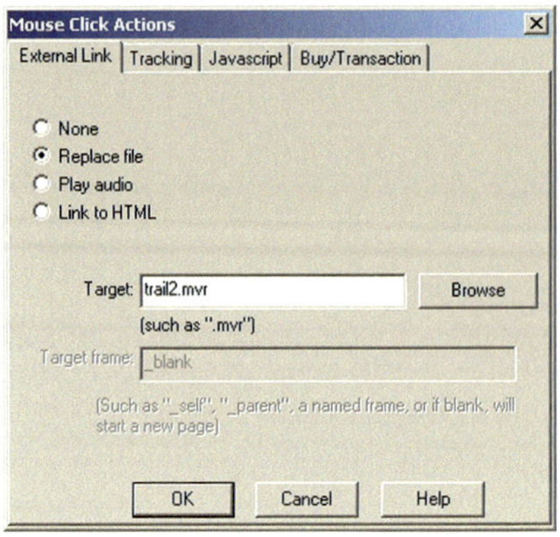

Figure 9.23
Panoramas are linked to each other in the *External Link* tab in the *Mouse Click Actions* window

Once the hot spots have been set and the target files linked, additional panoramic properties can be defined using the *Options* function the main window (see Figure 9.18). Display properties are defined in *View Limits* (see Figure 9.24).

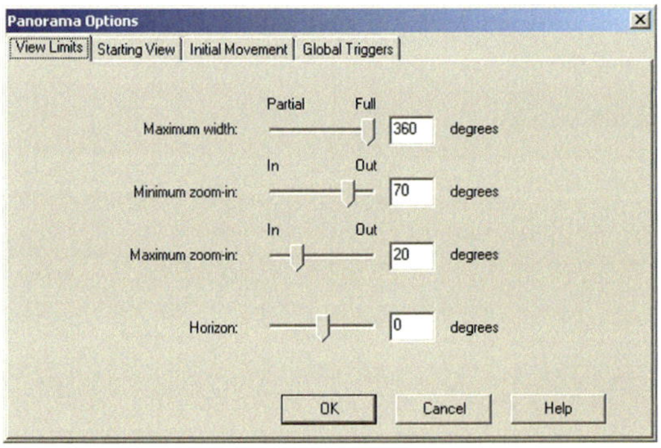

Figure 9.24
Playback properties can be defined in *View Limits*

By *Maximum Width,* you can determine whether you would like to display a complete 360° panorama (*Full*) or only a section thereof (*Partial*). The largest and smallest zoom factors that the observer is able to select in the subsequent panorama are set via the *Minimum zoom-in* and *Maximum zoom-in* functions. If the tilt angle of the panorama should be changed, enter the degree amount in the *Horizon* field.

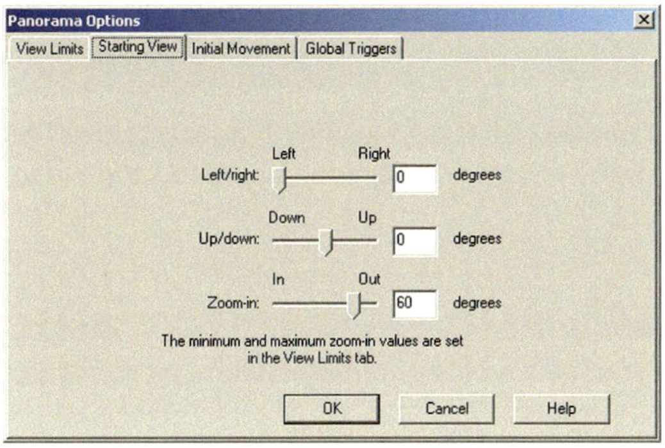

Figure 9.25
The initial viewpoint of the panorama is defined in the *Starting View* tab

The initial viewpoint of the panorama when it is started in the browser is defined in the *Starting View* tab (see Figure 9.25).

In the *Initial Movement* tab (see Figure 9.26), the movement of the panorama when it is first called up in the viewer can be set. To achieve a continuous rightward sweep of the panorama, enter a positive value by *Left/right velocity.* A negative value effects movement in the leftward direction.

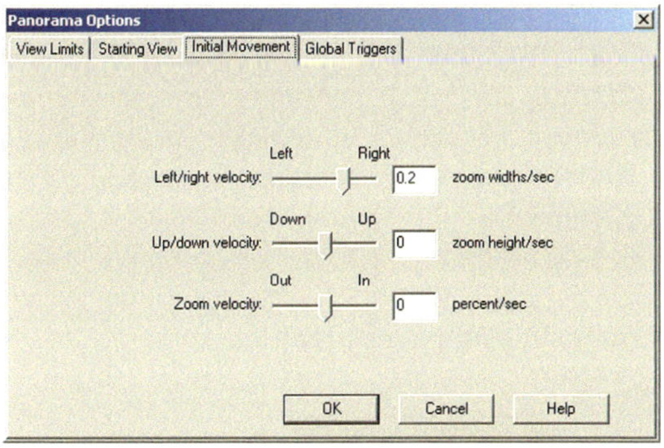

Figure 9.26
Continuous rotational movement is set in the *Initial Movement* tab

The *Global Triggers* tab is where the invoking of additional actions is configured. Here, optional extras such as the addition of sound and the playback properties of the sound can be defined. For more information on how to add sound, please refer to chapter 10.4.2.

The HotMedia file is saved by tracing to *File > Save As.* At this point, you also have the option of creating an HTML file with the embedded HotMedia applet and associated panoramic file. This function is activated with *File > Publish.* For a virtual tour, it is imperative that all interlinked panoramas be assigned hot spots in this fashion. More information on the HotMedia viewer is found in chapter 10.4.

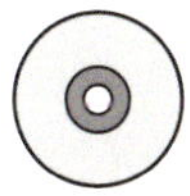

You will find the tour shown here on the CD at the following path:
\Workshop\
09 Virtual tours\
9_3_3 HotMedia

Advantages

- Easy to use and the individual functions are intuitive in scope.
- The software supports the linking of panoramas and objects and offers additional functions such as the integration of graphics, sound and video.

Disadvantages

- HotMedia no longer is offered by IBM as a stand-alone product. The software is now an integral component in the company's Homepage Builder and Web Sphere Studio applications.

9.3.4 iLinker

More information on the iLinker software an be found online at: http://infomedia.ipix.com/products/software/ilinker/

iLinker allows you to link several iPIX panoramas into tours. In addition, text information and sound can be added to hot spots. This tool is bundled with the iPIX Interactive Studio Enhancer level product or can be purchased as a stand-alone application. The following chapter shows how iPIX panoramas are linked to create a virtual tour.

The first step involves importing the initial panorama for the tour by tracing to *File > Open*. The respective panorama appears in the viewer window, at which point you can freely navigate. Now move across the picture until the desired area is displayed in the window. Trace to *Hot Spot > New Hot Spot* and lasso the area (see Figure 9.27).

Figure 9.27
Hot spots are lassoed in red

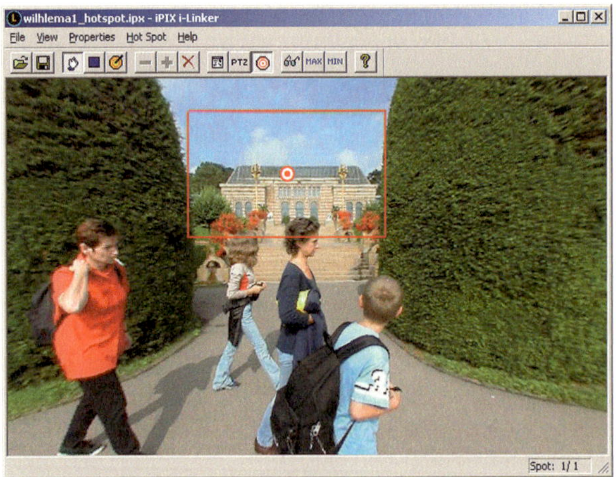

Double click on this hot spot to open the *Hot Spot Properties* window, where you can define the properties of the hot spot (see Figure 9.28).

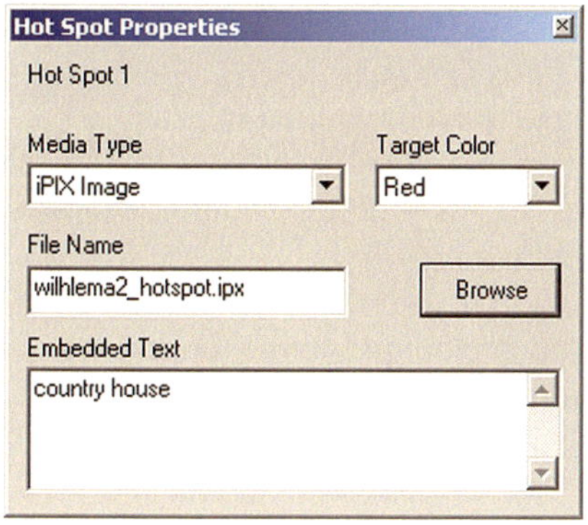

Figure 9.28
Hot spot properties are defined in the *Hot Spot Properties* dialog window

By *Media Type,* you can specify which action should be linked to the hot spot. If two iPIX panoramas are being linked, select *iPIX Image* from the pull-down menu. The *Browse* function allows you to define which panorama will be loaded when the hot spot is activated. Additional text information can be displayed in the viewer when the hot spot is traveled over by going to *Embedded Text* and making your entry.

If required, you can redefine the playback properties of the respective panorama prior to saving. If these settings are not changed, the playback properties of the underlying iPIX panorama are applied. To access the editing area for these settings, trace to the *Properties* menu. The initial viewpoint can be changed via the *Set Default Viewpoint* function. Additionally, the minimum and maximum zoom factors can be defined with the *Set Minimum Field-of-View* and *Set Maximum Field-of-View* functions, respectively. In the *Properties* menu, the background sound and GPS data also can be entered.

You will find the tour shown here on the CD at the following path:
\Workshop\
09 Virtual tours\
9_3_4 iLinker

Finally, the iPIX panorama is saved with hot spots by tracing to *File > Save As*. For a virtual tour, it is imperative that all interlinked panoramas be assigned hot spots in this fashion.

Advantages

- Easy to use and the individual functions are intuitive in scope.
- The software supports the linking of panoramas and offers additional functions such as the integration of graphics and sound.

Disadvantages

- Only iPIX tours can be created; other file formats are not supported.

9.3.5 PTViewer

Cylindrical or spherical panoramic filmstrips are required in order to produce virtual tours using PTViewer. In chapter 6, you learned how cylindrical panoramic filmstrips are created, while chapter 7 explained the production process associated with spherical panoramic pictures.

An HTML file with an embedded virtual PTViewer tour can be found on the CD at the following path: \Workshop\09 Virtual tours\9_3_5 PTViewer

The filmstrips appear only in conjunction with the PTViewer Java applet, integrated in an HTML file as an interactive panorama for the observer. Hot spots can be defined and controlled via the applet's parameters. This, however, requires a basic knowledge of the numerous parameters in the PTViewer applet. As such, reference is made here to chapter 10.2, which provides more information on PTViewer. Chapter 10.2.1.2 is dedicated to the linking of panoramas into virtual tours.

Advantages

- PTViewer is free of charge (freeware).
- The viewer can be adapted to individual layouts as desired. As such, static hot spots, for example, can be introduced to create various navigation bars.
- PTViewer allows you to play QTVR movies without having to install the QuickTime plug-in. The PTMViewer extension is used for this purpose.

Disadvantages

- A version of PTViewer different than the one used for Web publication is required to display panoramas in the stand-alone viewer. In a typical Internet publication, the filmstrips appear as interactive panoramas or tours for the observer only in conjunction with the PTViewer Java applet, integrated in the HTML file. The stand-alone version should be used for offline publications.

10. Publication

When it comes to Internet publication, there are many options for displaying panoramas and object movies by way of so-called viewers. The following focuses on some of the most common viewers used on the Web. You also will learn about the possibility of publishing cylindrical panoramic pictures to paper as well. For Internet publication, there are other solutions available than just those viewers covered in this book. A list of suppliers of viewer software can be found in the list of manufacturers (see chapter B.1.7). Chapter 13 provides an overview of the software described here as well as a table that lists the features of each product.

10.1 QuickTime VR

QTVR stands for "QuickTime Virtual Reality" and is an extension of Apple's QuickTime technology. QTVR allows the user to interactively explore a photo-realistic virtual world. Unlike other virtual reality systems, the observer does not need to wear a helmet, special glasses or gloves; the virtual world can be experienced by using an ordinary mouse and keyboard.

You will find the QuickTime player on the CD at: \Viewers\Mac and \Viewers\PC

QuickTime VR has been an integral component of QuickTime since January 1997. From this version (2.5) up through version 4, the only style of panoramic presentation supported was that of the cylindrical panorama. The launch of QuickTime 5 in April 2001 brought about initial support for cubic panoramas (cubic QTVR). The most recent version of QuickTime - QuickTime 6 - features a variety of improvements in audio and video compression as well as carries all of the QTVR functions. QuickTime supports the following media: video, audio, pictures, text, MIDI files, 3-D and VR (objects and panoramas).

In order to be able to open the QTVR format, Apple's QuickTime player must be installed. The QuickTime plug-in can be downloaded at: http://www.apple.com/quicktime/download [status: April 2, 2004].

With QuickTime, a number of codecs can be selected for data compression. Here is a list of the video codecs that are currently supported by QuickTime: Animation, BMP, Cinepak, Component Video, DV PAL, DV/DVC

Pro NTSC, DVC Pro PAL, Graphics, H.261, H.263, JPEG 2000 (currently only on Mac OS X), Motion JPEG A, Motion JPEG B, MPEG-4 Video, Photo JPEG, Planar RGB, PNG, Sorenson Video, Sorenson Video 3, TGA, TIFF.

If a panorama is to be produced for Web presentation, the type of compression is an important factor to consider, as transmission bandwidth on the Internet is limited. Not every form of compression listed above is best suited for QTVR. Codecs with good QTVR properties are explained in more detail as follows.

Cinepak

Cinepak was developed back in 1990 and was used to play small films on 2x CD-ROM drives. As such, the biggest advantage of this codec is its low CPU load; practically every computer can easily play films compressed using Cinepak. The downside, however, is that picture quality is somewhat poorer than with other codecs, such as Sorenson Video. When a high compression quality is selected, the file becomes considerably larger in size as compared to the remaining two codecs.

Photo-JPEG

The Photo JPEG codec uses the JPEG algorithm for image compression. Despite the fact that the algorithm automatically means a reduction in image quality, this codec is well suited to compressing panoramas and object movies. Due to the high computational load placed on processors, however, QTVR movies compressed using Photo JPEG may present a problem when run on older, less powerful computers; rotational movements can lead to a "jerky" picture.

Sorenson Video

The Sorenson Video codec has been supported by QuickTime since version 3 of the software. This codec is exceptionally well suited to QTVR applications. Although picture quality is better than with the Cinepak codec, the CPU load is also greater. Given the clock rates of today's processors, however, this is almost a non-issue. If QTVR movies are to be backwards compatible with QuickTime versions 1 or 2, the Sorenson Video codec should not be chosen.

Figure 10.1 uses the REALVIZ Stitcher software to show a number of settings required in order to render a QTVR movie. In addition to the form of compression used (otherwise known as a codec), the quality for rendering the QTVR can be specified. Both factors exert a great influence on the size of the file. The higher the compression quality selected, the better the picture quality of the panorama or object movie. The downside, of course, is that better picture quality makes the QTVR file substantially larger. The trick is to find a solution that combines good picture quality with a relatively small file size.

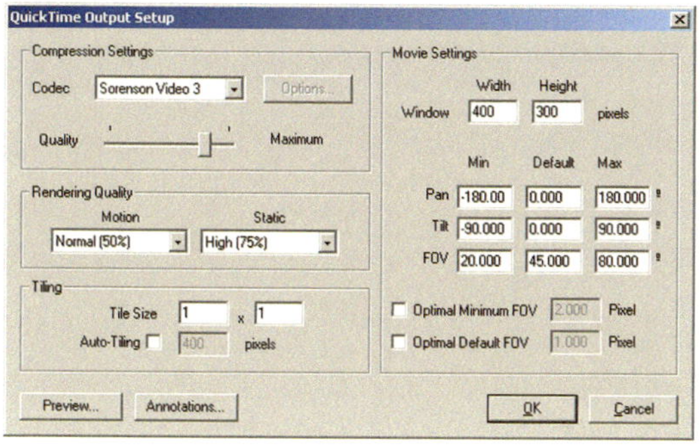

Figure 10.1
QuickTime settings

Under *Rendering Quality*, the picture quality during rotation (*motion*) and at a standstill (*static*) can be set. Typically, the highest setting is not used for motion.

In the *Tiling* field, the panoramic picture is divided into quadratic sections (tiles) so that only the visible areas of the picture are loaded in the viewer when playing the QTVR movie. This allows the load placed on the CPU to be kept to a minimum during playback. Additionally, the use of *tiles* gives the user the option of navigating in the panorama during the download process. Each downloaded tile can be immediately played.

In the *Movie Settings* section, you can specify the size of the *Window* for the QuickTime player. The *Pan, Tilt* and *FOV* fields are used to define the initial angle of the QTVR panorama as well as the minimum and maximum zoom factor.

It is best to determine the optimal settings for the respective motif and the desired form of use by way of a test series.

10.1.1 Integration in HTML code

The following must be observed when embedding QTVR panoramas in an HTML page: Using Netscape-specific EMBED tags leads to compatibility problems with versions 5.5 and 6.0 of Internet Explorer for Windows. The EMBED tag never was officially included as part of the HTML standard and no longer should be used. Alternatively, QTVR movies can be embedded using the OBJECT tag; however, as older versions of Netscape (4.x) do not recognize this OBJECT tag, it is recommended that both tags be included in the source code.

The following example shows how the QTVR file is embedded using both HTML tags:

```
<OBJECT
classid="clsid:02BF25D5-8C17-4B23-BC80-D3488ABDDC6B"
width="400"
height="316"
```

You can find an HTML file with embedded QTVR movie on the CD at: \Workshop\10 Publication\ 10_1 QuickTime

```
codebase="http://www.apple.com/qtactivex/qtplugin.cab">
<param name="src" value="panorama.mov">
<param name="autoplay" value="true">
<param name="controller" value="true">
<EMBED
src="panorama.mov"
width="400"
height="316"
autoplay="true"
controller="true"
pluginspage="http://www.apple.com/quicktime/download/">
</EMBED>
</OBJECT>
```

The size of the QTVR movie used here measures 400 x 300 pixels. If you want the QuickTime controller to be visible at the bottom of the movie, an additional 16 pixels are added to the height of the QTVR. For this example, the QuickTime movie (here: panorama.mov) must be located in the same directory as the respective HTML file.

10.1.2 Specials

QuickTime is capable of playing back panoramas, video and sound. QuickTime films can be linked to form a tour via hot spots, without the need to install an additional plug-in.

In addition to a QTVR movie, you can embed a simple sound loop into the HTML file. The sound file needs to be in QuickTime format, however. With the professional version of the QuickTime player (QuickTime Pro), you can convert virtually any sound file into this format.

The following example shows how to embed a background sound loop into an HTML file:

You can find an HTML file with embedded QTVR movie and sound loop on the CD at: \Workshop\ 10 Publication\ 10_1 QuickTime

```
<OBJECT
classid="clsid:02BF25D5-8C17-4B23-BC80-D3488ABDDC6B"
hidden
codebase="http://www.apple.com/qtactivex/qtplugin.cab">
<param name="src" value="sound.mov">
<param name="autoplay" value="true">
<param name="controller" value="false">
<param name="cache" value="true">
<param name="loop" value="true">
<EMBED
src="sound.mov"
hidden
```

```
autoplay="true"
controller="false"
cache="true"
loop="true"
pluginspage="http://www.apple.com/quicktime/download/">
</EMBED>
</OBJECT>
```

For this example, the sound file (here: sound.mov) must be located in the same directory as the respective HTML file. The disadvantage of this simple solution is that the user does not have the option of stopping the sound playback. The sound can only be turned off by deactivating the loudspeakers or by closing the Web site window.

Tips for combining QuickTime with various media can be found at: http://developer.apple.com/documentation/QuickTime/VirtualReality-date.html [status: April 29, 2004].

Additional extras such as surround sound, linked maps or automatic rotation of the panorama are provided by special software released by the Squamish Media Group. Tools include “SoundSaVR”, “MapSaVR”, “NodeSaVR” and “RevolVR”. More information can be found at: http://www.smgvr.com [status: April 5, 2004].

LiveStage Pro is capable of modifying the full range of QuickTime features. Audio and video tracks can be added and altered and new user interfaces can be generated. For more information and a downloadable demo version, point your browser to: http://www.totallyhip.com/lo/products/lsp [status: April 5, 2004].

10.2 PTViewer

PTViewer is a Java applet that can be used to display panoramic pictures and play object movies on the Web. It is also possible to play QTVR movies without the user needing to install the QuickTime plug-in. Here, the PTMViewer extension is used.

In order to be able to view object movies with PTViewer, Java must be installed and running in your browser (rule of thumb). If you are working on Windows XP or higher, Java is not automatically supported. Instead, Microsoft has integrated their own substitute technology known as JUMP to .NET. One way for Windows XP users to get around this problem is to install an older version of Internet Explorer (i.e. less than version 6), which still has an embedded Java engine. The other solution is to download the latest Java engine right from the developers (Sun Microsystems) at: http://www.java.com/en/download/manual.jsp [status: March 10, 2004].

PTViewer can be found on the CD at the following paths: \Viewers\Mac and \Viewers\PC

10.2.1 Integration in HTML code

10.2.1.1 PTViewer for panoramas

Panoramas are embedded in a Web site using the PTViewer Java applet. The following example shows how a panoramic picture saved in JPG format is embedded in an HTML file using the Java viewer:

You can find an HTML file with embedded PTViewer applet on the CD at: \Workshop\10 Publication\10_2 PTViewer\10_2_1_1 Panorama

```
<APPLET
name=ptviewer
archive=ptviewer.jar
code=ptviewer.class
width=400
height=300>
<param name="file" value="panorama.jpg">
<param name=pan value="45">
<param name=tilt value="50">
<param name=fov value="80">
<param name=fovmin value="30">
<param name=fovmax value="120">
<param name=auto value="0.5">
</APPLET>
```

For this example, the panoramic picture (here: panorama.jpg) and the Java applet (ptviewer.jar) must be located in the same directory as the HTML file.

Parameters of the PTViewer Java applet

- width

  Specifies the width of the viewer window in pixels.

- height

  Specifies the height of the viewer window in pixels.

- file

  The name of the panoramic picture that is to be displayed by PTViewer.

- pan

  Horizontal position of rotation when the panorama is started. You can enter values from -180 to 180. If this parameter is not listed, the angle of rotation automatically is zero.

- tilt

  Vertical position of rotation when the panorama is started. You can enter values from -90 to 90. If this parameter is not listed, the angle of rotation automatically is zero.

- fov

  Zoom factor when the panorama is started. You can enter values from 12 to 165. If this parameter is not listed, the picture automatically is set to a zoom factor of 70.

- fovmin

  Minimal zoom factor. You can enter values from 12 to 165. If this parameter is not listed, the minimal zoom factor automatically is set to 12.

- fovmax

  Maximum zoom factor. You can enter values from 12 to 165. If this parameter is not listed, the maximum zoom factor automatically is set to 165.

- panmax

  Maximum horizontal panning range. You can enter values from 0 to 180.

- panmin

  Minimum horizontal panning range. You can enter values from 0 to -180.

- tiltmin

  Minimum vertical tilt range. You can enter values from -90 to 0. If this parameter is not listed for spherical panoramas, the minimum tilt range automatically is -90.

- tiltmax

  Maximum vertical tilt range. You can enter values from 90 to 0. If this parameter is not listed for spherical panoramas, the minimum tilt range automatically is 90.

- wait

  There is the option of embedding a preview picture in JPG or GIF format that is displayed during the loading process. Absolute and relative path details are possible.

- auto

  The auto parameter is used to automatically rotate the panorama at startup. Values ranging from -360 to 360 can be entered, whereby negative values affect a leftward rotation and positive values a rightward rotation.

The PTViewer can be configured for individual layouts based on the parameters used. Additional information on the functions of the PTViewer can be found at: http://www.all-in-one.ee/~dersch/PTVJ/doc.html [status: May 12, 2004] and http://home.no.net/dmaurer/~dersch/PTVJ/doc.html [status: May 12, 2004]

A modified version of the PTViewers is capable of playing panoramas with a high dynamic range (HDR). More information on this panoramic viewer can be found at: http://webuser.fh-furtwangen.de/~dersch/ [status: May 17, 2004].

10.2.1.2 PTViewer for virtual tours

Hot spots can be defined with the PTViewer applet to create a virtual tour from several panoramas. Using an example, this chapter shows you how to link spherical panoramas using PTViewer.

Two fundamentally different scenarios must be noted when linking panoramas with this tool. The first scenario involves the hot spot referring to a URL. Here, the particular Web site is loaded in the browser window when the hot spot is clicked. The second scenario allows different panoramas to be loaded in the original HTML file. As such, only the panoramic picture needs to be reloaded; the HTML content and Java applet remain identical. This is the more refined solution, as all parameters can be controlled and changed via one file. This approach is explained in more detail shortly.

Once the hot spot is defined, a 24 x 24 pixel mark appears in the panorama at the location given by x and y coordinates. When this hot spot is clicked, the viewer is brought to the next panorama. The exact position of a hot spot can be conveniently determined using an image editing program. To do this, open the respective image file and note the x and y coordinates of the desired area of the picture. The unit of measure used by the program must be set to pixels.

The following example shows how the PTViewer applet (including hot spots) is embedded into an HTML file:

```
<APPLET
name=ptviewer
archive=ptviewer.jar
code=ptviewer.class
width=400
height=300>
<param name=file value="ptviewer:0">
<param name=preload value="panorama2.jpg">
<param name=pano0 value="
{file=panorama1.jpg}
{auto=0}
{pan=-20}
```

```
{tilt=7}
{fov=70}
{fovmax=100}
{fovmin=20}
{hotspot0=x1887y392n'Panorama2'qu'ptviewer:newPanoFromList(1)'}">
<param name=pano1 value="
{file=panorama2.jpg}
{auto=0}
{pan=0}
{tilt=8}
{fov=75}
{fovmax=100}
{fovmin=20}
{hotspot0=x1013y629n'Panorama1'qu'ptviewer:newPanoFromList(0)'}">
</APPLET>
```

An HTML file with an embedded PTViewer tour can be found on the CD at: \Workshop\10 Publication\10_2 PTViewer\10_2_1_2 Virtual tour

For this example, all panoramic pictures of the tour (here: panorama1.jpg, panorama2.jpg) and the Java applet (ptviewer.jar) must be located in the same directory as the HTML file.

Important parameters in connection with the hot spot tag

Here, only the parameters of the PTViewer applet that are relevant to virtual tours are mentioned. All additional parameters such as “pan”, “tilt” and “auto” are explained in chapter 10.2.1.1.

- file

  Defines the panorama loaded first. As such, *ptviewer:0* for calling up the panorama is listed as *pano0*.

- preload

  The sequence of panoramas that are to be loaded in the background for a tour is entered by “preload”. Here, the exact file names of the panoramas are entered (e.g.: *panorama2.jpg*).

- hotspot0=x1887 y392 n'Panorama2' q u'ptviewer:newPanoFromList(1)'

  x and *y* coordinates are used to create a 24 x 24 pixel circular mark. If the *x* and *y* coordinates are listed in lowercase letters, the parameter values refer to absolute pixels. If the coordinates appear in uppercase letters (*X* and *Y*), the information on the width and height of the panoramic picture is percentage-based.
  If the hot spot is to display the name of the target panorama, the desired text is entered in apostrophes after *n*. This text is displayed in the status line of the browser.
  The *q* parameter defines the respective hot spot as being permanently visible. If this parameter is not set, the hot spots only can be seen under certain circumstances, such as by pressing the spacebar when playing a panorama.

The *u* parameter specifies the location (path) of the target file, which is enclosed in apostrophes. Absolute and relative path details are possible. The *new-PanoFromList()* function is a practical option for virtual tours, whereby the figure in parentheses defines which panorama (*pano0, pano1,* etc.) will be loaded in the viewer window when the hot spot is clicked.

The PTViewer can be configured for individual layouts based on the parameters used. As such, static hot spots, for example, can be introduced to create various navigation bars. More information can be found at: http://www.all-in-one.ee/~dersch/PTVJ/doc.html [status: March 26, 2004] and http://home.no.net/dmaurer/~dersch/PTVJ/doc.html [status: March 24, 2004].

A modified version of the PTViewers is capable of playing panoramas with a high dynamic range (HDR). More information on this panoramic viewer can be found at: http://webuser.fh-furtwangen.de/~dersch/[status: March 10, 2004]

10.2.1.3 PTViewer for objects

Object filmstrips are embedded in a Web site using the PTViewer Java applet and the PTObject applet extension.

The following example shows how a filmstrip saved in JPG format is embedded in an HTML file using the Java viewer:

An HTML file with an embedded PTObject applet can be found on the CD at: \Workshop\10 Publication\10_2 PTViewer\10_2_1_3 Object

```
<APPLET
name=ptviewer
archive=ptviewer.jar
code=ptviewer.class
width=400
height=300>
<param name="applet0" value="
{code=ptobject.class}
{file=object.jpg}
{nhor=36}
{nver=1}">
<param name="inits" value="ptviewer:startApplet(0)">
</APPLET>
```

For this example, the filmstrip (here: object.jpg) and the Java applet (ptviewer.jar) must be located in the same directory as the HTML file. A version of PTViewer that contains the "ptobject.class" file must be used to play the object movie.

Parameters of the PTObject Java applet

This section only introduces the parameters of the PTObject applet. All additional parameters such as “pan”, “tilt”, “auto” and “wait” are explained in chapter 10.2.1.1.

- file

  The name of the object filmstrip that is to be displayed by PTObject.

- nhor

  The number of pictures in the horizontal direction.

- nver

  The number of pictures in the vertical direction.

More information on PTViewer extensions (PTObject, PTMovie, PTZoom, etc.) can be found at: http://www.all-in-one.ee/~dersch/PTVJ/helpers.html [status: February 26, 2004]

10.2.2 Specials

Sound also can be embedded in an HTML file using PTViewer. The observer does not need an additional plug-in for this. Anyone who has Java activated can benefit from all of the extensions PTViewer has to offer. Audio files in au, aiff, wav and midi formats are able to be played. The following example shows how a sound loop in au format is embedded, as this type of audio file can be played on any computer that has Java installed. Here, it is recommended that the audio file be limited to a resolution of 8 bits and a sample rate of 8 kHz.

An HTML file with embedded sound can be found on the CD at: \Workshop\ 10 Publication\ 10_2 PTViewer\ 10_2_2 Sound

The audio file can be embedded in an HTML file using the Java applet as follows:

<param name = sound0 value = soundloop.au>
<param name= inits value = ptviewer:PlaySound(0)>

More information on the additional functions and extensions of PTViewer can be found at: http://www.all-in-one.ee/~dersch/PTVJ/helpers.html [status: February 24, 2004]

10.3 iPIX

You will find the iPIX plug-in and the iPIX Java viewer on the CD at the following paths: \Viewers\Mac and \Viewers\PC

There are two ways to display iPIX pictures on a Web site. If the iPIX image is used without a Java applet, the visitor of the site will need to install the iPIX plug-in. The plug-in can be downloaded at: http://infomedia.ipix.com/support/download/alt_plugin.shtml [status: April 2, 2004]. This option provides better picture quality and increased rotational speed of the panorama. The second option is to integrate the iPIX image using the iPIX Java viewer. A plug-in is not required here, however Java must be installed and activated in the visitor's browser. If Java has not yet been installed, the current Java version can be downloaded directly from the developers at Sun: http://www.java.com/en/download/manual.jsp [status: March 10, 2004].

10.3.1 Integration in HTML

Any iPIX file can be used for publishing with the iPIX plug- in and the iPIX Java applet. If you want to embed iPIX panoramas that are to be played using the plug-in into an HTML site, please observe the following:

Using Netscape-specific EMBED tags leads to compatibility problems with versions 5.5 and 6.0 of Internet Explorer for Windows. The EMBED tag never was officially included as part of the HTML standard and no longer should be used. Alternatively, iPIX panoramas can be embedded using the OBJECT tag; however, as older versions of Netscape (4.x) do not recognize this OBJECT tag, it is recommended that both tags be included in the source code.

The plug-in version is embedded in HTML using the following code:

An HTML file with an embedded iPIX file can be found on the CD at: \Workshop\10 Publication\10_3 iPIX\10_3_1iPIX plugin

```
<OBJECT
ID="IpixX1"
width=400 height=300
classid="clsid:11260943-421B-11D0-8EAC-0000C07D88CF"
codebase="http://www.ipix.com/download/ipixx.cab#version=6,2,0,5">
<!-- For MSIE 3,4+ -->
<param name="ipixfilename" value="panorama.ipx">
<!-- For Netscape 3,4+ -->
<EMBED
src="panorama.ipx"
border=0
width=400 height=300
palette="foreground"
type="application/x-ipix"
pluginsPage="http://www.ipix.com/cgi-bin/download.cgi">
</EMBED>
</OBJECT>
```

For this example, all iPIX files (here: panorama.ipx) must be located in the same directory as the respective HTML file.

The iPIX Java applet is embedded into the HTML page using the following code:

```
<APPLET name="IpixViewer"
code="IpixViewer.class"
archive="IpixViewer.jar"
width="400" height="300">
<param name="url" value="panorama.ipx">
<param name="toolbar" value="on">
<param name="splash" value="wait.jpg">
<param name="splashbg" value="#000000">
<param name="initfov" value="80">
<param name="spinspeed" value="6">
<param name="spinstyle" value="flat">
</APPLET>
```

An HTML file with an embedded iPIX applet can be found on the CD at: \Workshop\10 Publication\10_3 iPIX\10_3_2 iPIX java

For this example, the iPIX applet (IpixViewer.jar) must be located in the same directory as the iPIX image (here: panorama.ipx) and the respective HTML file.

Parameters of the iPIX Java applet

- width

  Specifies the width of the viewer window in pixels.

- height

  Specifies the height of the viewer window in pixels.

- url

  The path where the iPIX file is located. Absolute and relative path details are possible.

- spinspeed

  The spinspeed parameter is used to automatically rotate the iPIX panorama at startup. Values ranging from -10 to 10 can be entered, whereby negative values affect a leftward rotation and positive values a rightward rotation.

- spinstyle

  The spinstyle parameter is used to specify the type of rotation. When flat is selected, the panorama rotates at the horizontal level; when wave is selected, the horizontal and vertical levels are incorporated.

- splash

  There is the option of embedding a preview picture in JPG or GIF format that is displayed during the loading process. Absolute and relative path details are possible.

- splashbg

  A background color can be selected for this preview picture, whereby the color values must be entered as hexadecimals (e.g. FFFFFF for white).

- toolbar

  This parameter is used to define whether the navigation bar should be visible or not. Select on if the bar is to be visible and off if the bar is to be hidden. If this parameter is not listed, the navigation bar automatically appears.

10.3.2 Specials

In order to be able to add sound or hot spots to iPIX pictures, an additional program called iLinker must be used. This tool is bundled with the iPIX Interactive Studio Enhancer level product. To learn how to merge several iPIX panoramas to form a virtual tour, refer to chapter 9.3.4. The HotMedia Java applet can be used as well to embed iPIX panoramas with sound and hot spots into Web sites (see chapter 10.4).

10.4 HotMedia

HotMedia is a Java applet developed by IBM that can be used to publish panoramas, object movies and virtual tours to the Web. Additional media such as video and sound can be incorporated as well. More information on HotMedia and a demo version of the software can be found at: http://www-3.ibm.com/software/awdtools/hotmedia [status: April 2, 2004].

This Java applet must be embedded in an HTML file in order to display the image. Likewise, it is necessary for Java to be installed and activated in the visitor's browser. If Java has not yet been installed, the current Java version can be downloaded directly from the developers at Sun: http://www.java.com/en/download/manual.jsp [status: March 10, 2004].

10.4.1 Integration in HTML code

Panoramas and object movies are embedded in a Web site using the HotMedia applet. It is possible to generate an HTML file directly from HotMedia (see chapter 9.3.3).

The following example shows how a panoramic picture saved in MVR format is embedded in an HTML file using the Java viewer:

```
<APPLET
code="hm35.class"
name="HotMedia"
width="400"
height="300">
<param name="mvrfile" value="panorama.mvr">
</APPLET>
```

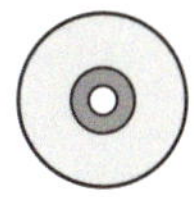

An HTML file with an embedded HotMedia applet can be found on the CD at: \Workshop\10 Publication\10_4 HotMedia

For this example, the HotMedia applet (hm35.class) and all classes used (e.g.: hm35player.class) must be located in the same directory as the HotMedia file (here: panorama.mvr) and the respective HTML file.

10.4.2 Specials

Panoramas, object movies, video and sound can be played using the HotMedia applet. You can include a sound loop in the HotMedia file. In the following example, a background sound is added to the panorama shown in chapter 9.3.3. In order to do this, the respective file must be opened from HotMedia.

From the main window, click the *Background Audio* checkbox under *Audio Media* (see Figure 10.2).

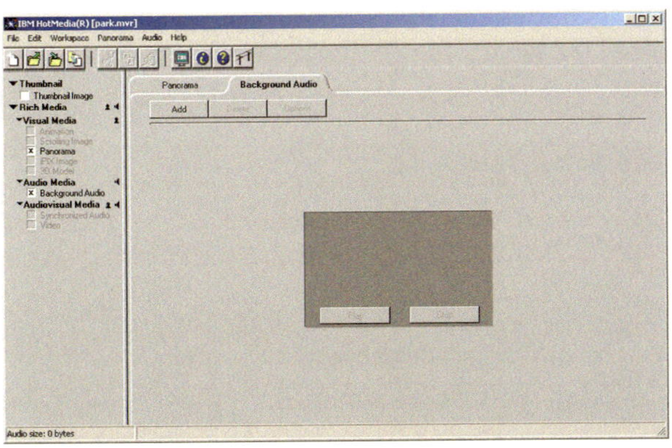

Figure 10.2
The *Background Audio* feature is used to embed a background sound

Now click the *Add* button to open the window for selecting the respective sound file. Several audio formats are supported (aiff, au, avi, mov, wav).

The audio file is compressed prior to importing (see Figure 10.3), whereby three different quality levels can be selected.

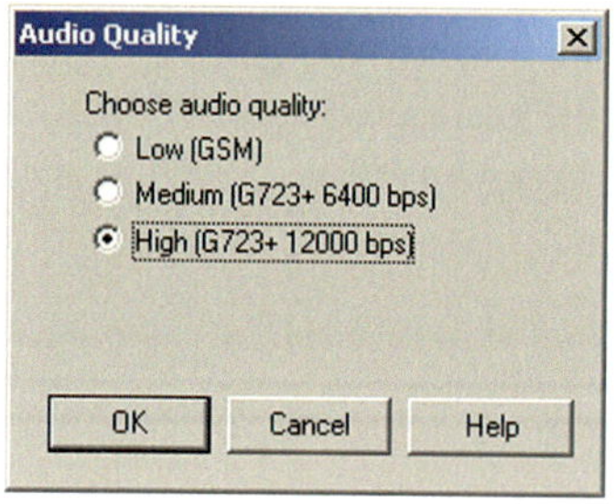

Figure 10.3
Compression can be set in the *Audio Quality* field

Additional properties for the sound file can be defined in the *Background Audio* tab by pressing the *Options* button (see Figure 10.4).

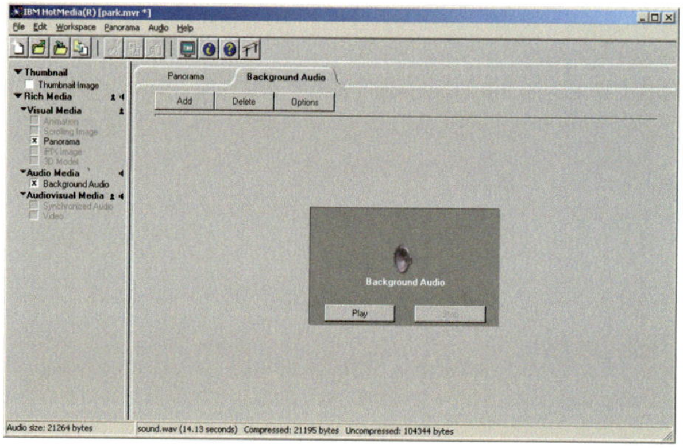

Figure 10.4
Additional properties of the audio file can be defined via the *Options* button

In the *Audio Options* (see Figure 10.5) dialog box, you can configure the sound file to repeat, for example. This feature is selected by clicking the *Loop continuously* checkbox. In the *Automatically start playing audio* field, you can configure the sound file to automatically play when the HTML file is called up.

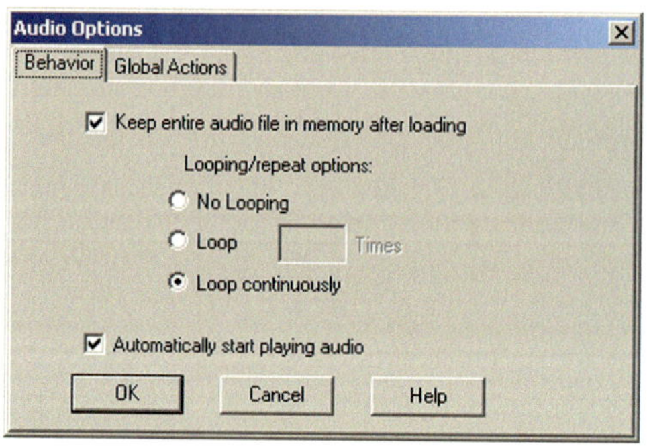

Figure 10.5
Properties such as looping can be defined in the *Audio Options* dialog box

The combined file is saved from the main window by clicking *File > Save As*. If desired, an HTML file can be directly created by tracing to *File > Publish*. The resulting file with integrated sound is embedded in the HTML code as with every other HotMedia file (see chapter 10.4.1). The sound file does not need to be explicitly "attached", as it is embedded in the HotMedia file, however the file size increases relative to the size and compression of the embedded audio file. An audio control interface appears at the bottom of the viewer for picture files containing sound. This interface allows the user to modify the sound output to his/her preference.

An HTML file with an embedded HotMedia applet can be found on the CD at: \Workshop\ 10 Publication\ 10_4 HotMedia

10.5 Cortona VRML viewer

VRML stands for Virtual Reality Modeling Language and was developed to display virtual worlds on the Internet. VRML files for 3-D display of data are programmed using the VR Modeling Language. Using VRML allows the user to individually set the color of an object, for example.

Not only objects can be displayed, however; VRML also can be used for panoramic presentations. VRML viewers use the cubic projection technique, whereby the sides of the cube for the projection are individually saved and called up by the viewer for presentation on the Web. A VRML viewer must be installed on your computer in order to be able to view a VRML file. Several VRML viewers currently are on the market. For an overview, please refer to chapter B.1.7. The Cortona Player has been introduced here as an example and can be found on the Internet at http://www.parallelgraphics.com/products/cortona [status: April 2, 2004].

You will find the Cortona VRML Client on the CD at the following paths: \Viewers\Mac and \Viewers\PC

10.5.1 Integration in HTML code

The following must be observed when embedding VRML panoramas in an HTML page: Using Netscape-specific EMBED tags leads to compatibility problems with versions 5.5 and 6.0 of Internet Explorer for Windows. The EMBED tag never was officially included as part of the HTML standard and no longer should be used. Alternatively, a VRML file can be embedded using the OBJECT tag; however, as older versions of Netscape (4.x) do not recognize this OBJECT tag, it is recommended that both tags be included in the source code.

The following example shows how the VRML file is embedded using both HTML tags:

```
<OBJECT
classid="clsid:86A88967-7A20-11d2-8EDA-00600818EDB1"
codebase="http://www.parallelgraphics.com/bin/cortvrml.cab#Version=
4,0,0,76"
width="400"
height="300">
<param name="src" value="panorama.wrl">
<param name="vrml_background_color" value="#000000">
<param name="vrml_dashboard" value="true">
<param name="vrml_splashscreen" value="true">
<param name="contextmenu" value="true">
<EMBED src="panorama.wrl"
width="400"
height="300"
vrml_splashscreen="true"
vrml_dashboard="true"
vrml_background_color="#000000"
contextmenu="true"
type="x-world/x-vrml"
pluginsPage="http://www.parallelgraphics.com/products/cortona">
</EMBED>
</OBJECT>
```

An HTML file with an embedded VRML file can be found on the CD at: \Workshop\10 Publication\10_5 Cortona VRML

The VRML file (here: panorama.wrl) and the embedded sides of the cube must be located in the same directory as the corresponding HTML file for this example.

Additional functions such as sound or the definition of a specific initial view for panoramas only can be programmed using the VR Modeling Language. More information can be found at: http://www.parallelgraphics.com/products/cortona [status: April 23, 2004] and http://www.vrmlsite.com [status: April 23, 2004]

10.5.2 Specials

Additional viewer functions can be loaded by way of so-called VRML extensions. Objects and panoramas created using a camera or 3-D software can be displayed. With these 3-D renderings, observers frequently can change properties such as color, size and movement of the panoramas or objects. The factors that define this interactivity are specified using the Virtual Reality Modeling Language (VRML). More information can be found at: http://www.parallelgraphics.com/developer/products/cortona [status: May 12, 2004].

10.6 Panoramas on paper

10.6.1 Making printouts with an ink-jet printer

The cylindrical panoramic format is suited to paper-based printouts. If the underlying panoramic picture for panoramic projection in a viewer has been saved, the picture can be printed out without any distortion. Spherical panoramic pictures also can be saved and printed, however such pictures have severe distortion at the top and bottom. These flat and "printer-friendly" panoramic pictures can be created using almost any stitching software program. For more information, please refer to the software comparison table in chapter 12.

Paper sizes

Panoramic pictures can be printed out on most commercially available ink-jet printers. Due to its oblong size, a panoramic picture only can be printed out on traditional A4 or A3 paper with a proportionately high amount of white at the edges. Depending on size of the picture (s) and the paper used, two panoramic pictures can be placed on a single sheet, thereby making optimal use of the available space.

Banner paper

Photo paper manufacturers such as Epson, Canon and Agfa make so-called banner paper that is ideal for printing out panoramic pictures. The maximum picture width differs from manufacturer to manufacturer. Typical dimensions of panoramic paper for A4 printers are 9.8 x 3.9" (24.8 x 10 cm) and 23.4 x 8.3" (59.4 x 21 cm).

Continuous paper

If larger-sized panoramic pictures are to be printed out, it is recommended that you use what is known as continuous paper. Continuous paper can be obtained for A4 and A3 printers. The maximum picture height for A3 continuous paper is 16.5" (42 cm), whereas the width depends on the length of the roll and can measure 20 meters, for example. Manufacturers of continuous photo paper include Epson, Hewlett Packard and Fuji.

In order to make printouts on continuous paper, a suitable ink-jet printer with a continuous paper holder is required. Special models are offered by Epson, Canon, Hewlett Packard and other manufacturers.

10.6.2 Professional developing

To date, you still have to really look to find a laboratory that offers professional development of pictures in the special oblong panoramic size. You of course have the option of getting the panoramic pictures developed in traditional sizes with an aspect ratio of 2:3 and cutting off the exposed white perimeter later on. Most digital laboratories offer a maximum picture size of 8 x 12" (20 x 30 cm).

At ez prints (http://www.ezprints.com [status: May 6, 2004]), however, professional development is possible up to 20 x 30" (50.8 x 76.2 cm). This laboratory also offers panoramic prints with a height of 12" (30.5 cm), whereby the width is determined according to your individual panorama. More information can be found at: http://www.ezprints.com/ezdirect/products.asp?Type=Panorama [status: May 6, 2004].

The colormailer laboratory (http://www.colormailer.com [status: April 6, 2004]) offers a number of different standard sizes, the largest of which is 8 x 12" (20 x 30 cm). Special panoramic sizes up to 10 x 30" (25.2 x 75.5 cm) also are supported. This laboratory operates on an international scale and mails prints throughout Greater Europe.

Roundshot laboratory

Special Roundshot panoramic laboratories are located in the U.S. (http://www.roundshot.com [status: April 27, 2004]), in Australia and in Germany (http://www.roundshot-labor.de [status: May 27, 2004]). Here, paper printouts of digital panoramic pictures as well as enlargements of analog panoramic film can be submitted for further processing. Scanning and print services also are offered. To date, the maximum picture width for enlargements (up to 40 x) is 80 m and 50 m for prints.

11. Comparing photo technology and techniques

It is more practical to invest time in comparing photographic technology and techniques for panoramic photography than doing the same with object movies. With object movies, a distinction is made between single-row and multi-row technique, however the use of various cameras and lenses does not bring about quite the difference in effect as with panoramic photography. As such, this chapter focuses exclusively on comparing the technology and techniques associated with photographing panoramas.

Digital panoramic camera

There are a number of options at your disposal for producing panoramas, depending on which motif you would like to photograph and how much money you can spend. If you have a large budget and would like to photograph scenes without any movement, a digital panoramic camera with a scanning feature is recommended. For spherical panoramas, a fisheye lens with at least a 180° field of view should be used. Those who are looking to produce a cylindrical panorama can use a lens with a smaller field of view. If the overall illumination of the motif is sufficient, a complete panorama can be photographed quickly and easily with a single revolution of the camera using this technique. Due to the scanning technology employed, however, digital panoramic cameras are not well suited to taking pictures involving motion. Undesired photographic defects that appear as narrow strips of color for fast-moving objects become evident. Slower moving objects cause wider strips of color. These results of course can (and should) be taken into account when photographing experimental creative panoramas. If the motif to be captured is too dark and cannot be sufficiently illuminated using special lighting systems, it may take 15 minutes or more to scan a panorama at the highest resolution. A night session taken at the highest resolution would require an exposure time of a few hours with such a camera. The resulting image may turn out to be promising for special effects, however this technique is rather fruitless if attempting to make a realistic depiction of dark surroundings. When subjected to direct sunlight, scanning cameras frequently produce so-called “blooming” errors (depending on the exposure setting), which can be seen as white vertical bands. The application range of these cameras focuses on panoramic photography, not on traditional applications. Additionally, the camera only can be controlled and pictures saved when connected to a notebook computer running the corresponding software. With a total weight of approximately six kilograms, the complete equipment is relatively heavy and, compared to other methods, takes some time to set up. This, in turn, limits the application possibilities. It only makes sense to acquire such a special camera if panoramas of still scenes (e.g. virtual tours of real estate) need to be produced on a frequent basis.

HDR camera

Spheron makes a digital scanning camera that is additionally equipped with an HDR function. With this camera, you can quickly and easily take spherical HDR shots with a high range of contrast. This model costs around US $ 60,000 and likewise is only suited for professional photographers who have specialized in panoramas.

Analog panoramic camera

Analog panoramic cameras offer better results when it comes to exposure time. Here, a scene can be photographed in a matter of seconds. As a result, moving objects also do not pose a problem and, depending on the camera setting used, can be captured in remarkable clarity . The vertical tilt range of the panorama in progress still, of course, is dependent on the field of view provided by the lens used. Application, however, typically is limited to cylindrical panoramas. As the panoramic picture is captured on physical film, additional time must be factored in for developing and digitalizing in the production process. Another point to consider is the increased cost associated with the wider film format.

Motifs involving motion

For scenes involving motion, it is advantageous to take as few pictures as possible. If the objects in motion are toward the edge of a picture, the result will be unpleasant cross fading during the stitching process. A portion of the object may even be missing. This can happen when the object moves outside of the camera's field of view while the photographer is adjusting the tripod head for the next picture.

Fisheye method with two individual pictures

In addition to panoramic cameras, a good way to photograph moving objects for a panorama is to use the fisheye method. Here, a spherical panorama is created by way of an 8 mm fisheye lens, whereby two exactly opposed pictures are taken. The large 180° field of view makes it quite feasible to capture moving objects, provided that they are not located near the perimeter of an individual picture. With iPIX, using two such pictures is preferred. The iPIX Rotator tripod head, which is offered in a special design for a few camera models, allows you to capture both hemispheres relatively quickly and without having to make any complex adjustments (see chapter 7.2.4). This approach is a very flexible one and, due to the reduced setup time, panoramas also can be photographed at locations that require fast reaction times, such as in densely populated downtown areas. When using this technique, attention should be paid to taking pictures at the highest possible resolution, as the reduced number of individual pictures also leads to a lower pixel count in the panorama and thereby reduces the picture quality, which is not as high as with other techniques that require a higher number of pictures.

Two and more fisheye pictures can be used to create a spherical panorama. Using eight fullframe fisheye pictures provides more picture information and higher picture quality. In addition, the distortion associated with fisheye lenses is less intense, as the individual pictures overlap each other more than with the iPIX technique.

Fisheye method with eight individual pictures

As with iPIX, the equipment required here also can be set up relatively quickly. When lightweight components are selected, transporting all of the equipment is easier, especially when traveling to out-of-the-way sites such as a mountain top. Fisheye lenses have the advantage that they cover a large field of view, which enables the photographer to take a comparatively low number of individual pictures for a spherical panorama. The eight pictures in total provide enough material for the subsequent image editing as well as the advantage that a complete spherical panorama can be created relatively quickly.

Multi-row technique

The multi-row technique allows for both cylindrical and spherical panoramic shots to be taken. When only two series of pictures are used, for example, a cylindrical panorama can be produced with an increased vertical tilt range. A spherical panorama requires several series of pictures to be taken in order to capture the entire scene. The number of pictures associated with the multi-row technique yields a high resolution, however this technique also has the disadvantage that moving objects sometimes are only partially visible in the stitched panorama. The latter can pose a problem with passersby or in surroundings involving road traffic. This effect can be intentionally used to include people "several times over" in a single panorama, for example. The people in question, however, must change their position only when instructed to do so by the photographer. The number of pictures taken here increases the time required to film the complete panorama. A major advantage of the multi-row technique is that no expensive camera equipment is required; good results even can be achieved using a compact digital camera. Regardless of the camera, it is recommended that a multi-row tripod head be used (see chapter 7.2.4). This type of tripod head makes it easier to find and adjust the nodal point, allowing for precise setting of the horizontal and vertical camera position.

Single-row technique

The single-row technique is the simplified version of the multi-row technique, whereby only a single series of pictures is taken. This technique typically is used for the production of cylindrical panoramas. The nodal point can be adjusted with the panoramic tripod heads introduced in chapter 6.2.5, allowing a series of panoramic pictures to be taken quickly and effectively.

The number of individual pictures influences the result

In addition to the type of projection, the photo technology and technique used and the number of pictures have a great influence on the picture quality and the overall impression made on the observer. The more pictures taken, the less the apparent degree of distortion the panorama has on a monitor. A general rule of thumb is that higher resolution pictures used in the panoramic projection produce a higher quality interactive panoramic experience. When stitching, it is also better to have a higher resolution than you think you need, as you then have more picture information at your disposal for defining the so-called overlapping points.

12. Comparing software applications

In this chapter, the software products introduced in this book for stitching panoramas and creating object movies are compared to each other. Special software that comes with panoramic cameras or parabolic mirrors whose application is only practical in conjunction with the respective products is not covered here.

REALVIZ Stitcher

REALVIZ Stitcher is a stitching software application for editing panoramas and virtual tours. Object movies cannot be created with this software. Instead, you can stitch pictures that were taken using a rectilinear lens. Fish-eye pictures cannot be edited with REALVIZ Stitcher. Pictures are manually overlapped, at which point the software automatically merges the individual images into a panoramic picture. If desired, differences in color and illumination can be balanced out. It is better to use special image editing software for this purpose, however, as more precise setting options can be configured. REALVIZ Stitcher also is capable of correcting distortion associated with wide angle lenses; undesired areas of a picture can be removed by calling up the "Stencil" function. REALVIZ Stitcher supports a wide variety of panoramic formats. Cylindrical and cubic QTVR movies as well as cylindrical, spherical and cubic pictures can be created in various file formats. There also is the option of exporting Shockwave files for Director and VRML files for VRML viewers. What's more, pictures can be very easily converted from one panoramic format to another. Besides stitching panoramas, this software can be used to define hotspots in order to link individual panoramas to create virtual tours.

PanoTools

The Panorama Tools (PanoTools) software suite enables the user to perform such activities as correcting distortion errors, stitching panoramas and creating object movies. PanoTools software is not particularly user-friendly for beginners, however it offers a great deal of editing functions. Graphical user interfaces such as PTGui or PTMac are recommended for stitching panoramas. This add-on software makes it easier to work with PanoTools, as it automatically calls up the PanoTools application required for the task at hand. PanoTools is controlled by a script in which the exact parameters of the individual pictures, including the panoramic and file format, field of view, size and position are specified. This script is specially saved and can be viewed using any text editor program, making the underlying algorithm very transparent. The other programs introduced here do not allow this; everything is done in the background. With PanoTools, specification of the overlapping areas occurs by way of stitching points that are set at all seams of the bordering pictures. It is recommended that you set three points per seam. The more points that are defined, the more precise the overlapping edges. These stitching points should reveal a high range of contrast, as otherwise they cannot be used as reference pixels for stitching. As such, large monochrome areas (e.g. the night sky) are difficult to edit with PanoTools. The coordinates of the individual pictures determine a large portion of the script, which is used by the PTStitcher application of PanoTools to stitch the pictures together. In addition to the actual stitching of the pictures to create a panoramic picture, PanoTools includes a variety of bonus software for image editing purposes. Among the things that can be done are to correct the optical distortion of individual pictures, reduce digital noise and create object movies. PanoTools offers a number of different panoramic formats, with support for cylindrical, spherical and cubic presentations. Additionally, when PanoTools and the corresponding PTViewer Java applet are used, hot spots can be defined and, ultimately, virtual tours created.

iPIX Interactive Studio

iPIX Interactive Studio software enables spherical panoramas to be produced from two or three fisheye pictures. A convenient auto stitch function is included for stitching the individual pictures together. These automatic settings, however, can be corrected if needed. Here, the positions of both hemispheres can be defined in the x and y directions for editing purposes, as well as the radii increased or decreased in size. The more exact the position of both fisheye pictures is defined and the less visible the seam edge appears, the less touch-up work needs to be done afterwards. Simpler image editing steps can be carried out directly in the software. iPIX Interactive Studio includes an integrated High Dynamic Range (HDR) function that allows you to generate a panorama with increased dynamic range from a series of pictures of the same motif. Numerous file formats are available for saving, giving the user the opportunity to generate not only iPIX panoramas, but also QTVR panoramas, for example. The iLinker add-on program can be used to set hot spots and thereby create virtual iPIX tours.

VR Worx

VR Worx software is capable of editing panoramas and object movies. In addition, it is possible to create virtual tours. VR Worx is comprised of three components: VR PanoWorx for stitching cylindrical panoramas, VR ObjectWorx for producing object movies and VR SceneWorx for linking panoramas and object movies to create virtual tours. VR Worx supports the QTVR format and allows panoramic filmstrips to be saved in different file formats. This complete software suite offers a variety of application options. The workflow is intuitively learned and is consistent in all three software areas. The stitching process in the panoramic stitching area is automatic, with the pictures automatically overlapped. The positions of the individual pictures, however, can be manually optimized. Many different effects can be used when producing an object movie that decisively improve the display quality of the object. During the editing stage of linking panoramas and object movies to create virtual tours, support can be drawn on in the form of a floor plan. This way, it is considerably easier to “keep your bearings”, especially when working on large tours.

QTVR Edit Object

QTVR Edit Object is only suited to producing object movies in QTVR format. From a series of object displays, a simple QuickTime film first is generated using the QuickTime Pro player. The film does not yet contain any interactive elements and only can be played normally. Using QTVR Edit Object, this QuickTime movie can be converted into an interactive QTVR object presentation, whereby various settings can be made with respect to play properties.

The following table provides a brief comparative overview of the software available for producing interactive panoramas and object movies.

Comparing software applications (table format)

Functions	REALVIZ Stitcher 4.0	PanoTools 2.6	iPIX Interactive Studio
Platforms	Mac, Win	Linux, Mac, Win	Mac, Win
Price	580 US $	Freeware (PTGui: 50 US $ PTMac: 60 US $)	899 US $ (for 12 months of use)
Form of use	Panoramas, virtual tours	Panoramas, object movies, virtual tours	Panoramas, virtual tours (only via the iLinker add-on software)
Stitching technique	Single-row, multi-row	Single-row, multi-row	Single-row (fisheye)
Lens types	Only rectilinear lenses (no fisheye lenses)	Rectilinear lenses and fisheye lenses	Only 8 mm fisheye lenses
Correction of distortion errors	Yes	Yes	No
Import formats	bmp, cin, iff, jpg, pgm, pict, png, pnm, ppm, rgb, sgi, tdi, tga, tif	bmp, jpg, png, pict, ppm, tif	bmp, jpg, tif
Export formats	iff, jpg, pic, png, ppm, psd, sgi, tga, tif	bmp, jpg, png, psd, tif	bmp, ipix, jpg
Projection formats	Planar, cylindrical, spherical, cubic	Planar, cylindrical, spherical, cubic	Planar, cylindrical, spherical, cubic
Conversion of projection formats	Yes	Yes	Yes
Panoramic formats	cylindrical QTVR, cubic QTVR, Shockwave 3D, VRML, Cylindrical, Cubical, Spherical	Cylindrical, Equirectangular, QTVR, VRML, Live Picture Java	iPIX Image, cubic QTVR, Equirectangular, Shockwave 3D

Comparing software applications (table format)

Functions	**VR Worx 2.5**	**QTVR Edit Object 2**
Platforms	Mac, Win	Mac
Price	299 US $ (complete) 89-149 US $ (separate)	Freeware
Form of use	Panoramas, object movies, virtual tours	Object movies
Stitching technique	Single-row	–
Lens types	Rectilinear lenses and fisheye lenses (excluding 8 mm)	–
Correction of distortion errors	Yes (with VR PanoWorx)	–
Import formats	bmp, jpg, psd, pict, png, sgi, tga, tif	QuickTime
Export formats	bmp, jpg, psd, pict, png, sgi, tga, tif	QTVR
Projection formats	Cylindrical	–
Conversion of projection formats	Yes	–
Panoramic formats	cylindrical QTVR, Object QTVR	Object QTVR

13. Comparing viewers

The various different forms of publication as well as their integration in Web sites are explained in greater detail in chapter 10. This chapter focuses on providing a comparative overview of the most common viewer solutions and includes a table-based comparison of the viewers presented here.

QuickTime-Player

Version 5 or higher of the QuickTime plug-in is required in order to view cubic QTVR movies. Older QuickTime versions only support cylindrical panoramic projection; cubic QTVR movies are displayed here with limited vertical tilt range. The QuickTime plug-in can be downloaded from the Internet free of charge. The installation file is approximately 500 KB. In addition to just displaying panoramas, QuickTime offers the option of integrating other media such as video and sound. Hot spots for virtual tours also can be integrated without a problem. The QuickTime viewer supports all of these additional functions, eliminating the need for installing extra software.

Compared to other viewer solutions, QuickTime provides exceptionally good picture quality, whereby quality and file size are a function of the compression codec selected. It is easy to navigate in the panorama; movements of the mouse are responded to with a high degree of accuracy. This allows the user to get a very realistic impression. Depending on the settings used when creating the QTVR file, the complete panorama can be seen right as it is being loaded (fading from fuzzy to a sharp image). The more picture information that is loaded, the clearer the picture. As navigation is possible during this download process (providing a certain level of entertainment), the user is more likely to wait out the time until the panorama is complete on the user's hard disk. Object movies are a different story. Here, the first picture of the movie appears only after the file has been executed. The remaining pictures are then consecutively loaded. As such, it is not possible to view the object in full 360° format until after the loading process has completed.

Java solutions

Java viewers do not require an extra plug-in, however Java must be installed and activated in the visitor's browser. This is usually the case. If you are working on Windows XP or higher, Java is not automatically supported. Instead, Microsoft has integrated their own substitute technology known as JUMP to .NET. One way for Windows XP users to get around this problem is to install an older version of Internet Explorer (i.e. less than version 6), which still has an embedded Java engine. The other solution is to download the latest Java engine right from the developers at Sun Microsystems. The installation file is approximately 10 MB. Java programs are translated on a computer into byte code, the execution of which requires a so-called interpreter. This is why resource-intensive applications such as panoramic viewers require relatively long processing times and do not react as quickly to movements of the mouse as compared to plug-in solutions. This effect is especially problematic on older computers with slower processors.

PTViewer

With Java applications, the corresponding viewer applet must be downloaded in addition to the image file and the remaining page contents every time the Web site is called up. The file size of the PTViewer applet is 35 KB. The observer is only able to view the panoramas and objects once the loading process has completed, at which point navigation can begin. Sound and other specials can be added to the PTViewer via an additional applet. The PTViewer can be configured for individual layouts based on the parameters used. As such, static hot spots, for example, can be introduced to create various navigation bars. A modified version of the PTViewer is capable of playing panoramas with a high dynamic range (HDR).

iPIX

There are two ways to display iPIX panoramas on a Web site: via the plug-in or a Java applet. If the iPIX image is used without a Java applet, the visitor of the site will need to have the iPIX plug-in installed. The installation file for the iPIX plug-in is approximately 800 KB. If the Web site is viewed using the plug-in, better picture quality and increased rotational speed of the panorama are obtained. Any iPIX file can be used for publishing with the iPIX plug-in, irrespective of the resolution and compression. The second option is to integrate the iPIX image using the iPIX Java viewer. A plug-in is not required for this solution, however Java must be installed and activated in the visitor's browser. The Java viewer places a high load on CPUs, making it slower in performance compared to the plug-in solution. Also, the 47 KB Java applet must be loaded here, too, along with the iPIX image and the remaining page contents every time the Web site is called up.

Only after the Java applet and the iPIX picture have been loaded in their entirety can navigation begin. With the plug-in version, previewing is handled similarly to that of QuickTime; as soon as enough picture information has been loaded, the observer begins to see the panorama forming and can move around in it right up until the file has been completely loaded. iPIX solutions allow for the integration of sound and hot spots. This is done using iLinker add-on program or HotMedia software and an additional Java applet. The observer does not need any extra software in order to be able to use these additional features.

HotMedia

HotMedia is a so-called rich media application developed by IBM that was specially designed for Web use in the form of a Java applet. Panoramas, object movies, graphics, video and sound can be linked using the HotMedia applet. Hot spots are outlined in red and can be combined with text. This visual indication allows the hot spots to be easily located and even makes it a breeze for inexperienced users to navigate their way through a tour. The observer is only able to view the panoramas and objects once the loading process has completed, at which point navigation can begin. The HotMedia applet is between 10 and 12 KB (depending on the version) and is transferred along with the contents every time the Web site is called up.

Virtual Reality Modeling Language (VRML)

A VRML viewer must be installed on your computer in order to be able to view a VRML file. This viewer can be downloaded as a browser plug-in from a number of Web sites. In this book, the Cortona VRML Client is introduced as an example. VRML viewers use the cubic projection technique, whereby the sides of the cube for the projection are individually saved and called up by the viewer for presentation on the Web. Navigation in the panorama is possible during the download process, whereby each side of the cube is displayed in the viewer once it has been loaded. The Cortona Player installation file is approximately 1.5 MB. Additional viewer functions can be loaded by way of so-called VRML extensions. Additional functions such as sound or the definition of a specific initial view for panoramas only can be programmed using the VR Modeling Language. Objects and panoramas created using a camera or 3-D software can be displayed. With these 3-D renderings, observers frequently can change properties such as color, size and movement of the panoramas or objects. The factors that define this interactivity are specified using the Virtual Reality Modeling Language (VRML).

Navigation

Navigation in all of the viewers introduced here is very similar. When the left mouse key is depressed and moved in a particular direction, the panoramic picture or object is rotated in this direction. The position of the mouse is displayed as a circle (panorama) or as a hand (object) with QTVR files; PTViewer shows the current position of the mouse using the traditional mouse pointer icon. iPIX viewers show different mouse icons, depending on the type of publication. The Java solution shows the position of the mouse as an arrow. With plug-in based display, the direction of the mouse is shown as a hand and the zoom option as a magnifying glass. Although this permanent display of the mouse eases navigation for the observer, the large navigation pointer is viewed by some people as an element that takes away from the panoramic experience.

Zoom

Except for the Cortona VRML Client, all viewers offer a zoom function for panoramic presentations. The zoom factor typically is defined in the panorama file. With QTVR, this occurs at the point of publishing, whereby the zoom range can be numerically entered. With iPIX, the zoom range is defined in the software; only the starting zoom factor can be defined by selecting the initial angle of view before saving the panoramic file. The magnitude of the zoom for PTViewer is defined in the applet and can be changed by entering the desired parameters in the HTML file. In order to allow the user to enlarge and decrease the size of the picture, an average value of the entire zoom range should be selected when defining the starting zoom factor

Automatic rotation

Almost all solutions provide the option of automatically rotating panoramas and objects in one direction (autorotation) when the application is started. This makes it easier for inexperienced users to familiarize themselves with this form of interactive image display.

In order to be able to reach as many users as possible (whose computers all are configured differently), it is recommended that you offer a panorama in different formats. For example, you could offer a Java-based solution and a corresponding plug-in version. It is best to give the user the option of selecting the file size (i.e. large/small) that is right for them when visiting the Web site.

The following table briefly compares the viewer software, especially with regard to application functionality. More information can be found at: http://www.panoguide.com/publish/viewers.html [status: March 15, 2004].

Viewer comparison table

Functions	**QuickTime 6.5**	**Cortona Player 4.2**	**iPIX Player 6.2**
Viewer type	Plug-in / ActiveX	Plug-in / ActiveX	Plug-in / ActiveX
Stand-alone player	Yes	Yes	Yes
Form of use	Panoramas, object movies	Panoramas, object movies	Panoramas
Projection format	Cylindrical, cubic	Cubic	Spherical
Zoom	Yes	Yes (however not for panoramas)	Yes
Hot spots	Yes	No	Yes (via iLinker or HotMedia)
Autorotate	Yes	No	Yes
Integration of other media	Sound, video, pictures	Sound (via VRML)	Sound (via iLinker or HotMedia)
Navigation during loading time	Yes	Yes	Yes

Viewer comparison table

Functions	**iPIX Java Viewer 4.0**	**HotMedia 3.5**	**PTViewer 2.5**
Viewer type	Java	Java	Java
Stand-alone player	No	No	Yes (with stand-alone version 0.4)
Form of use	Panoramas	Panoramas, object movies	Panoramas, object movies
Projection format	Spherical	Cylindrical, spherical	Cylindrical, spherical, cubic
Zoom	Yes	Yes	Yes
Hot spots	Yes (via iLinker or HotMedia)	Yes	Yes
Autorotate	Yes	Yes	Yes
Integration of other media	Sound (via iLinker or HotMedia)	Sound, video, pictures	Sound, video, pictures
Navigation during loading time	No	No	No

14. Application possibilities

Documentation of architecture

For architects and appraisers, documentation of the current state of development of buildings and physical structures is gaining in importance. When traditional photographic or film-based technologies are used, usually only a certain angle of view can be captured. As such, these methods are not well suited to neutrally depicting a spatial environment. Interactive panoramas, however, provide for complete documentation of rooms and areas. When spherical panoramas are used, every physical detail in the camera's environment can be recorded.

Art and culture

Such panoramas find application not only in the architectural and interior design fields; many other sectors are discovering the benefits as well. Other viable areas of application include cultural projects and activities, museums, tourism, e-learning, trade shows and sales-promoting illustrations such as interior views of automobiles. Artistic panoramas are a special form of application, whereby pictures that didn't originally "go together" are stitched, for example. This approach gives rise to interesting artificial worlds.

Securing of evidence

In Great Britain and in the United States, panoramic cameras are occasionally used to secure evidence and document crime scenes. There is a time limit for restricting access to crime scenes, which is why police normally only take pictures of details that are directly related to the crime. If, however, spherical panoramas are taken of every room in an apartment in which a crime has occurred, various different details can be examined in the panoramic pictures as the case progresses.

Interactive maps with GPS data

When photographing panoramas, GPS (Global Positioning System) can be used to determine the exact positioning data of a particular photographic site. This gives rise to so-called mapping systems. Mapping systems involve interactive maps that additionally show the exact navigation data for each panoramic picture. Mapping systems basically are extended virtual tours. Here, panoramas can be linked to graphics, sound, video and GPS data.

HDR panoramas serve as the basis for image-based lighting

In 3-D graphics, natural illumination of a computer-generated 3-D scene is critical in order to create a realistic impression. Panoramas that were taken using the High Dynamic Range (HDR) technique can serve as the basis for illuminating 3-D objects. This technique finds application in the production of science fiction films, for example. Here, model scenes such as moon landscapes are filmed using special spherical HDR cameras (SpheroCam HDR). The HDR picture obtained in this way can be used as a so-called light map for the realistic illumination, or lighting, of a computer-generated spaceship. This illumination effect based on HDR pictures used for 3-D renderings is known as image-based lighting.

Object movies

The areas of application for object movies are quite diverse, making it possible to present products ranging from technical appliances to furniture. Such object movies also are used in the fashion world and sometimes even include real models, who are photographed on enlarged turntables. Online shopping sites represent the classic application area of object movies. The presentation of products from all sides and the sense of touch invoked when rotating objects produce added value that can motivate customers to making a purchase.

15. Outlook

Software with automated stitching process

The stitching programs presented in the previous chapters only are capable of stitching pictures of the same size and focal length. Additionally, most techniques require that the overlapping areas be manually specified. At the Wilhelm Schickard Institute for Computer Science in the Graphical-Interactive Systems (GRIS) department at the University of Tübingen (Germany), a software is currently being developed that allows the user to stitch pictures with varying focal lengths. The software also is capable of automatically stitching pictures. Overlapping areas are automatically detected, provided that the pictures have a sufficiently high range of contrast. The latter allows the software to detect corresponding points in the individual pictures for the stitching process. Currently, the software application is used to create planar pictures, however capacity for cylindrical and spherical projection of these panoramas is in progress. More information on the status of the software development can be found at: http://www.gris.uni-tuebingen.de/~biber [status: May 12, 2004].

Video panoramas

In addition to the panoramas presented here (which are created from still shots), there are motion picture panoramas based on video pictures. With motion picture panoramas, the observer is presented the video in picture format and can easily navigate within this video using a mouse. An example of this is offered by iMove Spherical Video. The required plug-in can be downloaded from the company's Web site (http://www.imoveinc.com [status: March 31, 2004], where a number of sample videos can be viewed. The system uses a 6-lens video camera that captures the complete environment (360 degrees) in a single session. All six separate videos are then stitched with special software to create a spherical video. Immersive Media also offers a very similar system. More information can be found at: http://immersivemedia.com [status: March 31, 2004].

Not to be outdone, iPIX sells a system for spherical video panoramas, or so-called iPIX movies. Here, the 8 mm fisheye principle typical for iPIX is used. There are special double fisheye lenses available for video cameras that allow both fisheye video tracks to be simultaneously recorded. When the iPIX movie software is used, these video hemispheres are stitched to create a spherical iPIX movie. The iPIX Web site (http://infomedia.ipix.com/products/services/movies/ [status: March 31, 2004]) offers a few sample movies for viewing purposes.

Application areas for video panoramas

There are many possibilities for such video applications. Discussion rounds, sporting events and concerts, where various activities occur at the same time, represent potential application areas for 360° video recording. As such, the observer can be presented an individualized view behind the scenes that, at concert events, for example, would not be possible under normal circumstances. Additional application areas include music clips, advertising spots and company presentations. Here, the observer has the opportunity to navigate in the video and discover something new, even after viewing the same clip several times.

Photogrammetry

Spheron currently is developing a software application that will allow rooms and objects to be measured with a high degree of accuracy based on two spherical panoramic pictures. This photo-based measuring system is known as photogrammetry. While planar photogrammetry has been practiced for a while now, the developments being made in spherical photogrammetry represent an interesting alternative. Various distances in the respective rooms can be accurately measured from two fully spherical pictures using batch compensation. Photogrammetry is applied in the fields of architecture, culture and archeology, however it also is used to measure landscape, for example. When the software will be available on the market unfortunately was not able to be determined during the research stage. More information can be found at: http://www.spheron.com [status: March 29, 2004].

HDR viewer

A new HDR viewer has been announced that supports the spherical high dynamic range panoramic format. The special HDR function allows the observer to switch between the various levels of light in the panorama at any time. In this way, very bright and very dark areas of the picture can be viewed in detail. In addition to providing traditional functions such as sweeping and zooming, this viewer makes it possible to pivot the image vertically up and down. In other words, the observer can move upwards and downwards in parallel from a particular point, which is comparable to the visual impression one has when knee-bending. More information on this HDR viewer can be found at: http://www.spheron.com [status: March 29, 2004]. After the test phase has been concluded, the HDR viewer will be available for download from Spheron.

There is another new viewer for HDR panoramas, developed by Helmut Dersch (developer of PanoTools). With this HDR Java viewer, it is possible to always have the right illumination in every area of a panoramic picture. You can brighten the picture by pressing "B" or darken it by pressing "D" on your keyboard. Alternatively, it is possible to blend the brightness automatically while panning the panorama. More information about this new HDR viewer (PTViewer 3.1.2) can be found on the Internet at: http://webuser.fh-furtwangen.de/~dersch/ [status: April 29, 2004]).

Computer-generated object movies from two individual pictures

Recently, simpler solutions for creating computer-generated object movies have been offered as an alternative to using a large number of individual pictures. With special software such as 1-2-3D, for example, it is possible to automatically generate a 3-D lattice model based on just two pictures of an object, whereby these pictures also can serve to provide the object's surface texture. This makes for a realistic impression. In addition, the object can be shown from all sides relatively easily. Additional information on 1-2-3D can be found at: http://www.motionparallax.com/1-2-3Dinstructions.htm [status: April 28, 2004].

Lattice models based on spherical panoramas

A similar technique currently is being developed by Spheron for the display of interior rooms. Here, spherical panoramic pictures serve as the basis for editing complete rooms in 3-D programs. With special software, the panoramic picture is used to automatically create a lattice model of the room inclusive of all objects contained therein. The panoramic picture also is used to create the surface texture for this lattice model. In this way, rooms can be modeled quicker than previously was possible. A prerequisite for this time-saving production path, however, is the use of a digital panoramic camera. Unfortunately, at the time research was conducted, it was not possible to determine when the software will make its market debut. More information can be found at: http://www.spheron.com [status: March 29, 2004].

Combination of panoramic and 3-D displays

SceneWeaver from REALVIZ allows the user to integrate moving 3-D objects in virtual panoramic displays. For example, a train station with an incoming train can be depicted. While the train station is based on a genuine photographic panorama, the incoming train is created and rendered in a 3-D program. Both sources can be combined using the SceneWeaver software. In the time that the train enters, stops and leaves the station, the observer is able to freely move within the complete panoramic picture. You can find this train station panorama on the Internet at: http://www.realviz.com/gallery/spec.php?id=104&&offset=1&&product=sw# [status: February 12, 2004]. More information on SceneWeaver is available at the manufacturer's Web site: http://www.realviz.com/products/sw/index.php [status: February 12, 2004].

A. Bibliography

A.1 Reference literature

- Altmann, Ralph: Digitale Fotografie & Bildbearbeitung
  Midas / PRO, Zürich 2001
- Apple QuickTime Authoring Studio User's Manual
  Apple Computer Inc., Cupertino 1997
- Biere, Julien: Professionelle Dia-AV
  Photographie-Verlag, Schaffhausen 1998
- Comment, Bernard: "The Panorama" Reaction Books, 1999
  John Wiley & Sons: Seeing the light, 1986
- Gulie, Steven: QuickTime for the Web
  Morgan Kaufmann, London 2001
- Häßler, Ulrike u.a.: Digitale Fotografie
  Springer-Verlag, Berlin 1998
- Hedgecore, John: Meine große Fotoschule
  Christian-Verlag, München 1995
- iPIX Builder Manual
  Internet Pictures Corporation, Oak Ridge 2001
- Kastenholz, Frank u.a.: QuickTime 6
  Galileo Press, Bonn 2003
- Kneißl, Michael: Scannen wie die Profis
  dtv / KNO, München 2000
- Koren, Gerhard: Adobe Photoshop 7
  Galileo Press, Bonn 2003
- McClelland, Deke: Photoshop 6 Bible
  John Wiley & Sons, 2001
- Nischke, Michael: Panoramafotografie
  Augustus-Verlag, Augsburg 1994
- REALVIZ Stitcher User Guide
  REALVIZ, S.A., Valbonne 2002

- Richter, Günter: Foto-Handbuch
  vfv-Verlag, Gilching 1991
- Richter, Günter: Weitwinkelfotografie
  vfv-Verlag, Gilching 1988
- Roundshot 28/220 user guide
  SEITZ Phototechnik AG, Lustdorf 2002
- Roundshot Super Digital II user guide
  SEITZ Phototechnik AG, Lustdorf 2002
- Schmidt, Udo: Digitale Fotografie
  Franzis / PRO, Poing 2002
- Spheron Cam User Manual
  Spheron VR AG, Waldfischbach-Burgalben 2003
- Strutz, Tilo: Bilddatenkompression
  Vieweg Verlag, Wiesbaden 2000
- VR Worx Manual
  VR Toolbox Inc., Pittsburgh 1999

A.2 Internet sources

- http://360vr.com/ptvr/anasazi.html [status: March 8, 2004]
- http://developer.apple.com/documentation/[status: March 27, 2004]
- http://developer.apple.com/documentation/QuickTime/VirtualReality-date.html [status: March 27, 2004]
- http://developer.apple.com/referencelibrary/API_Fundamentals/QuickTime-api-date.html [status: March 27, 2004]
- http://frog.netperson.net/~wiz/lens_table_1.htm [status: May 10, 2004]
- http://home.no.net/dmaurer/~dersch/Index.htm [status: March 9, 2004]
- http://home.no.net/dmaurer/~dersch/html/Micros.html [status: March 9, 2004]
- http://home.no.net/dmaurer/~dersch/PTVJ/doc.html [status: May 2, 2004]
- http://immersivemedia.com [status: March 31, 2004]
- http://infomedia.ipix.com/ [status: March 30, 2004]
- http://infomedia.ipix.com/support/download/ [status: April 2, 2004]
- http://infomedia.ipix.com/products/services/movies/[status: May 1, 2004]
- http://java.com/en/download/manual.jsp [status: March 10, 2004]
- http://java.com/en/index.jsp [status: March 20, 2004]
- http://michel.thoby.free.fr [status: March 19, 2004]
- http://www.360texas.com/tips/nodalpts.htm [status: March 10, 2004]
- http://www-3.ibm.com/software/ad/hotmedia/about [status: May 2, 2004]
- http://www-3.ibm.com/software/awdtools/hotmedia [status: May 2, 2004]
- http://www.adobe.com/digitalimag/main.html [status: May 1, 2004]

- http://www.all-in-one.ee/~dersch/barrel/barrel.html [status: May 3, 2004]
- http://www.all-in-one.ee/~dersch/PTVJ/doc.html [status: April 8, 2004]
- http://www.all-in-one.ee/~dersch/PTVJ/helpers.html[status:May1,2004]
- http://www.alteredearth.com/vr/cubicvr/shaft1.htm [status: May 2, 2004]
- http://www.apple.com/hardware/gallery [status: March 8, 2004]
- http://www.apple.com/quicktime/download [status: March 10, 2004]
- http://www.apple.com/quicktime/gallery/cubicvr [status: April 18, 2004]
- http://www.atlantanation.com/cyclorama.html [status: March 15, 2004]
- http://www.cirkutpanorama.com [status: April 3, 2004]
- http://www.clickheredesign.com.au [status: March 29, 2004]
- http://www.colormailer.com [status: April 6, 2004]
- http://www.cyclorama.com [status: February 14, 2004]
- http://www.debevec.org [status: March 6, 2004]
- http://www.debevec.org/HDRShop [status: March 24, 2004]
- http://www.digitalkamera.de/Info/Workshop/Panorama/NodalPoint3-de.asp [status: March 10, 2004]
- http://www.eyesee360.com/photowarp [status: May 13, 2004]
- http://www.ex.ac.uk/bill.douglas/collection/panorama/barker.html [status: May 10, 2004]
- http://www.ezprints.com [status: May 6, 2004]
- http://www.fh-furtwangen.de/~dersch/ [status: May 17, 2004]
- http://www.gregdowning.com [status: March 6, 2004]
- http://www.grigull.com [status: April 1, 2004]
- http://www.gris.uni-tuebingen.de/~biber [status: May 12, 2004]
- http://www.imoveinc.com [status: March 31, 2004]
- http://www.ipixstore.com/cart/index.cfm [status: May 14, 2004]
- http://www.kaidan.com [status: March 15, 2004]
- http://www.kaidan.com/nightri.html [status: March 8, 2004]
- http://www.kekus.com [status: February 21, 2004]
- http://www.kodak.com [status: March 8, 2004]
- http://www.manfrotto.com [status: April 21, 2004]
- http://www.metmuseum.org/works_of_art/viewone.asp?dep=2&view-mode=0&item=52.184 [status: March 12, 2004]
- http://www.microsoft.com [status: February 24, 2004]
- http://www.motionparallax.com [status: April 28, 2004]
- http://www.netscape.com [status: February 23, 2004]
- http://www.nps.gov/gett/gettcyclo.htm [status: February 14, 2004]
- http://www.outline.be/quicktime/musee3d.html [status: March 8, 2004]
- http://www.panoguide.com [status: February 19, 2004]
- http://www.panoguide.com/publish/viewers.html [status: May 3, 2004]
- http://www.panoramaguth.com.au/panorama.shtml [status: May 2, 2004]
- http://www.panoscan.com [status: February 20, 2004]
- http://www.parallelgraphics.com/developer [status: May 29, 2004]
- http://www.parallelgraphics.com/products/cortona [status: May 3, 2004]
- http://www.path.unimelb.edu.au/~bernardk/tutorials/360/readme/scripts.html [status: April 15, 2004]
- http://www.pbs.org/wnet/newyork/hidden [status: March 8, 2004]

- http://www.ptgui.com [status: February 21, 2004]
- http://www.realviz.com [status: May 8, 2004]
- http://www.roundshot.ch [status: March 21, 2004]
- http://www.roundshot.com [status: March 21, 2004]
- http://www.roundshot-labor.de [status: April 19, 2004]
- http://www.selfhtml.org/ [status: January 28, 2004]
- http://www.smgvr.com [status: May 5, 2004]
- http://www.soh.nsw.gov.au/virtual_tour/vrtour.html [status: May 5, 2004]
- http://www.sorenson.com [status: February 10, 2004]
- http://www.spheron.com [status: February 20, 2004]
- http://www.totallyhip.com/lo/products/lsp [status: June 5, 2004]
- http://www.vrhotwires.com/beetle-pano.mov [status: March 8, 2004]
- http://www.vrtoolbox.com [status: May 7, 2004]
- http://www.vrmlsite.com [status: June 3, 2004]
- http://www.worldserver.com/turk [status: March 29, 2004]

- QuickTime VR mailing list. Here you can read tips offered by professionals as well as search for specific topics in the archive. Registration and infos at: http://lists.apple.com/mailman/listinfo/quicktime-vr [status: May 12, 2004]

- Immersive Imaging mailing list. Here you have access to information and tips for panoramic production using PanoTools. Registration at: http://groups.yahoo.com/group/PanoTools [status: May 15, 2004]

A.3 Image sources

The illustrations in chapters 4.1.1, 4.1.3 and 4.1.4 are screenshots of the PanoTools software. Copyright © 1998 - 2001 Helmut Dersch. All rights reserved.

The illustrations in chapter 4.2 are screenshots of the HDR Shop software. Copyright © 2001 University of Southern California. All rights reserved.

The illustrations in chapters 6.3.1, 6.3.2, 8.3.3 and 9.3.2 are screenshots of the VR Worx software. Copyright © 2003 VR Toolbox, Inc.
All rights reserved.

The illustrations in chapters 6.3.4, 7.3.1, 7.3.2 and 9.3.1 are screenshots of the REALVIZ stitcher software. Copyright © 2003 REALVIZ, S.A. All rights reserved.

The illustrations in chapters 6.3.3 and 7.3.4 are screenshots of the PTGui software.Copyright © 2002 New House Internet Services, B.V. All rights reserved.

The illustrations in chapter 7.2.1.1 are screenshots of the Roundshot Super Digital software. Copyright © 2003 SEITZ Phototechnik AG. All rights reserved.

The illustrations in chapter 7.2.1.2 are screenshots of the SpheronCam software. Copyright © 2003 Spheron VR AG. All rights reserved.

The illustrations in chapter 7.3.3 are screenshots of the iPIX Interactive Studio software. Copyright © 2003 Internet Pictures Corporation. All rights reserved.

The illustrations in chapter 8.3.2 are screenshots of the QTVR Edit Object software. Copyright © 2003 Apple Computer, Inc. All rights reserved.

The illustrations in chapter 9.3.3 are screenshots of the HotMedia software. Copyright © 2003 IBM Corp. All rights reserved.

The illustrations in chapter 9.3.4 are screenshots of the iPIX iLinker software. Copyright © 2003 Internet Pictures Corporation. All rights reserved.

The illustrations of the Roundshot cameras (Figs. 6.1 and 7.3) were kindly provided by Werner Seitz (Roundshot).

The illustration of the SpheroCam HDR (Fig. 7.6) was kindly provided by Marcus Weiß (Spheron).

The panoramic pictures in chapter 6.2.2 were kindly provided by Torben Ohme.

The panoramic pictures in chapters 6.2.1.1 and 7.2.1.1 were kindly provided by Marc Kairies.

The panoramic picture in chapter 7.2.1.2 was kindly provided by Tim Kondermann.

The 3-D model shown in chapters 8.2.2 and 8.3.3 was kindly provided by Amazing 3D Graphics.

All additional pictures have been provided by the author.

B. List of manufacturers

B.1 Software

B.1.1 Software for cylindrical panoramas

3D Vista
http://www.3dvista.com [status: May 12, 2004]

Corel Photo-Paint
http://www.corel.com [status: May 12, 2004]

D Vision Works D Joiner
http://www.d-vw.com [status: May 12, 2004]

iSeeMedia PhotoVista Panorama (component of Reality Studio)
http://www.iseemedia.com [status: May 12, 2004]

PanaVue Image Assembler
http://www.panavue.com [status: May 12, 2004]

Panorama Factory
http://www.panoramafactory.com [status: May 12, 2004]

Panorama Tools (PanoTools)
http://www.path.unimelb.edu.au/~dersch [status: May 12, 2004]
http://www.all-in-one.ee/~dersch [status: May 12 2004]

PixAround PixMaker
http://www.pixaround.com [status: May 12, 2004]

Pixtra OmniStitcher
http://www.pixtra.com [status: May 12, 2004]

PTMac, PTGui and PTAssembler (user interfaces for PanoTools)
http://www.kekus.com [status: May 12 2004]
http://www.ptgui.com [status: May 12, 2004]
http://www.tawbaware.com/ptasmblr.htm [status: May 12, 2004]

QTVR Authoring Studio
http://www.apple.com/quicktime/qtvr/authoringstudio [status: May 2, 2004]

REALVIZ Stitcher
http://www.realviz.com [status: May 7, 2004]

Ulead Cool 360
http://www.ulead.com/cool360 [status: May 12, 2004]

VR PanoWorx (component of VR Worx)
http://www.vrtoolbox.com [status: May 12, 2004]

B.1.2 Software for spherical panoramas

D Vision Works D Joiner
http://www.d-vw.com [status: May 12, 2004]

easyPanoram
http://www.easypanoram.de [status: May 12, 2004]

iMove Spherical Photo Solution
http://www.kaidan.com [status: May 12, 2004]

iPIX Interactive Studio
http://infomedia.ipix.com/products/software/iis/ [status: May 12, 2004]

PanaVue Image Assembler
http://www.panavue.com [status: May 12, 2004]

Panorama Tools (PanoTools)
http://www.path.unimelb.edu.au/~dersch [status: May 12, 2004]
http://www.all-in-one.ee/~dersch [status: May 12, 2004]

Panoweaver
http://www.easypano.com [status: May 12, 2004]

PTMac, PTGui and PTAssembler (user interfaces for PanoTools)
http://www.kekus.com [status: May 12, 2004]
http://www.ptgui.com [status: May 12, 2004]
http://www.tawbaware.com/ptasmblr.htm [status: May 12, 2004]

REALVIZ Stitcher
http://www.realviz.com [status: May 12, 2004]

B.1.3 Software for object movies

3D Vista
http://www.3dvista.com [status: May 12, 2004]

iSeeMedia PhotoVista 3D Objects
http://www.iseemedia.com [status: May 12, 2004]

Panorama Tools – PTStripe
http://www.path.unimelb.edu.au/~dersch [status: May 12, 2004]
http://www.all-in-one.ee/~dersch [status: May 12, 2004]

PixAround PixMaker
http://www.pixaround.com [status: May 12, 2004]

QTVR Authoring Studio
http://www.apple.com/quicktime/qtvr/authoringstudio [status: May 1, 2004]

QTVR Edit Object
(conversion of a QuickTime movie to a QTVR object movie)
http://developer.apple.com/quicktime/quicktimeintro/tools [status: May 12, 2004]

QuickTime-Player Pro
(conversion of a picture sequence to a QuickTime movie)
http://www.apple.com/quicktime/upgrade [status: May 12, 2004]

SpinimageDV (offers software plus turntables)
http://www.spinimagedv.com [status: May 12, 2004]

VR ObjectWorx (component of VR Worx)
http://www.vrtoolbox.com [status: May 12, 2004]

B.1.4 Software for virtual tours

3D Vista
http://www.3dvista.com [status: May 12, 2004]

CubicConnector
http://www.clickheredesign.com.au [status: May 12, 2004]

HotMedia
http://www-3.ibm.com/software/ad/hotmedia [status: May 12, 2004]

iLinker
http://infomedia.ipix.com/products/software/ilinker/ [status: June 2, 2004]

Panorama Tools – PTViewer
http://www.path.unimelb.edu.au/~dersch [status: May 12, 2004]
http://www.all-in-one.ee/~dersch [status: May 12, 2004]

Photovista Virtual Tour (component of Reality Studio)
http://www.iseemedia.com [status: May 12, 2004]

QTVR Authoring Studio
http://www.apple.com/quicktime/qtvr/authoringstudio [status: May 1, 2004]

REALVIZ Stitcher
http://www.realviz.com [status: May 12, 2004]

VR SceneWorx (component of VR Worx)
http://www.vrtoolbox.com [status: May 12, 2004]

B.1.5 Software for converting panorama formats

Cubic Converter
http://www.clickheredesign.com.au [status: May 12, 2004]

Panorama Factory
http://www.panoramafactory.com [status: May 12, 2004]

PanoPost
http://www.kaidan.com/Detail.bok?no=75 [status: May 12, 2004]

Panorama Tools (PanoTools)
http://www.path.unimelb.edu.au/~dersch [status: May 12, 2004]
http://www.all-in-one.ee/~dersch [status: May 12, 2004]

PTMac, PTGui and PTAssembler (user interfaces for PanoTools)
http://www.kekus.com [status: May 12, 2004]
http://www.ptgui.com [status: May 12, 2004]
http://www.tawbaware.com/ptasmblr.htm [status: May 12, 2004]

QTVR Authoring Studio
http://www.apple.com/quicktime/qtvr/authoringstudio [status: May 2, 2004]

REALVIZ Stitcher
http://www.realviz.com [status: May 12, 2004]

B.1.6 HDR (High Dynamic Range) software

Full Dynamic Range Exposer
http://andreas-schoemann.de/fdrtools/fdrtools_e.php [status: May 1, 2004]

HDR Shop
http://www.debevec.org/HDRShop [status: May 1, 2004]

Photogenics HDR
http://www.idruna.com/photogenicshdr [status: May 1, 2004]

Photomatix
http://www.multimediaphoto.com/photomatix [status: May 1, 2004]

B.1.7 Viewer software

HotMedia
http://www-3.ibm.com/software/awdtools/hotmedia [status: May 7, 2004]

iPIX-Plug-in
http://infomedia.ipix.com/support/download/plugin.shtml [status: May 12, 2004]

Java
http://www.java.com/en/download/manual.jsp [status: May 12, 2004]

PTViewer
http://www.all-in-one.ee/~dersch/PTVJ/doc.html [status: May 2, 2004]
http://home.no.net/dmaurer/~dersch/PTVJ/doc.html [status: May 2, 2004]

QuickTime-Player
http://www.apple.com/quicktime/download [status: May 12, 2004]

VRML Cortona-Player
http://www.parallelgraphics.com/products/cortona [status: May 7, 2004]

VRML Blaxxun Contact
http://www.blaxxun.com/en/products/contact/ [status: May 3, 2004]

VRML Cosmo-Player
http://www.cai.com/cosmo [status: May 12, 2004]

Zoomify
http://www.zoomify.com/zoomifyer [status: May 12, 2004]

Zoom Image Server (iSeeMedia plug-in)
http://www.iseemedia.com/products/zoom [status: May 12, 2004]

B.1.8 3-D software

3D Studio Max
http://www.discreet.com/products/3dsmax [status: May 12, 2004]

Cinema 4D
http://maxon-computer.com [status: May 12, 2004]

Maya
http://www.aliaswavefront.com [status: May 12, 2004]

Softimage
http://www.softimage.com [status: May 12, 2004]

B.1.9 Software for image editing

Gimp
http://www.gimp.org [status: May 12, 2004]

Lens Doc
http://www.andromeda.com [status: May 12, 2004]

Microsoft Digital Imaging
http://www.microsoft.com/products/imaging/products/default.asp [status: May 12, 2004]

Panorama Tools (PanoTools)
http://www.path.unimelb.edu.au/~dersch [status: May 12, 2004]
http://www.all-in-one.ee/~dersch [status: May 12, 2004]

Photo Impact
http://www.ulead.com/pi/runme.htm [status: May 12, 2004]

Photoshop
http://www.adobe.com/products/photoshop/ [status: May 12, 2004]

PTMac, PTGui and PTAssembler (user interfaces for PanoTools)
http://www.kekus.com [status: May 12, 2004]
http://www.ptgui.com [status: May 12, 2004]
http://www.tawbaware.com/ptasmblr.htm [status: May 12, 2004]

B.2 Equipment

B.2.1 Camera manufacturers

Agfa
http://www.agfa.com [status: May 12, 2004]

Canon
http://www.canon.com [status: May 12, 2004]

Contax
http://www.kyoceraimaging.com [status: May 12, 2004]

Fuji
http://www.fujifilm.com [status: May 12, 2004]

Kodak
http://www.kodak.com [status: May 12, 2004]

Konica
http://www.konica.com [status: May 12, 2004]

Leica
http://www.leica-camera.com/index_e.html [status: May 12, 2004]

Minolta
http://konicaminolta.com [status: May 12, 2004]

Nikon
http://www.nikon.com [status: May 12, 2004]

Olympus
http://www.olympus.com [status: May 12, 2004]

Pentax
http://www.pentax.com [status: May 12, 2004]

Sigma
http://www.sigmaphoto.com [status: May 12, 2004]

Sony
http://www.sony.com [status: May 12, 2004]

B.2.2 Lens manufacturers

Canon
http://www.canon.com [status: May 12, 2004]

Carl Zeiss
http://www.zeiss.com [status: May 12, 2004]

Contax
http://www.kyoceraimaging.com [status: May 12, 2004]

Leica
http://www.leica-camera.com/index_e.html [status: May 12, 2004]

Minolta
http://konicaminolta.com [status: May 12, 2004]

Nikon
http://www.nikon.com [status: May 12, 2004]

Olympus
http://www.olympus.com [status: May 12, 2004]

Pentax
http://www.pentax.com [status: May 12, 2004]

Rollei
http://www.rollei.com [status: May 12, 2004]

Sigma
http://www.sigmaphoto.com [status: May 12, 2004]

Tamron
http://www.tamron.com [status: May 12, 2004]

Tokina
http://www.tokina-usa.com [status: May 12, 2004]

B.2.3 Manufacturers of parabolic mirrors

EyeSee 360
http://www.eyesee360.com [status: May 12, 2004]

Behere
http://www.behere.com [status: May 12, 2004]

Remote Reality
http://www.remotereality.com [status: May 12, 2004]

B.2.4 Manufacturers of panoramic cameras

Eyescan
http://www.kst-dresden.de [status: May 12, 2004]

Panoscan
http://www.panoscan.com [status: May 12, 2004]

Roundshot
http://www.roundshot.ch [status: May 12, 2004]

Spheron
http://www.spheron.com [status: May 12, 2004]

B.2.5 Manufacturers of panoramic tripod heads

Accupan
http://www.accupan.com [status: May 12, 2004]

Bogen / Manfrotto
http://www.manfrotto.com [status: May 12, 2004]

Kaidan
http://www.kaidan.com [status: May 12, 2004]

Peace River Studios
http://www.peaceriverstudios.com [status: May 12, 2004]

Roundshot
http://www.roundshot.ch [status: May 12, 2004]

B.2.6 Manufacturers of turntables for object movies

Accupan
http://www.accupan.com [status: May 12, 2004]

Anything 3D
http://www.anything3d.com [status: May 12, 2004]

Corybant West
http://www.corybantwest.com [status: May 12, 2004]

Kaidan
http://www.kaidan.com [status: May 12, 2004]

Peace River Studios
http://www.peaceriverstudios.com [status: May 12, 2004]

Roundshot
http://www.roundshot.ch [status: May 12, 2004]

CD-ROM with sample files

This book comes with a CD including sample files (under "Workshop") and demo versions of the software (under "Demo versions" and "Viewers"). Throughout the book there is reference made to the CD, which contains the same pictures as those found in the respective book chapters. In addition to the pictures, already processed project files using the respective software are included to aid workflow comprehension. The "raw pictures" included can, of course, also be used in conjunction with other software products (offering similar features) for test purposes. This is relatively easy for object movies, with all of the programs introduced here having the capacity to create such movies using the single-row and multi-row techniques. When it comes to producing cylindrical panoramas, the raw pictures also can be easily stitched using all of the programs introduced. Only when spherical and cubic panoramas are desired are some programs not able to process "normal" and fisheye pictures or pictures from panoramic cameras. Chapter 12 provides a table view of the functions included in the individual software products.

In order to be able to view the interactive panoramas and object movies, you will need the QuickTime plug-in, the iPIX plug-in and a VRML viewer (e.g. the Cortona Player); additionally, Java should be activated in your Web browser. Refer to the "System requirements" section below and the readme files on the bundled CD to learn where you can download the required plug-ins. A number of software manufacturers kindly provided us the installation file for their plug-in. You will find these files in the "Viewers" folder on the CD.

Demo versions of almost every software product introduced in this book can be downloaded from the manufacturer Web sites. The links are listed in the respective chapters so that you can download the software for testing purposes. A number of software manufacturers have given us permission to publish demo versions of their products on the book CD. You will find these programs in the folder labeled "Demo versions".

Software products are improved and updated all the time. As such, it is highly recommended that you pay a visit to the respective manufacturer's Web site prior to installing their program(s) from the book CD. It is possible that more recent versions of the software are available here.

System requirements:

PC:

Windows 98 and higher, 128 MB RAM, 400 MHz processor, 4x CD-ROM drive, minimum 100 MB of free hard disk space, sound card, color monitor with 24-bit color depth and a minimum resolution of 800 x 600 pixels (1,024 x 768 pixel resolution is recommended).

MAC:

Mac OS 8.6 and higher, 128 MB RAM, 400 MHz processor, 4x CD-ROM drive, minimum 100 MB of free hard disk space, sound card, color monitor with 24-bit color depth and a minimum resolution of 800 x 600 pixels (1,024 x 768 pixel resolution is recommended).

The following viewers are needed in order to be able to view panoramas and object movies. The download links are provided as follows:

- QuickTime plug-in from version 5
  http://www.apple.com/quicktime/download [status: May 1, 2004]
- iPIX plug-in
  http://infomedia.ipix.com/support/download [status: May 1, 2004]
- VRML Cortona Player
  http://www.parallelgraphics.com/products/cortona [status: May 1, 2004]
- Additionally, Java must be installed and activated in your browser
  http://java.com/en/download/manual.jsp [status: May 1, 2004]

Glossary

Blooming

Blooming refers to an undesirable oversaturation of light in the image, typically in the form of streaks. Any element of the **CCD chip** that needs to absorb a great quantity of light (due to the motif being photographed) is subjected to an extremely high electrical load. This load is then passed on to the neighboring elements. The picture information that is read out later on always appears white without any other delineation.

CCD chip

CCD stands for **C**harge **C**oupled **D**evice. The CCD chip is a component consisting of multiple photocells. These photocells release a certain amount of voltage relative to the amount of light that contacts them. This voltage is then stored in the CCD chip as an electrical charge.

Chromatic aberration

Chromatic aberration occurs when rays of light are refracted differently by a lens (depending on the wavelength) and, as a result, do not meet at exactly the same point in the focal plane. This type of distortion is associated with blurriness and color fringing.

CMOS chip

CMOS stands for **C**omplementary **M**etal **O**xyde **S**emiconductor. The CMOS chip is an energy-saving image recording sensor that stores an electrical charge with respect to the light conditions.

Codec

Codec stands for **Co**mpressor / **Dec**ompressor. Codecs typically are used in video applications in order to compress image material. One example of a codec is the Sorenson codec.

Coefficient

The multiplicator of variable factors in mathematical functions.

Cubic

Cubic-shaped projection that uses a quadratic picture for each of the six sides of a cube.

Cylindrical

Cylindrical projection noted for its limited vertical range. A cylindrical picture is suited for making printouts.

Distortion

A frequently occurring lens error that causes straight lines to appear arched. If the distortion is convex towards the observer, we speak of pincushion distortion. If the distortion is convex away from the observer, we speak of barrel distortion.

DPI

DPI stands for **D**ots **P**er **I**nch. As the term implies, dpi refers to the number of pixels per inch (1 inch = 2.54 cm) on an output device (i.e. a monitor or a printer).

Equirectangular

Rectilinear display of a spherical view, also known as a spherical picture.

Field of View (FOV)

FOV stands for **F**ield **o**f **V**iew. The field of view is the area captured by a camera lens and is relative to the picture format and the focal length of the lens. The field of view always is given in degrees, with 360° representing a full circle.

Gamma value / gamma curve

The gamma value describes the tonal value range (the distribution of color between the black and white points) of a picture. Monitors, camera chips, film material, etc. typically have specific gamma curves that can be adapted to each other (or at least approached) via a so-called gamma correction process.

Global Positioning System (GPS)

A system designed to globally position a location by the user via satellite. GPS is finding increased application in nautical and motor vehicle navigation systems.

High Dynamic Range (HDR)

Dynamic range refers to the range of light and dark areas in a picture. HDR is a technique in which the range of contrast saved on a recording medium approaches the true contrast of a scene. When HDR pictures are created, not only color information is saved for each pixel, but also the sum of the light that meets this particular area.

HTML

HTML stands for **H**yper**T**ext **M**arkup **L**anguage. HTML is the language in which Web sites are written. HTML is not a true programming language, as there are no loops, conditions or other control elements involved. Commands are known as **tags**, while the constituent parts of a site are referred to as objects or elements.

Image-based lighting

The natural lighting of a 3-D scene is critical in order to make a realistic impression. With image-based lighting, the light information captured in the form of an HDR picture is used to illuminate a computer-generated scene.

Interlacing method

A display method used in video applications, whereby the image is not formed line-by-line; instead, all even horizontal lines are written first, followed by all odd horizontal lines. Interlacing requires only half the image frequency as compared to non-interlaced display. Pictures generated in this way, however, tend to flicker.

Interpolation

The calculation of an unknown value from a minimum of two known values. This method frequently is used to magnify and scale down the size of pictures by adding or eliminating pixels, respectively. The type of interpolation method used determines the resulting picture quality.

Java applet

Applets are nothing more than “dependent” Java programs integrated in a Web site. Java applications, on the other hand, are complete programs that run on their own.

Nodal point

The point around which a camera and lens must be rotated in order to avoid **parallax errors** from cropping up between the foreground and background of a picture. The foreground and background must not be shifted in relation to each other while swiveling. The optical center of a camera/lens combination is known as the nodal point.

Parallax error

The parallax is the angle formed by two straight lines directed at a certain point from two different locations. This angle and the distance between both objects must remain the same. If this is not the case, a parallax error has occurred. This error especially becomes evident when moving objects are filmed relatively close to the camera. This error can be avoided by affixing the camera on the tripod such that the optical center of the camera/lens combination is directly over the tripod's rotating axis.

Photogrammetry

Photogrammetry is a measuring system used to determine the shape, size and position of an object based on photographs, not the object itself.

PPI

PPI stands for **P**oint **P**er **I**nch. This unit refers to the number of displayable pixels per inch (1 inch = 2.54 cm) for input devices (scanners).

Rectilinear

A right angle depiction lens also is known as a rectilinear lens, whereby rectilinear means that the lens captures straight lines and angles as such. In general, these lenses most often are referred to as “normal”, or standard lenses.

Rendering

Rendering is the computer process of generating digital pictures. In CAD and 3-D applications, models are displayed on the monitor screen in simple quality while being edited. For image output, selected areas of the picture are optically enhanced via rendering.

Resolution

Resolution simply refers to the number of pixels in the horizontal and vertical directions. The higher the resolution, the greater the visual detail of the picture displayed. Resolution can be given as an absolute value (1,024 x 768 pixels) or as a relative value (72 **dpi**). Relative resolution specifies how many pixels per unit of length (inch) are available in a picture.

Spherical

Spherically shaped projection, whereby the entire scene is displayed in a panoramic picture.

Stitching

Stitching is the seamless converging of individual pictures to form panoramas.

Tag

The Web sites on the Internet are formatted using the **HTML** language. Individual commands are known as tags (markers) and are enclosed in pointed brackets: <Tag>.

Thumbnail

A thumbnail is a small preview of a digital picture. Thumbnails typically are used to provide an overview of a large number of pictures. When a thumbnail is clicked, the larger version of the picture usually is displayed.

URL

URL stands for **U**niform **R**esource **L**ocator. A URL is the exact address of a file on the Internet. This address gives the online file its unique identity and makes it able to be located.

Vignetting

Vignetting refers to a frequent effect, whereby the corners of a picture are darkened. While the center of the picture is properly lit, the surrounding scene dims with increasing intensity the farther it extends from this point. This type of image distortion primarily affects wide angle lenses.

VRML

VRML stands for **V**irtual **R**eality **M**odeling **L**anguage. VRML is a language that is used to describe three-dimensional computer-generated scenes for displaying virtual worlds on the Internet.

Index

Q

R

S

T

U

V

W

Z

Printing: Appl, Wemding
Binding: Appl, Wemding

System requirements:

PC:
Windows 98 and higher, 128 MB RAM, 400 MHz processor,
4x CD-ROM drive, minimum 100 MB of free hard disk space, sound card, color monitor with 24-bit color depth and a minimum resolution of 800 x 600 pixels (1,024 x 768 pixel resolution is recommended).

MAC:
Mac OS 8.6 and higher, 128 MB RAM, 400 MHz processor,
4x CD-ROM drive, minimum 100 MB of free hard disk space, sound card, color monitor with 24-bit color depth and a minimum resolution of 800 x 600 pixels (1,024 x 768 pixel resolution is recommended).

The CD contains

a) Installation files for the following plug-ins and packages (see: Viewers):
- Cortona VRML Client 4.2
- iPIX® Java® Viewer4.0
- Java™ 2, Standard Edition (J2SE) Java Runtime Environment (JRE), Version 1.4.2_04
- PTViewer
- QuickTime 6.5.1

b) Demo versions of the following products (see: Demo versions):
- iPIX® Interactive Studio™ v1.1
- PanoTools 2.6b1
- PTGui 3.6
- Realviz® Stitcher V4.0
- VR Worx

c) Pictures and project files (see: Workshop):
The CD is referred to by the book in the respective chapters and includes examples covered therein. The same pictures that are shown in the different chapters in the book also can be found on the CD.
- In addition to the pictures, already processed project files using the various software products are included to aid workflow comprehension. The pictures can, of course, also be used in conjunction with other software products (offering similar features) for test purposes. (see: Workshop)

Before installing software packages, please read the files Readme_PC.txt and Readme_Mac.txt respectively.